Kim Ruger

COMMUNICATING
PROJECT MANAGEMENT

COMMUNICATING PROJECT MANAGEMENT

THE INTEGRATED VOCABULARY OF PROJECT MANAGEMENT AND SYSTEMS ENGINEERING

HAL MOOZ
KEVIN FORSBERG
HOWARD COTTERMAN

JOHN WILEY & SONS, INC.

*To the professional organizations and their volunteers
who work tirelessly for the benefit of their membership
and the industries represented.
We trust that this book will make their job easier.*

ACKNOWLEDGMENTS

The content of this book has been a labor of love for over a decade, starting with Len Malinowski who insisted on a concise vocabulary for his government agency.

Increasing emphasis on systems management has fueled the need for better communications among the contributing disciplines. This trend is exemplified by the National Aeronautics & Space Administration's initiative in establishing systems management offices at the eight NASA centers. We wish to acknowledge the important contributions of Dr. Ed Hoffman and Dr. Pat Patterson for their leadership in providing relevant and effective training to NASA.

We acknowledge the SEI-authorized CMM® and CMMI^SM appraisers, evaluators, and assessors at the Center for Systems Management for their valuable contributions taken directly from their daily practice of systems management process improvement.

We are pleased to acknowledge our many clients, instructors, and students who, over the years, provided suggestions and encouraged us to make this work available to the systems management community.

We appreciate the foresight of Larry Alexander at John Wiley & Sons for recognizing the need for *Communicating Project Management* as a companion to *Visualizing Project Management*. We acknowledge Paula Sinnott and the production and manufacturing team for making it all happen.

H.M.
K.F.
H.C.

CONTENTS

FOREWORD

To emphasize the multidisciplinary approach required to effectively communicate in the Systems Management environment, we invited three experts, each a world leader in his field, to share their views and experiences related to a common vocabulary—one that integrates the disciplines of Project Management, Systems Engineering, and Software Engineering.

Stephen Cross is the director and CEO of the Software Engineering Institute (SEI) at Carnegie Mellon University in Pittsburgh, Pennsylvania. He started his professional career designing software for embedded computer systems, and now he heads one of the most influential software organizations in the world. The software Capability Maturity Model® (CMM®), developed by the SEI, is now in use worldwide. Dr. Cross's goal is to help organizations "get it right the first time." He also recognizes that software does not exist in a vacuum, and any software system is part of a larger system. For this reason, the SEI has expanded and revised their capability model to encompass systems engineering as well. The new models are known as the Capability Maturity Model® Integration℠ Product Suite.

William R. Duncan is one of the founders of the American Society for the Advancement of Project Management (asapm) where he is now the director of Standards. He is also a Principal in the consulting firm Project Management Partners. Mr. Duncan was a principal editor and contributor to Project Management Institute's Project Management Body of Knowledge (PMBOK®) and he continues to participate in an Australian-led international group with the objective of developing an International Project

Management Body of Knowledge. His extensive experience and global contributions to the profession of project management have made him an internationally recognized and respected leader in project management.

Heinz Stoewer is the president-elect of the International Council on Systems Engineering (INCOSE). Professor Stoewer started his career in aerospace, working with both European and U.S. aerospace firms. He was the program manager for the Spacelab at the European Space Agency in the 1970s. As a professor at the Technical University of Delft in the Netherlands, he initiated the highly successful space systems engineering program. Throughout his career, he has been aware of the need to communicate precisely with compatriots in other fields and in other countries and, as he observed, "a dictionary that provides a common vocabulary covering the management of projects, systems, and software engineering is urgently needed."

We are proud to have these three leaders as collaborative contributors to our Foreword. It is our hope that increased collaboration and cooperation will follow this milestone.

STEPHEN CROSS, Ph.D.

As a past systems and software architect and developer, I understand the perspective of the designer who feels that too much discipline can stifle creativity. At the same time, my experience demonstrates that, in most disciplines, 98 percent of engineering success is attributable to following routines that extend creativity rather than reinvent the wheel. Now, as an executive committee member and past chairman of the Information Science & Technology panel at the Defense Advanced Research Projects Agency (one of the terms you will find in this dictionary), together with my role as Director of the Software Engineering Institute, I enjoy a bird's-eye view of technical systems management and the forces that are shaping it. Those forces are reflected in the broad vocabulary of this book.

As system complexity continues to grow relentlessly, and more and more functions move to software, we have to ask ourselves: "Does it make sense to view software development as something very different from other system technologies? Can project budgets really be managed separately from the technologies they enable?" These technical and management issues are often aggravated and perpetuated by language barriers.

The SEI mission is to provide leadership in advancing the state of the practice of software engineering to improve the quality of systems that depend on software. We accomplish this mission by promoting the evolution of software engineering from an ad hoc, labor-intensive activity to an orderly discipline that is well managed and supported by technology. Our mission is not only to advance the practice of software engineering, but also to make predictable the acquiring, developing, and sustaining of software-intensive systems, from design and through operation. Our capability models—most prominently the CMMI^{SM} models—provide the primary means we use to accomplish our mission. The CMMI Product Suite, resulting from the Capability Maturity Model® Integration^{SM} Initiative and referenced extensively in this dictionary, represents a major cooperative effort. Representatives of government and commercial organizations were intimately involved in the development of the CMMI Product Suite, including the term definitions and the Standard CMMI Appraisal Method for Process Improvement (SCAMPI^{SM}). These organizations donated the time of senior technical people with expertise in software engineering, systems engineering, integrated product and process development, and acquisition.

Our goal is to make writing software as structured and disciplined as building bridges or houses, to which the terms in this dictionary apply equally well. The future of software should have more in common with the nuts-and-bolts fields of manufacturing and construction than with lone coders pulling all-nighters to build elegant new programs.

For software development to become truly reliable and predictable, programmers will also have to develop better ways to reuse existing code—something I like to call the Holy Grail. Making this approach the norm will require dramatic cultural shifts such as planning projects more thoroughly and setting up processes that enforce development schedules and that audit code during development to keep it focused on the project's goal.

We are at the threshold of merging multiple technical management disciplines. This dictionary is a milestone and a key to our adopting a vocabulary that is consistent across them. I encourage you and your teams to help in our quest for improved performance by first understanding these terms and then applying them in your workplace.

WILLIAM R. DUNCAN

The English-speaking comedian Steve Martin once observed "those Frenchmen—they have a different word for everything!" His sentiment is often true in project management as well where we use different words to mean the same thing, while in other circumstances, we use the same word to mean very different things. For example:

- The words relationship, dependency, and constraint all mean essentially the same thing—there is a schedule-affecting interaction between two work items in a project plan.
- The phrase *project charter* may refer to a simple, high-level authorization document, or it may refer to the post-feasibility project plan, replete with cost and schedule estimates.

Some individuals (and some organizations) reject consistency in language out of a belief that consistency somehow interferes with creativity. But I think that this belief is misguided—consistency *facilitates* creativity. When teams start out speaking the same management language, they can focus their creative talents on the work of the project.

Others reject consistency out of a belief that smart people will find a way to work out their problems. But whether we look at the *Challenger* disaster, the Enron melt-down, or our own most recent project, we are reminded that smart people can still make dumb mistakes. I don't expect that I will ever see an error-free project, but when teams start out speaking the same management language, they should have fewer time-gobbling misunderstandings.

One of the major obstacles to the development of a common language is our relative insularity. Despite the overall breadth of the project management profession, the fact remains that most practitioners have experience in only one application area. In the same way that physical isolation breeds language dialects, our intellectual isolation has bred project management (and systems management) dialects. Cross-border projects create yet another challenge: Even when all the participants are nominally English-speaking, we must "translate" terms such as tender, solicit, and table.

Over the past 12 years, I have devoted more hours than I can count to the development of a common project management language. As the primary author of the 1994 and 1996 versions of the Project Management Institute's *A Guide to the Project Management Body of Knowledge,* I believed that document's glossary would support greater consistency. But although there are an estimated 700,000 copies in circulation, even the Institute's own publications frequently fail to use these terms as they are defined!

I'm now involved with a relatively new organization, the American Society for the Advancement of Project Management (*asapm*). As *asapm*'s Director of Standards, I will continue to strive to promote greater understanding and consistency both within the profession of project management as well as between project and systems management. While it may not be practical to expect project teams to always speak *exactly* the same language, I would hope that this dictionary will support movement toward that goal.

HEINZ STOEWER, MSC

Anyone who has grown up with the multination and multicultural European Space Programme can immediately appreciate the objective of this book, namely to contribute toward commonly accepted definitions of terms in a set of complex technical fields.

Since the early 1970s, many of our space projects have been planned and successfully implemented in broad international cooperation. Having "lived through" some of these, I well understand the need for a common vocabulary to be applied across technical fields and countries.

It was rather fortunate, that prior to my European Space Agency appointment as Programme Manager for our first human space-flight enterprise "Spacelab" in the early 1970s, I had already spent a few years in U.S. industry with McDonnell-Douglas/Boeing. This gave me a sufficient understanding of the different engineering and project management approaches and terms prevailing in Bremen, Toulouse, Rome, Noordwijk, Houston, Huntsville, Los Angeles, or Washington to be able to understand and translate between the different groups trying to cooperate across the Atlantic.

Failures not only result from bad hardware engineering, software engineering, systems engineering, or project management, they can also result from differing interpretations of engineering, communications, or management terms and associated cultures.

As professor for Space Systems Engineering at the Technical University of Delft in the Netherlands, I had initiated a few years ago a new international postgraduate Master of Space Systems Engineering program for engineers with a focus on modern "end-to-end" systems engineering. This program contains essential components of cross-disciplinary engineering, communication, and management. We emphasize the importance of multidisciplinary interaction on the basis of a common use of terms, with commonly understood definitions. We also recognize that systems engineering needs to further evolve into a disciplined process and design driven profession. For this reason, I became interested in the International Council on Systems Engineering (INCOSE), especially when, in 1995, the organization became international in scope.

During my professional career, I have witnessed the growth of software from a tradecraft with a few gurus in the 1960s to a more disciplined, process-driven profession today. During the past decade, there has been a growing awareness that the system and software engineering communities share common processes and indicators of organizational maturity. Already in the 1970s, the European Space Agency, ESA, had issued software standards, which became widely accepted well beyond the aerospace community. (They are presently part of the European Space Standards System; Software Engineering; ECSS-E-40.) In the 1980s, the Software Engineering Institute (SEI) has gained a worldwide reputation for its Software Capability Maturity Model (CMM). In the early 1990s, INCOSE started to develop a Capability Maturity Model for Systems Engineering, while the SEI expanded their model to encompass systems and software engineering, now known as the SEI CMMI[SM]. SEI and INCOSE now have joint working groups reviewing content and application of this model.

The importance of a common vocabulary covering project-, systems-, and software-engineering cannot be overemphasized. I was hence delighted to have been invited to write a portion of the Foreword to this wonderful dictionary.

PREFACE

SYSTEMS MANAGEMENT—A REBIRTH

We sought simplicity in our definitions with the intention of capturing the essence of the terms within their systems management context. We begin by characterizing the systems management context, starting with the foundation definitions:

systems management

The integration of project management and systems engineering into a seamless process that is dedicated to ensuring system integrity.
See also **system integrity** and **project success.**

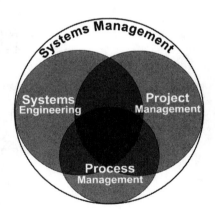

system integrity

Keeping the business, budget, and technical baselines congruent. A developing system has integrity when its baselines are in agreement or congruence, which results from establishing a balance among the three aspects (business, budget, and technical) at the outset of the project and then maintaining that balance as changes occur.
See also **project success.**

project success

Achieving the solution that does what it is supposed to; when it is supposed to; for the predicted development, operating, and replication costs; and with the reliability and quality expected.
See also **system integrity.**

Once established as congruent, project baselines have to be held in balance (easier said than done). The budget and schedule must allow achievement of the technical requirements. Conversely, the technical requirements must be achievable within the budget and schedule. There is continual pressure throughout a project to change baselined agreements. Schedules are compressed, available resources decreased, and technical functionality increased. The project team must be able to recognize and respond to serious inconsistencies. When change requests are considered, whether schedule, budget, or technical, the congruence needs to be reestablished.

All too often, projects proceed with their technical inventiveness and sophisticated development without paying heed to the evolving business case or the prevailing business and budget environment. Moreover, the managers of lower levels of decomposition often have little knowledge of the driving business case and of the derivative business cases at their level of decomposition. This lack of awareness of the driving business issues stems from inadequate collaboration between the business and technical disciplines and can lead to the wrong solution that is ultimately rejected by the user, customer, or marketplace. The concept and practice of *systems management* is a deliberate step to implementing knowledge, behavior, processes, and practices to correct this deficiency.

A LEGACY OF BARRIERS

It starts with the universities and other institutions of higher learning that separate their School of Business from their School of Engineering. New graduate engineers are ushered into the engineering environment and situated among other engineers—likewise with the new recipients of master's degree in business administration (MBAs). Engineering and business staffs are often in different buildings—possibly in different campuses or cities. Business and technical collaboration, if present at all, is not emphasized or facilitated. The barriers between disciplines begin to grow.

In many companies, organization structures keep technical and business management apart all the way to the second level of management. It is nearly impossible to bridge the gap without abandoning your career path. Historically, the professional organizations have further exacerbated this situation, with the Project Management Institute meetings not embracing systems engineering while the International Council on Systems Engineering does not emphasize schedule and business topics. The barriers grow even higher and stronger.

Finally, technical and business professionals establish their own independent customer contacts, each believing the other doesn't really know what the customer wants. Instinct replaces understanding, and when the product doesn't satisfy the customer, it's often attributed to the customer's "lack of appreciation for good work."

A TIMELY REBIRTH OF COLLABORATION

The concept of ensuring business-driven technical decisions throughout the project by integrating project management and systems engineering into systems management is not new. In the late 1960s, the U.S. Air Force Systems Command, in an attempt to improve project management practices, released AF SCM 375-1 through 375-5. It was called the *Systems Management Manual* and was focused on the "integration of management systems to effectively use technological knowledge" or the business-driven exploitation of technology. While it was an excellent concept with companion practices, it was just too progressive for the military industrial complex to digest at that time and it was successfully resisted and ultimately abandoned.

Later in the 1970s, the University of Southern California initiated a master's degree in Systems Management program that enjoyed high acclaim. The College of Notre Dame in Menlo Park, California, followed with a master's degree in Systems Management. More recently, the Massachusetts Institute of Technology established its joint business/engineering Systems Design and Management curriculum, together with a consortium that includes the Rochester Institute of Technology and the Naval Postgraduate School. The Technical University of Delft in the Netherlands now offers a Master of Space Systems Engineering programme, a cross-disciplinary engineering, communication, and management curriculum. Old Dominion University in the state of Virginia, jointly with the Center for Systems Management, recently introduced their Professional Certificate in Systems Engineering, which includes management courses.

The Software Engineering Institute, in its Capability Maturity Model® (CMM®) Integration Initiative, has contributed to the further blending of the engineering management disciplines and collaboration among the associated professional communities. The SEI provides comprehensive models for assessing software and systems development maturity. CMMI^{SM} is now used by commercial companies to increase their success rate as well as by government contractors seeking to increase their development efficiency and to reach the competitive proficiency threshold mandated by U.S. government buyers.

This book's publication, highlighted by the organizations and individuals contributing to the Foreword, demonstrates that a new era of collaboration has indeed begun.

USING THIS DICTIONARY

TERMINOLOGY DRAWN OR ADAPTED FROM OTHER SOURCES

This book is designed to promote seamless integration of the project management and systems engineering professions; therefore, our definitions are expressed in the context of the systems management field. At the end of each term that is related to a specific organization, we have identified that organization in brackets: [USG] for the U.S. government, [PMI®] for the Project Management Institute, and [SEI] for the Software Engineering Institute. These organizations provide their own term definitions in one or more glossaries. In the case of those designated as SEI terms, the definitions are from the SEI CMMI^{SM} -SE/SW/IPPD/SS, Version 1.1 Introduction, Chapter 2, and Glossary, except as noted. The latest versions of SEI models and term definitions can be found on the SEI Web site: http://www.sei.cmu.edu. The source documents can be found at http://www.sei.cmu.edu/cmmi/products/models.html. The Software Engineering Institute copyrights the SEI definitions as further defined in the Copyrights and Service Marks section.

PROVIDING CONTEXT THROUGH THE USE OF MODELS AND EXAMPLES

In keeping with our approach to use illustrations and examples to simplify potentially complex descriptions, we have included

Part 2, "Fostering Communication through Systems Management," includes a related set of process models to help clarify the terms in their context. Definitions that benefit from the context provided by these models are designated as [VPM], referring to the Visual Process Model, or [RPC], referring to the Reference Project Cycle.

COPYRIGHTS AND SERVICE MARKS

All terms denoted by [SEI] are Copyright 2002 by Carnegie Mellon University. Please refer to the Software Engineering Institute, Carnegie Mellon University, Pittsburgh, PA 15213-3890 or http://www.sei.cmu.edu, for permission to reproduce or to prepare derivative works. The following SEI service marks and registered marks are used in this book:

Capability Maturity Model®
CMM®
CMM Integration^{SM}
CMMI^{SM}
IDEAL^{SM}
SCAMPI^{SM}
SCE^{SM}

CMM and Capability Maturity Model are registered in the U.S. Patent and Trademark Office. CMM Integration, CMMI, SCAMPI, SCE, and IDEAL are service marks of Carnegie Mellon University.

PMI® is a service and trademark of the Project Management Institute, Inc. which is registered in the United States and other nations. PMBOK® is a trademark of the Project Management Institute, Inc. which is registered in the United States and other nations.

Vee+^{SM}, Vee++^{SM}, and Visual PM^{SM} are service marks of Center for Systems Management.

1

COMMUNICATING PROJECT MANAGEMENT

Communication is the soul of management: analysis and solid decisions translated into clear messages that influence people to act and feel good about their performance.

Dianna Booher
Communicate with Confidence!

As George Bernard Shaw once said, "The greatest problem in communication is the illusion that it has been accomplished." Many infamous project failures, such as the Space Shuttle Challenger disaster, can be attributed directly to just that illusion. Project success depends directly on achieving stakeholder understanding by communicating effectively.

We all know that communicating is difficult enough in familiar work, social, and family settings. The project environment can be particularly challenging. Projects, being temporary, often bring people together who were previously unknown to one another—reason enough for miscommunication, especially in the first project phases. A related reason is that projects represent a microcosm of a broad, general organization—one that integrates different technical specialties and people with very different backgrounds. Common labels such as *nerd, geek,* and *bean counter,* suggest some

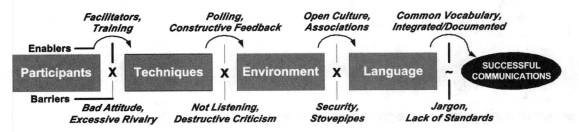

FIGURE 1.1 The project management communication model.

of the attitudinal barriers that interfere with project communications, not to mention the vocabulary ambiguities among the various disciplines. Referring to disparities between the technical and financial, Stephen Cross observed in his Foreword that technical and management issues are often aggravated and perpetuated by language barriers.

While much of this book is devoted to project language, it is but one major factor in the project communication equation. As illustrated in Figure 1.1, communications results are only as good as the least effective of the multiplication factors in this product:

Participants × Techniques × Environment × Language ~ Communication

This book consists of six parts. The main sections of Part 1 correspond to the four factors in the communications equation in Figure 1.1, emphasizing the first two: the participants and those techniques that are particularly important in the project environment. Part 2 broadens the discussion of techniques by defining the context for project communications in the form of visual process models, project integrity, and systems management. Part 3 focuses on the global professional environment and the organizations that shape it. Part 4 provides further context for the project vocabulary. Parts 5 and 6 address the language factor with a common project vocabulary consisting of terminology (Part 5) and acronyms (Part 6).

COMMUNICATIONS MODELS

Our models, summarized in Part 2, focus on projects. This section briefly describes several general models that have proven helpful in understanding the communication process itself. We also identify references that delve into the underlying theories that are outside this book's scope and purpose.

Many models dating from the late 1940s are referred to as *transmission* models since they approach communications as an information transfer problem based on some variation of four fundamental elements:

Sender (or Source) > Message > Channel (or Medium) > Receiver

One of the most popular models was created when Warren Weaver, a distinguished mathematician, applied Claude Shannon's concept of information transmission loss over telephone wires to interpersonal communication (Figure 1.2).

Shannon was a research scientist at Bell Telephone Laboratories trying to achieve maximum telephone line capacity with minimum distortion. Though he had never intended for his mathematical theory of signal transmission to be used for anything but telephones, the Weaver adaptations were very influential in information theory. Norbert Wiener, a renowned mathematician and founder of cybernetics, added the feedback loop to the Shannon-Weaver Model. We elaborate further on feedback in later sections.

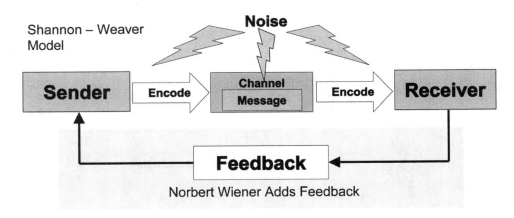

FIGURE 1.2 Shannon-Weaver Model with Weiner's feedback.

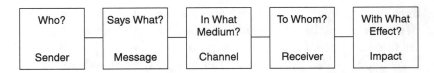

FIGURE 1.3   The Lasswell Formula.

The Lasswell Formula (Figure 1.3), another popular transmission model introduced a year later by sociologist Harold Lasswell, added the idea of impact or effect.

The transmission models have also influenced early studies of human communication, but many theorists now consider them to be misleading. These models and their derivatives focus more on the study of message-making as a process, rather than on what a message means and on how it creates meaning. The issues of meaning and interpretation are reflected in the models depicted in Figures 1.4 and 1.5, both of which emphasize the interpretive processes.

David Berlo, a well-known communication researcher who studied at the University of Illinois with Wilber Schramm, introduced the model in Figure 1.5 in 1960. Further emphasizing encoding and decoding, he defined five verbal communication

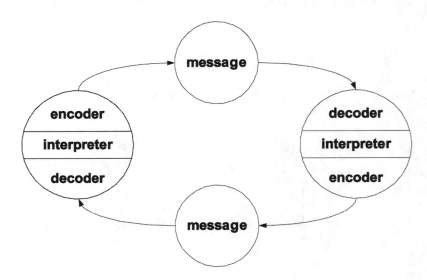

FIGURE 1.4   Osgood and Schramm circular model.

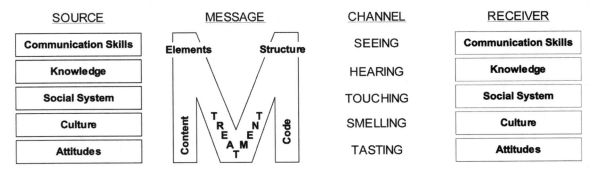

FIGURE 1.5   David Berlo SMCR Model.

skills: speaking and writing (encoding skills), listening and reading (decoding skills), and thought or reasoning (both encoding and decoding).

For those readers interested in a deeper understanding of the theories underlying these and other models, we offer these references:

- Stephen W. Littlejohn, *Theories of Human Communication* (Belmont: Wadsworth Publishing Company, April 1995). This book is considered the seminal text in the field.
- Richard L. Lanigan, *Phenomenology of Communication: Merleau Ponty's Thematics in Communicology and Semiology* (Pittsburgh: Duquesne University Press, 1988). Semioticians center their attention on semantics—what a message means and on how it creates that meaning.

The remainder of Part 1 addresses the communications issues of project teams by considering each of the four factors: participants, techniques, environment, and language.

PARTICIPANTS AND THEIR INFLUENCE ON PROJECT COMMUNICATIONS

We often think of project participants as being limited to the team members. But from total influence and broader communications viewpoints, the participants encompass a wide array of stakeholders, including:

- Functional and middle management.
- Executive management.
- Closely related stakeholders, such as contractors, customers, and potential users.
- Global stakeholders, such as professional associations and standards organizations.

Stakeholders all bring their own vocabulary, behaviors, communication styles, attitudes, biases, and hidden agenda to the project environment.

PERSONAL BEHAVIORS AND COMMUNICATION STYLES

To communicate effectively, we need to be aware of differing behaviors and styles and their potential impact. Leaders often need to adapt their own style rather than "shape up" the other person.

There are numerous texts and self-study guides for analyzing your own style tendencies and preferences. We summarize two models proven to be particularly effective. However, the details of any specific self-typing or group analysis scheme are less important than the process itself—exploring your own preferences and stretching your range of styles. To benefit from that process, you first have to be self-aware.

Wilson Learning Corporation's Interpersonal Relations Model (Eden Prairie, MN) has been widely used in the business environment for characterizing personal style. Your interpersonal style is determined by a blending of your peers' perceptions acquired through formal questionnaires similar in format to psychology and aptitude profiles. The process begins with the interpretation of your individual results relative to the four-quadrant model in Figure 1.6.

Combining your primary style—Analytical, Driver, Amiable, or Expressive—with your secondary or backup style (one of the same four quadrants in the basic model), places you in one of the 16 style categories (e.g., an Expressive/Driver) (Figure 1.7).

The utility of the Wilson model becomes clear when you consider the interactions among the various categories. The result is a much-improved insight and

Analytical	Driver
(technical or systems specialist)	(control specialist)
Amiable	Expressive
(supportive specialist)	(social specialist)

FIGURE 1.6   The basic Wilson model.

awareness, not only of your own styles, but of others' behavior patterns as well. Perhaps most important is this newly acquired means to recognize behavior patterns and then anticipate interactions so as to adapt by extending your own personal behavior boundaries.

Another model broadly supported in psychology and self-help, is based on the theory of psychological types described by Carl G. Jung (1875–1961). Jung theorized that people are different in fundamental and definable ways and that preferences for how people function and solve problems can be categorized. He believed that, while certain preferences are inborn, they can be changed over time. Jung's model places you in one of 16 categories based on determining your dominant traits. In the 1950s, Isabel Myers and Katharine Briggs devised the Myers-Briggs Type Indicator to further characterize and apply Jung's 16 categories. The Myers-Briggs model uses a questionnaire to help you determine your dominant trait in each of four pairs of traits:

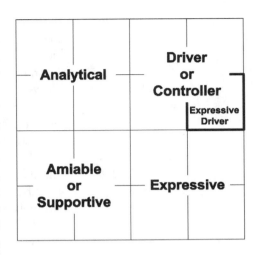

FIGURE 1.7   The 16 Wilson style combinations.

E/I   Extrovert or Introvert

N/S   Intuitive or Sensing

T/F   Thinking or Feeling

J/P   Judging or Perceiving

David Keirsey developed his related Temperament Sorter to help with personal action plans and communications. The characterizations in Figure 1.8 are adopted from David Keirsey and Marilyn Bates, *Please Understand Me, Character & Temperament Types* (Del Mar, CA: Promethius Nemesis Book Company, 1984), one of several guides for interpreting the results.

Rather than consolidating peer- and self-review into one composite result, you are encouraged to characterize yourself and to independently have others respond to the same questions about you. Additional insight can thus be gained by comparing your results

INFJ	INFP	ISTJ	ISFJ
Author	Questor	Trustee	Conservator
ENFJ	**ENFP**	**ESTJ**	**ESFJ**
Pedagogue	Journalist	Administrator	Seller
INTJ	**INTP**	**ISTP**	**ISFP**
Scientist	Architect	Artisan	Artist
ENTJ	**ENTP**	**ESTP**	**ESFP**
Field Marshall	Inventor	Promoter	Entertainer

FIGURE 1.8   Sixteen Meyers-Briggs categories.

for each trait with the perception of others. As with the Wilson model, most authors provide detailed advice and insight regarding the dynamics of one style interacting with another (e.g., an ENTN interacting with an ISFP), whether it be as team members, manager/subordinate, or spouses.

These models help discern cognitive preferences and do not represent behavioral absolutes. They provide insight into how we gather information, process it, and communicate. Regardless of your preferred style, your actual style at any time should be affected by factors such as the maturity level of team members and the gravity or priority of the situation. Variety and shifts in style are not only necessary—they're healthy. Communicating in projects requires flexibility and adaptability in dealing with the task at hand, the personalities involved, events, and the situation.

ATTITUDES AND BIASES CAN BUILD BRIDGES OF UNDERSTANDING OR DESTROY PROJECTS

We refer to negative personal biases regarding important project management techniques as the *hidden enemies*. For example, our surveys of some 20,000 managers regarding their attitude about red teams, revealed that only 20 percent of project participants have a positive attitude about this important communication technique. Please refer to the illustration under *bar chart* in Part 5 for more attitude survey data.

The Berlo SMCR Model (Figure 1.5) identifies attitude as one of five facets that affect personal communications (some models combine Berlo's social system facet with culture). An inappropriate attitude or bias regarding project subject matter or a specific technique, once understood, can usually be dealt with rationally and amicably. However, attitudes toward you or toward another in the communications loop is a much more significant barrier. If you have a low opinion of the person with whom you are dialoging, you will certainly formulate your message differently from the way you formulate it for your close collaborators. This person is a computer nerd. That one is a geek. You make sure that you don't smile too much and don't say any more than necessary in case it is interpreted as an invitation to strike up a friendship. It is regrettable that the type of productive dialog illustrated at the top of the mountain in Figure 1.9 is so unstable and susceptible to a sudden decline.

Constructive challenge (Figure 1.9) is a problem-resolving technique that depends on good communication skills and a positive attitude. Known as *constructive confrontation* in some circles, it can easily turn destructive without the right intentions, skills, or the commitment to immediately solve problems. To keep it constructive:

Go directly to the most likely solver—independent of organization structure.

Confront the problem not the person—use facts.

Exclude personalities from discussion.

Jointly work toward resolution—hold each other accountable.

Used with good intentions, this approach eliminates whining and solves problems fast. But when used in name only, as a weapon in rivalry or for other wrong purposes, it can destroy teamwork and the project.

Excessive rivalry can be just as destructive at the individual level as it is at the global level. As long-time participants in

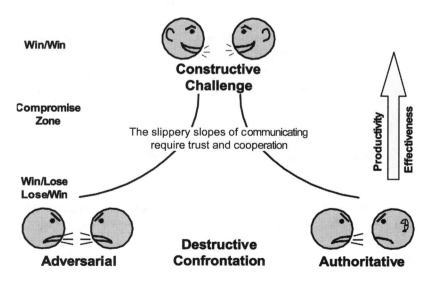

FIGURE 1.9   Attitude—the slippery slopes of communicating.

professional associations and industry standards organizations, we have observed a trend of increasing cooperation among the key project disciplines, which we address in the next section and in Part 3, The Collaborative Environment. But this industry-level collaboration frequently fails to permeate the very organizations and projects that form their constituency. Sometimes this is a result of competitive pressures. More often, it is ignorance or misdirected ambition.

In the face of management and global barriers, how can project managers ensure effective communications on their own project? Just like every other responsibility within a project, it starts at home—by taking responsibility for communicating skills, attitudes, and training at the individual and team levels. You, as project manager, need to assess the skills within your team and take the appropriate measures, which often starts with good guides, such as those we identify in the next section.

The participants have the greatest potential to promote understanding by proactively strengthening the other three communication factors. When you or other key stakeholders anticipate a communication breakdown or encounter a barrier, the best strategy may be to turn to a nonstakeholder for objective feedback or assistance. For example, the initial project planning session is often held before the new group of people has coalesced as a team; therefore, they may benefit greatly from an outside facilitator, one who is skilled in the subject matter as well as the art of communicating among disparate factions. Not only will this converge more quickly on a workable plan, but it also can provide valuable on-the-job communications skills training and experience while serving as a model for future conduct.

TECHNIQUES FOR COMMUNICATING IN PROJECTS

Exchange and *feedback* are key words in describing communication techniques. Whether engaged in a simple conversation or conducting a multifaceted design review, the most powerful techniques are those that result in some kind of exchange or feedback.

Since it is beyond the scope of this book to enumerate the thousands of communication techniques that can benefit projects of all sizes and complexity, we will occasionally refer to general guides that we have found especially valuable, such as:

- Dianna Booher, *Communicate with Confidence!* (New York: McGraw-Hill, 1994). This compilation of 1,042 tips, all with explanations, is directed toward better governance with words, both written and oral.
- Philip J. Harkins and Warren G. Bennis, *Powerful Conversations: How High-Impact Leaders Communicate* (New York: McGraw-Hill, 1999). This book describes proven communications techniques for improving growth and productivity.
- Robert Kegan and Lisa Laskow Lahey, *How the Way We Talk Can Change the Way We Work: Seven Languages for Transformation* (San Francisco: Jossey-Bass, 2000). This book offers practical solutions to several communications barriers.
- Juanita Brown and David Isaacs, "Conversation as a Core Business Process," *The Systems Thinker* (Cambridge, MA: Pegasus Communications, December 1996/January 1997), pp. 1–6. This article elevates the casual conversation to business process status.

While many of the suggestions offered in these sources may seem like common sense, they help you focus on critical points that you may take for granted, like preparing for a one-on-one conversation, testing a potentially touchy conversation, or actively listening to what other people say. In addition, they offer some helpful conversational strategies and tips for determining when your meeting is going off course.

We previously discussed the situational nature of communications, particularly in projects. In addition to being aware of your own and others' communication styles, you need to consider your purposes, such as:

- Social (entertainment, enjoyment, or passing time).
- Relationship (build rapport, teamwork, trust, and commitment).

- Information exchange (present, learn, and share).
- Collaborate (work towards common goals or outputs).
- Resolve problems (address issues, remove barriers, vent hostility).
- Influence (persuade, negotiate, or direct).

You may find it useful to identify your purposes and describe your situation in order to anticipate the way in which you and the others involved may respond. Start by identifying your motivation source (personal need served).

Over the course of a project, shifts in purpose and situations occur commonly. For example, you may start a project with heavy and generous support from the functional engineering department, only to see that support wane later when a new project competes for the same resources. When collaboration suddenly turns to negotiation:

- Identify or reinforce the common vision or expected outcome.
- Identify the interests of each party in the outcome.
- Have each party prioritize their interests.
- Generate alternative solutions.
- Choose the solution that satisfies the most interests of both parties.

We devote our discussion of techniques to those that are often overlooked or underutilized to the point of project failure.

VIEWING DIALOG AS A CORE PROCESS

"Talk is by far the most accessible of pleasures. It costs nothing in money, it is all profit, and it completes our education, found and fosters our friendships, and can be enjoyed at any age and in almost any state of health." This joy of talk articulated by Robert Louis Stevenson's witty remark is both a bane and blessing when we, as project team members, seek to employ talk in the form of conversation.

Fundamental communication techniques are brought into play whenever one project member engages another in conversation.

The potential impact of the ubiquitous one-on-one conversation is too often ignored or taken for granted. Figure 1.9 illustrates a few of the situations we have all been in—on one side or the other.

Hundreds of valuable and creative conversational techniques are explored in the sources listed earlier. Juanita Brown and David Isaacs cite research demonstrating that informal conversations can often be much more powerful and satisfying than formal communication processes. They offer this thesis: "Consider that these informal networks of learning conversations are as much a core business process as marketing, distribution, or product development. In fact, thoughtful conversations around questions that matter might be the core process in any company—the source of organizational intelligence that enables the other business processes to create positive results." We hasten to add that, while informal conversation techniques can certainly be used more effectively when properly supported, their utility and power is greatly diminished when they are practiced as a substitute or work-around for inadequate project visibility and statusing processes.

By definition, deep dialog goes beyond an informal conversation. It extends to the exchange of constructive feelings and attitudes in order to reach a common understanding. The practice of this communication technique is a good sign that an effective project team is in place. It also helps improve teamwork as challenges occur. Openness and sharing can elevate dialog to collaboration and create an environment for resolving conflict, but it does require a time investment. One useful technique is to schedule a meeting with no fixed agenda.

To promote dialog as a core process, consider these ground rules:

- Test assumptions and inferences.
- Share all relevant information.
- Focus on interests, not positions.
- Be specific, use examples.
- Agree on what important words mean.
- Explain the reason behind one's statements, questions, and actions.

- Disagree openly.
- Make statements, then invite questions and comments.
- Do not make disparaging or destructive remarks or otherwise distract the group.
- All members are expected to participate in all phases of the process.
- Exchange relevant information with nongroup members.
- Make decisions by consensus.
- Do self critiques.

BEING PROACTIVE BY WALKING AROUND

Management by walking around works on the assumption that a manager must circulate to fully understand the team's performance and problems. The best managers, according to Tom Peters, spend 10 percent of their time in their offices and 90 percent of their time talking and working with their people, their customers, and their suppliers.

Think about it: The most important job for the project manager or technical leader is to be in touch with the team members. Yet, project communications often suffer because team leaders spend too much time managing by PowerPoint. By occasionally circulating among team members in their work setting, you can resolve—or at least learn about—issues that may never make it to a formal review, address morale or even technical problems before they become issues, or simply enter into a brief conversation that helps maintain an open culture.

ACHIEVING UNDERSTANDING THROUGH BREVITY— WHEN LESS IS MORE

Very often, the real impact of communication doesn't occur until the information is recalled. As a rule of thumb, retention halves for each of five steps, which leaves us with eight minutes in the bank for a two-hour investment:

We *hear* half of what is said.	2 hours
We *listen* to half of what we hear.	1 hour
We *understand* half of what we listen to.	30 minutes

We *believe* half of what we understand.   15 minutes

We *remember* half of what we believe.   8 minutes

Beyond two hours in one session, another factor takes over—fatigue. As Anatole France put it, "The more you say, the less people remember."

Hiding problems by saying nothing is not a positive application of this technique.

OBSERVING AND LISTENING—ENCOURAGING COMMUNICATIONS BY REMAINING SILENT

Perhaps the most difficult communication technique of all is effective listening. We all know this from our own experiences and from the proliferation of great thinkers who have lamented the lost art of listening. We would all do well to heed Sydney Harris' admonition: "It's a tossup as to which are finally the most exasperating—the dull people who never talk, or the bright people who never listen." Those bright people are often in one of these roles:

- Dreamer—thinking of other things
- Actor—focusing on delivery rather than content
- Rehearser—formulating responses or rebuttals
- Placater—agreeing, just to be nice
- Derailer—switching
- Debater—discrediting or discounting the message
- Filterer—hearing selectively or with bias
- Know-it-all—succumbing to the "urge to talk"

One listening technique we favor begins by turning off your natural tendency to react to what you're hearing. Turn up the gain on your receiver—just remember to turn off your own sound to feel the power of remaining silent. Oscar Wilde quipped, "He knew the precise psychological moment to say nothing." Sometimes your silence can speak volumes.

This is especially difficult if you are an expert in your field or a high-level manager who believes you know it all. But that's one of the most critical listening situations for breaking barriers, experiencing fresh ideas, building rapport, and exerting positive leadership at the project level. Former Secretary of State, Dean Rusk, put it this way, "The best way to persuade others is with our ears."

POLLING TECHNIQUES—OVERCOMING THE DANGER OF REMAINING SILENT

Friedrich Nietzsche observed, "There are no facts, only interpretations." But what do you do when people withhold their interpretations for the wrong reasons?

In her Tip 40, Dianna Booher asserts that you need to hear silence as it is intended (and we add, not as you want to interpret it). She points out that people who believe that silence is consent are in for a big disappointment. She identifies 16 meanings for silence, including reflection, confusion, anger, revulsion, rebuke, shock, and powerlessness. We add one that often dooms projects: Fear.

Polling is a communication technique that has been traditional in aerospace programs for years. It consists of addressing individually each representative in a launch operation and recording their position as to proceeding with the launch. Every individual has the right and obligation to stop a launch if his or her area is not launch worthy.

The power of using this technique, and the danger of inappropriately omitting it, is illustrated by ABC Television's faithful reenactment of the Challenger launch decision by telephone conference between the NASA launch team and the solid rocket manufacturer, Thiokol. It shows a team of responsible Thiokol engineers being overpowered by their management who are determined to please NASA officials with a favorable launch decision even though the engineers believe that the low launch temperature was far too risky for the rocket booster O-rings. NASA attempted to ensure that Thiokol's decision was based on team consensus by asking over the conference call telephone, "Is there anyone in the room with a different opinion?" The engineers fearfully remain silent, their facial expressions and body language telling the true story of their discomfort with the reckless decision. NASA is unable to see the telling body language and the critical communication did not occur.

According to the Rogers Report ("Report of the Presidential Commission on the Space Shuttle Challenger Accident," W. P.

Rogers, Chairman, 6 June 1986), "The Commission concluded that there was a serious flaw in the decision-making process leading up to the launch of flight 51-L. A well-structured and managed system emphasizing safety would have flagged the rising doubts about the Solid Rocket Booster joint seal. Had these matters been clearly stated and emphasized in the flight readiness process in terms reflecting the views of most of the Thiokol engineers and at least some of the [NASA] Marshall engineers, it seems likely that the launch of 51-L might not have occurred when it did." On that basis we can conclude that, had NASA recorded a poll requiring those present to state their name and launch decision, the launch probably would have been postponed, possibly saving seven lives. The massive analyses of the Challenger disaster dwell on the O-ring failure with only brief mention of the communication failure, the root cause, and lesson learned.

MEETINGS MADE MEANINGFUL—DON'T NEGLECT TO FOLLOW UP

In *Visualizing Project Management,* we refer to meetings as the project manager's dilemma. High-value meetings are critical to project success while ineffective meetings can be worse than wasteful—they can destroy morale. "Whether one-on-one or involving the entire project, meetings are a significant technique for gathering and disseminating information. As such, they can easily consume 40 percent to 60 percent of a project manager's time." The book identifies a dozen types of useful project meetings and offers guidelines for their planning and execution.

Since entire books are devoted to effective meeting management, we look at one important aspect that is often underused: meeting follow-up techniques. Too many times an expensive meeting is concluded by published minutes that go into a file drawer or e-mail folder.

Take notes. Effective follow-up communication begins at the opening of the meeting by asking the attendees to make their own notes about specific issues or questions important to them. These need to be collected at the conclusion (these notes may be anonymous) for follow-up and may be just as important as the acknowledged action items. These items can range from an assessment of the meeting itself to issues that were triggered there, but unrelated to the meeting subjects. They can often spawn communications that have their own life and purpose.

Don't wait too long to follow up. In fact, a shortcut may often be appropriate. If you're not clear about an action item or message, play it back right in the meeting for the benefit of everyone involved.

If you're too busy to plan your meeting or the follow-up, reschedule it!

CONSTRUCTIVE FEEDBACK—ENSURING THAT THE EXCHANGE IS UNDERSTOOD BY ALL

You haven't fully communicated until your intended meaning is confirmed through your audience's response or by some other form of feedback. The importance of this communication technique is not only critical when eliciting requirements, but at every step in the project cycle. Feedback provides the basis for project decisions:

Fast feedback enables **fast** decisions.
Fast **honest** feedback enables fast **sound** decisions.

Agreement

Projects are driven by the project cycle with its reviews and control gates. Since these events bring together the key stakeholders, they offer one of the most powerful and efficient opportunities for project communications. However, unless that all-important feedback loop is reinforcing and constructive, the experience will be worse than no communication at all (see Figure 1.10).

Some situations can benefit greatly from a two-way feedback agreement:

"In order for us to be effective, I give you permission to be totally honest with me. (So long as you don't attack me as a person and focus solely on work content.)"

"I will do my best to comprehend your message and to remain calm and centered as we resolve the issues together."

"In turn, I will be honest and forthright with you."

Feedback works best as part of an organizational culture that encourages feedback to be given and received without reservation. All discussions should keep these positive objectives in mind, while avoiding their negative counterparts:

Effective	*Ineffective*
Frank and objective	Emotional and personal
Specific and complete	General and vague
Capable of being acted upon	Not actionable
Factual	Opinions
Timely	Ill-timed

According to Jack Welch of General Electric, "The secret of running a successful business is to make sure that all key decision makers have access to the same set of facts." But access is not enough. There must be confirmation that key decision makers are cognizant of the relevant facts and are bringing them to bear on decisions important to the project. This is best accomplished at control gates where proof of concept performance and proof of design producibility provide the basis for moving ahead. In the conduct of control gates, constructive challenge and constructive feedback are key to achieving confidence. Receivers must be open to this input and concentrate on hearing the suggestions and solution as best intentions. No matter how caustic the delivery may be, don't react as if you are attacked personally or you may end up shooting the messenger.

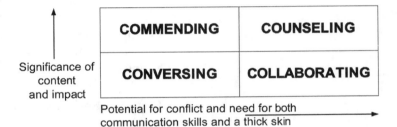

FIGURE 1.10   Feedback categories.

Control gates are not the only forum for constructive feedback. Others are personnel performance reviews, project status reviews, fee evaluation reviews, proposal evaluations, proposal debriefings, peer reviews, red team reviews, and tiger team reviews. There is no limit to the informal opportunities and methods for providing essential, on-going feedback, including discussions around the water cooler.

We have found peer reviews to be very effective when the review methods of all parties are aligned. There are three distinctive types of peer reviews for content and quality:

Type 1—Please Comment

- Author requests comments.
- Commenter provides comments without expectation of feedback.
- Author decides what will be incorporated and what will be ignored.

Type 2—Collaborate to Consensus (C2C)

- Author requests C2C.
- Commenter(s) provides comments and expects discussion until consensus is reached on the result.
- Both can then vigorously defend the result.

Type 3—Red Team Reviews

- Used when comparing to a standard such as an RFP or an industry standard.
- Reviewer(s) produce scoring against pre-established criteria.
- Reviewer(s) produce strengths and weaknesses assessments.
- Reviewer(s) produce recommendations for improvements.
- Author(s) discuss details with the reviewer(s) to ensure understanding of the scoring, strengths and weaknesses, and recommendations (but not to argue correctness of the reviewer(s) observations and recommendations).
- Author(s) unilaterally respond to the reviewer(s) suggestions as the author(s) deem appropriate.

THE ENVIRONMENT

This section considers the local project environment, which has about as much variation as does the world's governmental landscapes—from free and open to·dictatorial and suppressive. In Part 3, we address the global professional environment.

A BALANCED ENVIRONMENT ENCOURAGES FEEDBACK

An organization's culture and process should not become one where feedback providers must spend excessive time massaging the message so as not to irritate the receiver. Again, focus on facts and issues, not personalities. Speed and clarity must prevail in the interest of achieving swift but informed decisions.

Feedback receivers must develop an immunity to being offended in the interest of swift, clear communication. A thick skin helps. The receiver needs to give the provider some *slack*.

STOVEPIPES AND SILOS

As William Duncan notes in the Foreword, "One of the major obstacles to the development of a common language is our relative insularity. In the same way that physical isolation breeds language dialects, our intellectual isolation has bred project management (and systems management) dialects."

One form of organizational isolation is known as *stovepipes* or *silos* (see Figure 1.11). This jargon refers to virtual barriers proudly built by functional teams of a single discipline or power group. If not carefully managed, we might end up with "we creators" and "those bean counters" or as another example, "our night shift" and "that dazed shift" or any other equally derogatory division. These virtual barriers, so proudly built, not only partition and inhibit communication, but also foster negative communication that alienates and punishes. One of the authors would visit customers without informing his marketing personnel because he felt they were not technically qualified. This practice is seriously wrong and can be disastrous for any project depending on free and open communication to ensure the best decisions.

FIGURE 1.11 Silos.

THE PROJECT (OR COMPANY) GRAPEVINE: A BLESSING IN DISGUISE?

The simple human pleasure of talking can overcome any organizational barrier. But, as C. Northcote Parkinson sees it, that talk may not always be helpful to the project, "The vacuum created by a failure to communicate will quickly fill with rumor, misrepresentations, drivel, and poison."

Juanita Brown and David Isaacs take the opposite view. "Consider for a moment, that the most widespread and pervasive training in your organization may not be happening in the training rooms, or boardrooms, but in the cafeteria, the hallways, and the café across the street. Imagine that through e-mail exchanges, phone visits, and bull sessions with colleagues, people at all levels of the organization are sharing critical business knowledge, exploring underlying assumptions, and creating innovative solutions for key business issues." They assert that the organization's communication grapevine is "not a poisonous plant to be cut off at the roots, but a natural source of vitality to be cultivated and nourished."

Plato resolves the dichotomy very simply: "Moderation in all things." The secret is coming to a balanced environment where the informal channels of communications are supported for the good things they do, but not at the expense of the appropriate visibility and statusing facilities, which the grapevine should compliment, not replace.

LANGUAGE—THE MANY MEANS WE USE TO EXPRESS OUR THOUGHTS

We strongly agree with Samuel Johnson when he said, "Language is the dress of thought." Like clothing, language can also conceal thoughts, or worse yet, replace thinking altogether.

The answer to, "What was he thinking about when he selected that awful tie to wear to this meeting?" is probably, "Nothing." Your attire communicates—sometimes very loudly.

By language, we mean everything from a common vocabulary to appropriate attire and body language, and we include the effective use of silence, as well (Figure 1.12). Our simple advice regarding body language: Believe the body language you're seeing if it conflicts with the words you're hearing. Likewise, intonation speaks louder than words.

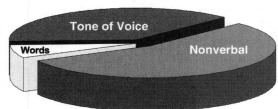

FIGURE 1.12   Elements of language.

Safeway, a major grocery chain, succeeded in making a remarkable marketplace shift from the low price leader to a high value and service image on the strength of a comprehensive, corporatewide language training program (called "Front-Line Leadership"). A store manager recently approached one of the authors waiting in his car that blocked a fire lane in front of the store. To encourage moving the car, the manager said, "May I help you with something, sir?" But the intonation said something very different: You need to move your car!

In addition, Safeway has set a new industry standard for communicating appreciation to its customers. Every credit card customer hears "Thank you for shopping at Safeway, Mr. Jones. Do you need help to your car?" This personalized "thank you" rarely goes unnoticed.

Here are a few word choices that can facilitate communications and project success:

Communication Killers	*Communication Enhancers*
We've tried that before.	That's an idea we can build on.
You have to be practical.	Why not? Let's put a timeline on it.
Let's form a committee.	Do it!

People consider and anguish over word choices. They may even think about their tone of voice. Seldom, however, do they think about or plan what the rest of their body is saying through crossed arms, stance, or facial expressions.

The study of nonverbal communication in psychology has its origins in the nineteenth-century writings of Charles Darwin on *The Expression of Emotions in Man and Animals* (1872) and in Wilhelm Wundt's nineteenth century work on gesture. It would take another 50 years for body language to become a central topic in social psychology.

Based on research done by Albert Mehrabain and published in his article "Communication Without Words" in *Psychology Today,* 93 percent of all communication is expressed nonverbally. Nonverbal communication includes eye contact, facial expressions, gestures, inflection, tone, and rate of speech. Body language makes up 55 percent of the communicated message, tone of voice accounts for 38 percent and words the remaining 7 percent.

The word *babel* was derived from an infamous project failure in the ancient town by that name. The Tower of Babel project was destroyed by lack of a common language. Here are a few language suggestions to help prevent such total destruction.

LANGUAGE ABUSES—ACRONYMS AND JARGON

Acronym abuses are legendary. Andy Rooney, a television commentator, once did a full-hour special video on the folly of acronyms and titles within the U.S. government. We are all guilty of AA—acronym abuse, and its close relative, JA—jargon abuse.

At one extreme, jargon is a lethal weapon. At the other, it provides the foundation for a uniquely meaningful project vocabulary. Unfortunately, specialists on the project team (whether rocket scientists or accountants) may consciously use jargon to confuse, confound, or obscure embarrassing or deficient information. Others, perhaps reluctant to reveal their ignorance, choose to ignore what could lead to project failure. The solution is easy to recognize, but often very hard to implement. Ferret out all jargon and either eliminate it from project communications or embrace it by defining it in the baseline project vocabulary document.

COMMUNICATION DISTORTION—THE NOISE FACTOR

This problem is vividly illustrated by performing the "pass the message around the table" exercise, a favorite at dinner parties and communication seminars. The problem starts with wording the message itself—using $5 words when 50 cent words will do. The fog factor (defined in Part 5) can destroy the message before it is even heard: What he said isn't what he meant to say or even what he thought he said. To distort matters more, what you thought he said is not what you said he said!

READING BETWEEN THE LINES—META MESSAGES

Meta messages (a term coined by Gerard Nierenberg, the author of *The Art of Negotiating*) refers to the messages between the lines—the ones that come from the context. Make sure that your own meta messages are the intended ones. For instance, when explaining how to fill out a task authorization form to an audience that includes small projects, use small values as examples to be consistent with their financial environment and avoid distractions.

A rather extreme meta message was conveyed by the NASA official who said he was "appalled" by Thiokol's recommendation not to launch the ill-fated Challenger mission. Unfortunately, the meta message suggesting that the recommendation be reversed got through and the launch recommendation was indeed reversed after 30 minutes of deliberation (subsequent events are described in the earlier Techniques section on polling).

Listen and respond to the meta-message, not to the words, but make sure that your meta-message is what you intend it to be.

THE PROJECT VOCABULARY DOESN'T EXIST UNTIL IT IS DOCUMENTED

Since we sometimes use the same word to mean very different things, each term that has multiple meanings needs to have multiple definitions, each documented in its own context. It is incumbent on both senders and receivers to clarify or to demand clarification when the context is missing or unclear. The best policy is to eliminate the ambiguity altogether and find (or invent) a substitute term. We address several ambiguities in our own vocabulary in the last section.

THE PROJECT VOCABULARY NEEDS TO HAVE CONTEXT

As Heinz Stoewer asserted, "Failures not only result from bad hardware engineering, software engineering, systems engineering, or project-management, they can also result from differing interpretations of engineering, communications, or management terms and associated cultures." Many terms can only be fully understood in their relationship with others and in the context of a specific project, process model, or project cycle. We included Part 2 for that very purpose. The cross-referencing we employ in Part 5 is another means to relate one term to another.

One way to provide the context is by incorporating examples or templates for use in the project. Part 5 provides examples or illustrations for the following terms that are some of the more widely used and important project management concepts and communication vehicles:

affinity diagram	product breakdown structure
cards-on-the-wall planning	project evaluation review technique
control chart	
critical path	project charter
decision tree	project office triad
earned value	requirements verification matrix
Gantt chart	
matrix management	schedule
network diagram	stakeholder
organization options	verification
performance measurement system	work breakdown structure

PRECISION IN COMMUNICATION—DEALING WITH AMBIGUITY

Some imprecise, confusing, or ambiguous terms have, through usage, become de facto industry standards. The very fact that they are commonly used can frequently interfere with communication on projects, leading to mistakes and costly delays. We draw your attention to them here and refer you to the definitions in Part 5.

In a project environment, the words *model* and *prototype* are not well understood, and common usage by technical people has distorted both terms to the point that they must be defined (or have an adjective modifier) with each use (but only if you want to be understood). Similarly, to be precise when you use *baseline* or *verification,* you should consider using the appropriate modifier to avoid miscommunication.

Quality, qualification, test, verification, and several combinations of these terms are frequently abused and misused. Consequently, our definitions for these terms are very detailed, some with examples or anecdotes to highlight subtleties.

The definition of *verification* as "proof of compliance with specifications" is generally understood. The reality that verification may be determined by test, inspection, demonstration, or analysis, is less well understood, as are the differences in these four methods since they sound similar. For instance, how does demonstration differ from test? *Verification by test* requires examination of performance data, whereas *verification by demonstration* means witnessing the operation and does not require data. When the team understands these subtle but important differences, precise communication is much more likely.

When referring to project cycle events, the terms *review* and *control gate* are often used interchangeably. This is unfortunate because they have very different meanings, purposes, and expected outcomes.

A *review* assesses status and, if the status is unsatisfactory, the review results in action items designed to achieve expected performance.

A *control gate* assesses work accomplished to determine if the results should be included in a new elaboration of the baseline and placed under formal change control.

Notice the very different expectations of these events and note also, that in much of the U.S. government environment, both status reviews and control gates are called reviews.

This confusion is further compounded by the very names of the control gates. For instance, the *Preliminary Design Review* known around the world as the PDR is not *preliminary,* does not review *design,* and to be precise, is not even a *review!* While this control gate does review evidence, the higher purpose is to approve concepts and their associated specifications. It is the obligation of the control gate event to prove that the specified performance is achievable within the state of the art and within the available schedule and resources. Laboratory testing and analysis are presented as evidence to support the claims. Hence, this "review" should be correctly titled, "Performance Guarantee Gate" where the concept and its performance is guaranteed by the offeror and is baselined.

Similarly, the *Critical Design Review* control gate known around the world as the CDR, is not a review, is no more critical than other control gates, and is certainly not more critical than the *System Concept Review* control gate. The CDR does review design but does so to ensure that the producers can do what is being asked for and that the results will be as expected. Production proof models and software feasibility prototypes are offered as evidence. Hence this "review" would be more appropriately titled the "Production Guarantee Gate."

Unfortunately, we are saddled with nomenclature issues such as these. Part 5 seeks further to clarify these and other ambiguities.

Periodic project reviews are often scheduled on a biweekly basis, but how often is the project review to occur? Twice a week or every other week? Unfortunately, consulting an English dictionary doesn't help. The consistent definition from the Merriam-Webster's Dictionary (2001), the Oxford American Dictionary (1999), and the American Heritage Dictionary (2000) is: "Biweekly, *adj., adv.,* 1. every two weeks. 2. twice a week." While all state that the first definition is preferred, confusion still occurs within project teams. Project management usage should be biweekly for every two weeks and semiweekly for twice a week, and likewise for monthly and yearly.

We'll close on a lighter note about a heavy substance, cement (which is not defined in Part 5). We frequently see newspaper articles about a new cement building or a newly completed cement highway. But driving down a cement highway would be a very dusty affair, since cement is a powdery ingredient in concrete (There are no cement highways, only concrete ones). We would never ask for a slice of flour to accompany our breakfast, so why has "cement" replaced "concrete" in our common vocabulary? Of course, it doesn't make any difference . . . unless you are in the building industry where it makes all the difference in the world.

2

FACILITATING COMMUNICATION THROUGH SYSTEMS MANAGEMENT

We ended Part 1 with the problems related to vocabulary context and ambiguity, which are two communication barriers that can be overcome with a frame of reference. To provide project context and language precision and to address many of the related ambiguities, we offer a reference communications infrastructure consisting of process models and ground rules. We have positioned these models in an environment that resolves an additional barrier to project communications: isolation between interfacing contributing disciplines. The defining framework is Systems Management.

SYSTEMS MANAGEMENT FUNDAMENTALS

Projects usually exist to address a business opportunity. Systems management is therefore rooted in the concept that, to achieve project success, all decisions must be business based. This concept demands collaboration between the business and technical aspects of the project. This may be difficult to achieve since business cases and technology often represent opposing forces that require compromise, usually through trade studies, negotiation, or similar processes. But developers often focus on what is possible technically regardless of what the customer wants, or the constraints of cost, or a limiting schedule.

It has been proven time and again that an attractive technical solution may not satisfy the business case. The English Channel Tunnel and two recent satellite-based mobile phone systems, Iridium and Globalstar (both of which filed for bankruptcy), are recent examples of wonderful technical solutions that failed financially. Each of these projects continued to press on to completion even though the original business justification had vanished and updated business case analysis would have projected financial disaster. "Iridium LLC collapsed after it could not find enough paying customers to repay its creditors," according to *SpaceNews*. Investors hoping for high returns lost most of their investment. A contrasting example and systems management case study is provided by the Øresund bridge between Copenhagen, Denmark, and Malmö, Sweden. This 10-year project finished in July 2000, two months early and on budget and, during its initial operations, it is meeting the business projections made almost seven years earlier.

Sometimes the technical need is valid, but the cost of achieving a solution is prohibitive. The newly formed Iridium Satellite LLC, for instance, is planning to launch an additional 96 satellites in 2004 or 2005, which is surprising until you realize that Iridium Satellite LLC was able to purchase the assets of its bankrupt predecessor, Iridium LLC, in 1999 for $25 million, less than half a percent of the $5 billion spent in developing and fielding the original system.

How do we understand the evolving business case so that the business case drives the technical and financial decisions throughout the project cycle?

The project cycle with its periods and phases provides the overall strategic and tactical management approach to achievement of the project's objectives. The project cycle's control gates provide the approval discipline for the evolving baseline. The evolving baseline must be continuously tested for business case viability. Systems management requires that for on-going system integrity the three aspects of the project cycle—business, budget, and technical—remain congruent at all times.

When systems management fundamentals guide the management of projects, the following ground rules apply:

- The business aspect of the project cycle must drive the overall management approach.
- The three aspects of the project cycle must start congruent and remain congruent as changes occur.
- The project's business case must be flowed down along with the requirements to all levels of solution decomposition.
- All design reviews and control gates, although heavy in technical content, must be conducted as business-driven reviews.
- All control gates must confirm that the team is:
  - (1) Building the right solution—in response to the business case at the level of decomposition under consideration and at least one level above.
  - (2) Building the solution right.

To implement a culture of systems management, these ground rules must become part of the culture just as CMM, CMMI, and ISO encourage practices and behavior conducive to achieving predictable results in building the solution right. The details of the project cycle and the implementation of these five basic rules of conduct are expanded in the following sections.

VISUALIZING SYSTEMS MANAGEMENT— THE VISUAL PROCESS MODELS

Imagine the challenges faced by a newly formed jazz group, composed of highly trained specialists, each capable of an excellent solo performance.

Consider further one of the freest expressions of creativity in music—improvisational jazz. One of the apparent mysteries is that, while it seems free and unstructured, it doesn't result in uncontrolled noise. Music is produced, just as surely as music is produced by a symphony orchestra, which clearly requires a musical score.

However, each jazz session is unique—just like a project. It is improvisational and thus being created at the time. The fact that music is reliably produced by the combined efforts of a group of jazz musicians suggests that there is an underlying process, which facilitates the musicians in a group setting.

The answer is that jazz has rules. For example, each piece has a time signature. The musicians both follow a process and also exercise controls that enable them to free their creativity within boundaries because they don't have to keep inventing basic rules.

When musicians of any kind come together for a short-term engagement, they depend on five essentials: a common music communications language; teamwork; a score or plan (cycle); guidelines, rules, and techniques (leadership and management elements); and resources and environment (organizational commitment). The process model for a successful project team is based on these same five essentials:

 Communication—The language and the techniques used by a particular person or group to achieve understanding. In project management, the essential that enables team members to interact effectively and function as a team.

 Teamwork— Efficiently working together to achieve a common goal, with acknowledged interdependency and trust, acceptance of a common code of conduct, and with a shared reward.

 Project cycle—The project's overall strategic and tactical management approach that is performed in periods and phases and is punctuated by baseline approval control gates. The cycle usually starts with the identification of user needs and ends with disposal. The project cycle contains three aspects: business, budget, and technical.

 Management elements—The 10 categories of interactive management responsibilities, techniques, and tools that are situationally applied in all phases of the project cycle by all organizations participating in the project to manage the project through the project cycle.

 Organizational commitment—The supporting foundation of the project that includes: (1) the project manager's charter to do the job; (2) an organizational culture responsive to the project manager's orchestration of the project; (3) the financial and other resources necessary to accomplish the job; and (4) the appropriate tools and training for efficient execution.

The model differentiates between practices that are ever present, those that are sequential, and those that are situational. As we visualize the structure of each essential and the relationships among them, communication, teamwork, and organizational commitment are seen as perpetual properties of a project, while the project cycle is sequential and the project management elements are situational.

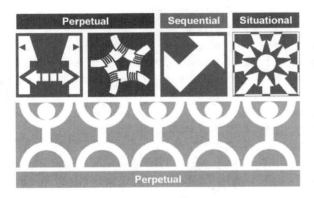

To illustrate the relationship between the situationally applied management elements and the sequential project cycle, a third dimension is required. The first nine management elements are:

1. Project Requirements
2. Organizational Options
3. Project Team
4. Project Planning
5. Opportunities and Risks
6. Project Control
7. Project Visibility
8. Project Status
9. Corrective Action

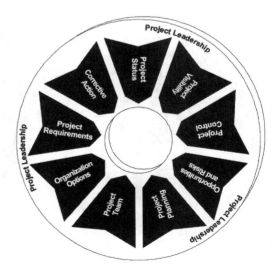

They are depicted as the spokes of a wheel, held intact by its rim, Project Leadership.

The project cycle is visualized as an axle with the three congruent aspects depicted as the core:

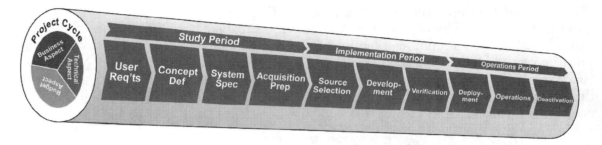

The wheel progressing along the axle represents the sequential process, while its dynamic rotation re presents the situational application of the techniques and tools of the ten management elements. This project management process is supported by the ever-present piers of communication and teamwork mounted on a solid foundation of organizational commitment.

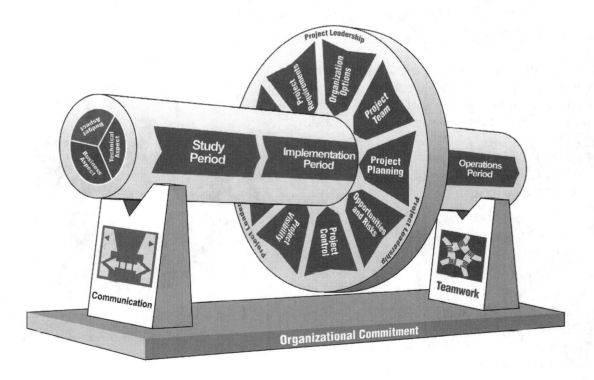

THE PROJECT CYCLE AND THE SYSTEMS MANAGEMENT GROUND RULES

Professional project management organizations usually have a standard or template project cycle that sequences their preferred management logic. This standard cycle is then tailored to the special characteristics of the project at hand. The resultant tailored project cycle becomes the parent or driver of the tactical logical project network that will be developed during planning.

As illustrated in Figure 2.1, the project cycle has Periods (such as Study, Implementation, and Operations), and Phases within the periods (such as Concept Definition and Verification). Phases include Activities such as Conduct Concept Trade Studies, Products such as Concept Trade Study Results and Concept Definition Document, and Control Gates or Phase Transition Reviews such as Concept Definition Control Gate.

The three aspects of the project cycle can be viewed as layers (Table 2.1). Each layer—business, budget, and technical—

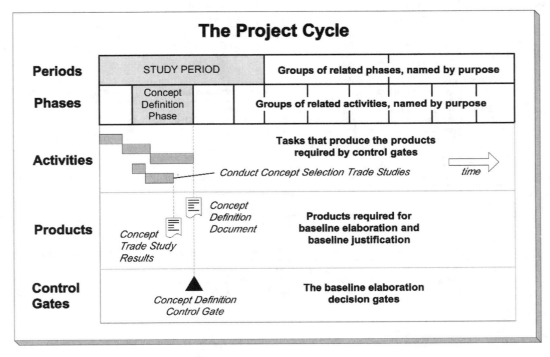

FIGURE 2.1   The project cycle.

SYSTEMS MANAGEMENT GROUND RULE 1

The business aspect of the project cycle drives the overall management approach.

In designing the project cycle, all three aspects must be conceived and charted in sync. The business aspect is the authority and the driver of the other two aspects. Budget and technical aspects must always be responsive to the business case to ensure solution viability.

The project cycle is the highest level parent of the tactical approach required to succeed in the project. Therefore, it is imperative that the project cycle represents the optimum overall management approach, which will then be responded to by all parties when planning the detailed logic and when executing the logic-driven plan.

TABLE 2.1   The Three Aspects of the Project Cycle

Period	Study				Implementation			Operations		
	Figuring Out What to Do				*Doing It*			*Using It*		
Phase	User Requirements	Concept Definition	System Specification	Acquisition Preparation	Source Selection	Development	Verification	Deployment	Operations and Maintenance	Deactivation
	What project is it? Is it worth doing? How do we acquire it?				*Are we getting value?*			*Are we glad we did it?*		
Business Aspect	Recognize opportunity	Develop business case	Prove business feasibility	Select acquisition approach	Select best value supplier	Manage suppliers In-process ROI projection		Manage doers	Continuous improvement and value	Evaluate ROI
	Can we afford to do it and is money available?				*Are financials on plan?*			*Was it financially worth it?*		
Budget Aspect	Determine resource availability and source	Predict should-cost and phasing	Refine should-cost and phasing	Ensure phased resource availability	Determine most probable cost	Manage budgets, funding and value		Manage value	Manage value	Provide closure
	What is the problem and the solution?				*How to do it and prove it?*			*Is the customer smiling?*		
Technical Aspect	Collect user requirements, user CONOPS and select system requirements	Select concept and develop system CONOPS	Prove technical feasibility and develop specification	Identify capable suppliers	Select capable supplier	Manage design-to, build-to; buy, build, code	Integration and verification	Ensure validation	Provide technical support	Provide technical support

contains its own logic set. The interwoven events for the three aspects constitute the total cycle, which can also be considered as the *project opportunity cycle*. The project cycle can span from user wants to project disposal or a reduced scope in accordance with the project objectives.

The business aspect drives the project and is based on the business case, which must justify the pursuit of, and the strategy for accomplishing the opportunity. The business aspect includes the proving of the business case complete with expected business results.

The budget aspect represents the management approach for resourcing the project and effective fiscal management. It includes development of the should-cost estimate for the concept under consideration, which must match the customer's target cost.

The technical aspect identifies the activities and events required to provide the optimum technical solution in the most efficient manner, a systems engineering responsibility. Development strategies, such as incremental or evolutionary, and delivery strategies such as single or multiple, should be decided on and reflected in the technical aspect of the cycle. In time-critical

---

SYSTEMS MANAGEMENT GROUND RULE 2

The three aspects must start congruent and be maintained so as changes occur.

As projects progress, it is quite normal for things to change. Requirements, schedules, funding, and technology all have a way of changing and often at the worst possible time. All too often these changes are accommodated without examining the impact to the other aspects of the project cycle.

To ensure that congruency exists, change boards must revisit all three aspects when considering baseline changes to take into account the associated drivers that influence or are influenced by the proposed change. This forces the necessary collaboration between the necessary disciplines. If changes to any of the project cycle aspects are required then they must be baselined and communicated to all stakeholders.

projects, the baseline elaboration control gates set the timing of the cycle.

The project cycle processes are best visualized when portrayed as a Vee format (Figure 2.2), rather than as purely horizontal. This format more accurately illustrates decomposition from system requirements and concepts down to detailed code, part, and assembly processes and then upward consistent with fabrication and integration of the system elements into the completed system.

The Vee Model is a system development model designed to help understand the complexity associated with developing systems. Predecessor software development models of the Waterfall and Spiral, while making important contributions to the understanding of software development, fall short in conveying several

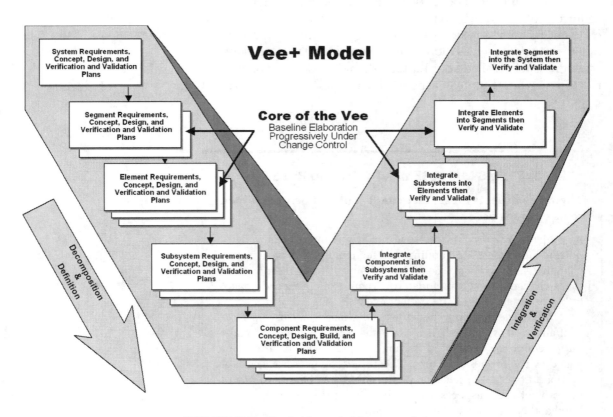

FIGURE 2.2   Project cycle Vee+ model.

SYSTEMS MANAGEMENT GROUND RULE 3

The project's business case must be flowed down along with the requirements to all levels of decomposition.

All projects are driven by the business case, usually in response to economic opportunity or threat (competitive or political). The business case (project opportunity) substantiates the need for the project and the expected return created by the deployment of the solution. Return on investment and the break-even point are metrics that are often estimated and quoted to justify the project. For commercial products and services, empirical data is acquired by precedence, competitive trends, or test marketing in sample market zones. This information is then extrapolated to the global business case for market share and availability projections. For government projects, the business case deals with threats and threat mitigation.

As the project solution is decomposed into segments, elements, and subsystems down to assemblies, the business case implications must also be correspondingly flowed down.

In doing so, the business case takes a different form and is represented by solution criticality, risk, budgets, and schedules. These drivers must be defined to the development manager as part of the User CONOPS for that element and should also be part of the Work Authorization (Internal Contract) against which the work will be performed. As control gates are held for each entity, satisfaction of these criteria must be assured.

important concepts necessary to doing system development right the first time and every time.

The Vee model is rooted in the project cycle, which is displayed from left to right to represent project time and maturity. Coupled with this depiction is the recognition of levels of decomposition, which are illustrated in the vertical dimension from top to bottom. The User is at the highest level and parts and lines of code are at the lowest.

At each level, there is a direct correlation between activities on the left and right sides of the Vee. This is deliberate. For example, the method of verification to be used on the right must be determined on the left—at the time requirements are defined—

for each set of requirements developed and documented at each decomposition level. This minimizes the chances that requirements are specified in a way that cannot be measured or verified.

In Figures 2.2, 2.3, and 2.4, the increasing thickness of the Vee (orthogonal to the paper) illustrates the number of entities at each level of decomposition, which relates to the complexity of the system. The concept of an evolving baseline, progressively increasing in depth and under change control is represented by the Vee core. The left leg of the Vee represents Decomposition and Definition and the right leg represents Integration and Verification.

An important attribute of the Vee diagram is the *Time Now* line, which explicitly highlights the iterative nature of the development process. Iterations between levels of decomposition are

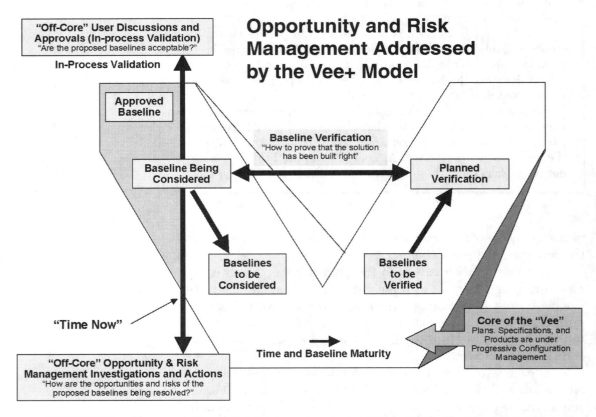

FIGURE 2.3   Opportunity and risk management addressed by the Vee+ model.

Integration and Verification Management Addressed by the Vee+ Model

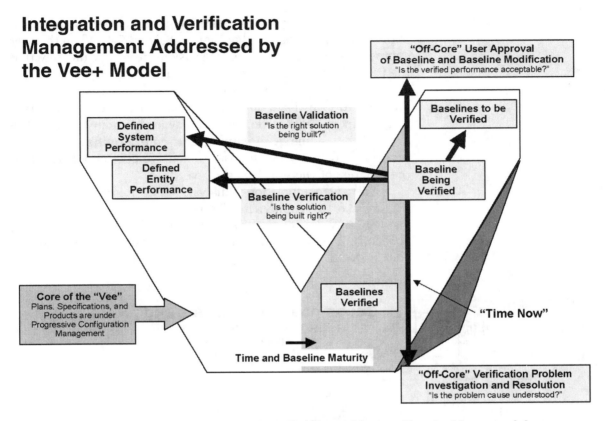

FIGURE 2.4   Integration and verification addressed by the Vee+ model.

an important part of system development and definition. Since one can never go back in time, all such iterations are vertical on the *Time Now* line.

The most significant contribution of the Vee is recognition of the off-core activities. Downward off-core activities on the left leg allow investigation of opportunities and risks to justify baseline decisions on the Vee core. The off-core results are not baselined but are essential to justifying the on-core decisions. Unlike the spiral model, these opportunity and risk investigations may be conducted in series with or in parallel with normal development activities.

Upward off-core activities encourage in-process validation with the user, as illustrated in Figures 2.3 and 2.4. When the user approves progressive baselining decisions, it is very unlikely that the user will ultimately be disappointed.

Downward off-core activities on the right side of the Vee are used to investigate and resolve anomalies discovered during integration and verification, which may lead to adjustment of the as-verified baseline. Again, upward off-core activities provide in-process validation with the user to achieve continuous buy-in to the progress of the solution as it is verified.

The Decomposition Analysis and Resolution Process (Figure 2.6) as applied in Figure 2.5, orthogonal to the left Vee leg, provides for the trade studies leading to the baselining decisions. This expansion of the Vee+ Model is known as the Vee++ Model.

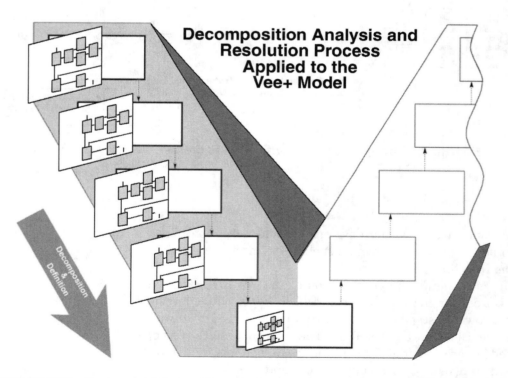

FIGURE 2.5   Decomposition and resolution process applied to the Vee+ model.

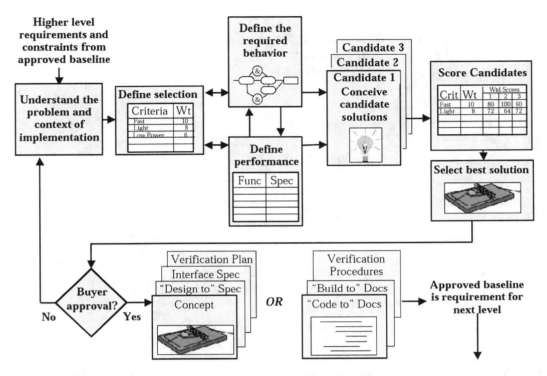

FIGURE 2.6 Decomposition analysis and resolution process.

The Verification Analysis and Resolution Process (Figure 2.8) as applied in Figure 2.7, orthogonal to the right Vee+ leg, provides for anomaly correction and/or baseline modification. (For more information regarding these processes see *Visualizing Project Management* published by John Wiley and Sons, 2000.)

THE IMPORTANCE OF CONTROL GATES

A control gate is a baseline approval event in the project cycle, sufficiently important to be defined and included in the schedule. Control gates represent the major decision points in the project cycle and ensure that new activities are not pursued until the required baseline elaboration on which new activities depend, are

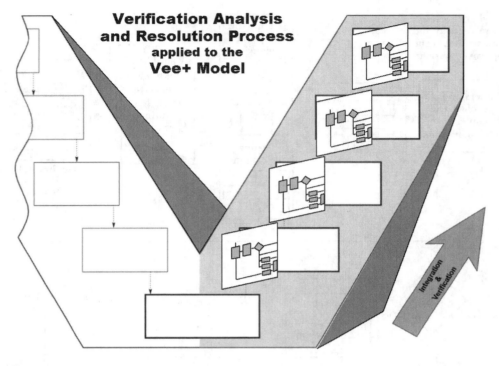

FIGURE 2.7   Verification analysis and resolution process applied to the Vee+ model.

satisfactorily completed. The primary objectives of control gates are to:

- Ensure that critical products are sufficiently complete to be baselined and placed under formal change control.
- Ensure that the team is prepared and that the risk of proceeding is acceptable.
- Promote a synergistic team approach

A control gate requires critical review to evaluate status and obtain approval to proceed according to the project plan. The work performed is examined and, if satisfactory, is approved and baselined. On successful completion of a control gate, the appropriate agreements (usually in the form of documents—products

SYSTEMS MANAGEMENT GROUND RULE 4

All control gates and design reviews, although heavy in technical content, are business reviews.

While many control gat e titles sound like technical reviews and they are often conducted as such, under the concept of systems management all control gates are business reviews. As such they must visit and answer these questions:

- Is it affordable?
- Can it be delivered when needed?

This approach keeps the focus on satisfying the business aspects of the project rather than becoming a technical hobby shop.

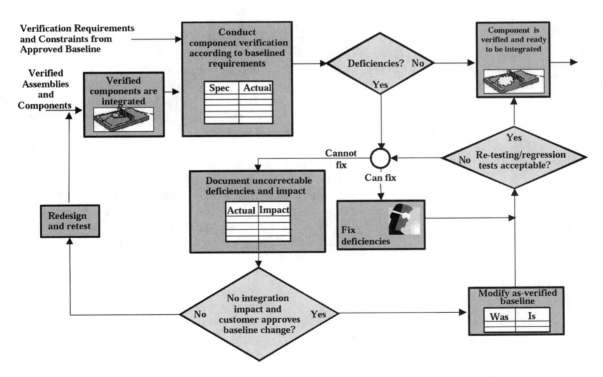

FIGURE 2.8 Verification analysis and resolution process.

SYSTEMS MANAGEMENT GROUND RULE 5

All control gates must confirm that we are *building the right solution* and that we are *building it right*.

Every control gate must answer two questions: *Are we building the right overall solution and are we building the overall solution right?* The first question must respond to the business case at the level of decomposition under consideration and one level above. This requires in-process validation with the users and customers of the system.

Once we are satisfied that as of the current control gate the overall solution is proceeding in the correct direction, then we must continue evaluating the cost and schedule aspects at each level of decomposition, where two additional key questions must be satisfied. *Are we building the right entity and are we building the entity right?* To answer these questions, the business case for each entity must be the current business case properly flowed down with accompanying criticality, risk, cost, and schedule.

To answer the question, "Are we building the right entity?," the review must address the latest, as-baselined configuration, one level up from that being reviewed. It also must address the evolving states of the entities being developed and in various stages of baselining at the same level of decomposition.

To answer the question, "Are we building the entity right?" while on the left side of the Vee, requires comparison to best practices and lessons learned from experts in the technology involved. When the project has progressed to the right side of the Vee, this question is answered by comparing the entity as-built configuration with the entity design specifications.

Had Iridium used this approach the concept of a satellite constellation to serve cell phones might have been abandoned before launch when it became apparent that the target markets were already being served by much lower cost ground based cells. For most users the wrong system was being built perfectly right—a system management failure of the worst kind. (Now with capital investments at a small fraction of the original, the new business case depends on competitive operational costs—a future systems management challenge with a much better chance for success.)

of a project cycle phase) will be put under configuration management, requiring change control authority to effect any changes.

A typical control gate is the Preliminary Design Review (design-to review) where the concept and specifications for the concept are guaranteed to be achievable. Laboratory test data and other evidence are offered to prove these claims.

A second typical control gate is the Critical Design Review (build to review) where the actual shop drawings, material and process specifications, and code-to documentation are offered for baselining. This is the review where the producers guarantee that they can build to the documentation offered. Evidence to prove these claims are work samples demonstrating specification achievement, process repeatability, and mitigation of other risky areas of compliance.

Too few control gates may allow the project to operate out of control. Too many may overburden the project with unnecessary administration.

CONCLUSION

Producing the right solution right is a formidable task. Systems management is a proven approach for visualizing, comprehending, implementing, and communicating the processes needed to empower and support the project team. The appropriate process scaling, tailoring, and training can make the difference between project success and failure.

3

THE COLLABORATIVE ENVIRONMENT

We have been viewing communications challenges from the perspective of the technical disciplines, management processes, and stakeholders involved in an active project or group of projects. Now we drop back and look at the global environment created by the professional associations and standards organization that frame those projects. To provide further context for the terms and definitions, we characterize the systems management communication environment by profiling the professional associations and standards organizations that have the greatest influence on the practice and the vocabulary of systems management and on the practitioners, individually. The first section provides an overview of the nine interrelated organizations, each of which is then described in alphabetical order.

RELATIONSHIPS AMONG THE MAJOR PROJECT MANAGEMENT, SYSTEMS ENGINEERING, AND SOFTWARE ENGINEERING ORGANIZATIONS

Table 3.1 is an overview of the nine organizations. The degree of shading for each column is explained in the sections that follow.

TABLE 3.1 Overview of Organizations

	Professional Associations	Standards and/or Models	Provide Certification
INCOSE	███		▨▨▨
SESA	███		
IPMA	**Individual Focus**		███
PMI	███	███	███
ASAPM	███		▨▨▨
SEI		███	▨▨▨
ISO		███	░░░
EIA		███	
IEEE	░░░	███	

ORGANIZATIONAL FOCUS

Those shaded in the first column are all professional associations. The black shading identifies those that focus on individual members, facilitating professional growth in specific disciplines. As a large professional association, the IEEE has a broad individual program, but also influences organizational practices through its industry standards activities. The others are not professional associations and focus on external organizations. The SEI, ISO, and EIA address the capability or practices of an organization, ranging from a functional unit to a company or government agency.

STANDARDS AND/OR MODELS

Table 3.2 identifies representative standards of practice, capability/competency criteria, or evaluation guidelines that are generally

TABLE 3.2 Overview of Standards and Models

Best Practices	Processes	Competency Models	Evaluation Guidelines
INCOSE	SE Handbook, *SE BOK*	SECAM	
IPMA		Four level model	
PMI	PMBOK®	PMP®	
ASAPM	Guidelines	*Development*	
SEI		CMM, CMMI	ARC, SCAMPI
ISO	12207, 15288		15504
EIA	ANSI/EIA-632	EIA/IS 731	
IEEE	1220, 12207.0		

accepted in the industry. Those in italics are under development at the time of this book's publication. For further details, refer to the later sections for each organization.

Figure 3.1 is one view of the genealogy of the SEI CMMI Product Suite. We use it to illustrate one of the major collaborative and integrative efforts among the organizations and disciplines involved in systems management.

CERTIFICATION

Table 3.3 identifies those organizations that provide some form of certification, either at the individual or organization level. Those shaded in black in Table 3.1 certify their members as qualified to provide professional services, usually by proficiency testing. The cross hatch indicates that the organization's certification program is under development. The SEI (dark gray in Figure 3.1), refers to its form of certification as authorization. It authorizes four classes of reviewers (see details below under Software Engineering Institute) to use its appraisal framework through a program of training, mentoring, observation, and performance criteria. The authorized appraisers rate organizations as to their competency level. The ISO (light gray in Figure 3.1) does not directly certify or authorize, but rather provides the certification criteria through its standards groups, such as ISO 9000. For further details, refer to the Certification section under the specific organization.

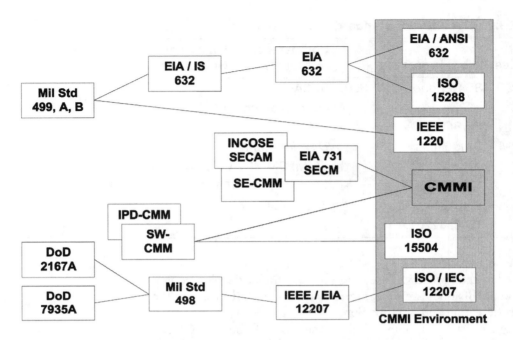

FIGURE 3.1 Standards relationships illustrated by CMMI genealogy.

TABLE 3.3   Overview of Certification

	Discipline Competency	Appraiser Competency	Certification Criteria
INCOSE	Developing		
IPMA	Four levels		Three stages
PMI	PMP®		
ASAPM	Developing		
SEI		Four classes	CMM. CMMI
ISO			ISO 9000

AMERICAN SOCIETY FOR THE ADVANCEMENT OF PROJECT MANAGEMENT (asapm)

The American Society for the Advancement of Project Management (asapm) is a not-for-profit professional society. It is dedicated to advancing the project management discipline through professional growth of both members and the profession, enhancement of the profession, and best use of practices, procedures, and techniques. Its mission is to provide opportunities for U.S. industry and individuals to improve their project management competencies through a series of programs and projects that share information and demonstrate best practices.

The asapm is a member-driven organization that encourages open resources and collaboration, and offers its members choices regarding their rights for each contribution of intellectual property.

MODELS, STANDARDS, AND CERTIFICATION

This organization develops Best Practice Guidelines to codify project initiation, planning, controlling, and implementing. The asapm Standards Development Program is open to all experience levels, members and nonmembers, practitioners and academics.

The asapm Competency Model is intended to advance learning opportunities beyond knowledge transfer and skill building into competency and is to be the basis for the Learning, Certification and Standards Program.

SCOPE AND IMPACT

The American Society for the Advancement of Project Management is focused on the United States with an ambitious program encompassing standards, competency models, and member certification.

If the asapm can achieve critical mass and industry recognition, it could directly raise the bar on project management professionalism. Through organizational competition, the new society might influence the practices and policies of the PMI®.

ELECTRONIC INDUSTRIES ALLIANCE (EIA)

In 1997, EIA changed from the Electronic Industries Association to the Electronic Industries Alliance, the primary industry association representing the U.S. electronics community and its six trade associations:

- Consumer Electronics Association (CEA)

  Represents over 1000 companies within the U.S. consumer technology industry, offering promotional programs and member certification in specific technologies.

- Electronic Components, Assemblies, and Materials Association (ECA)

  Represents the electronics industry sector comprised of manufacturers and suppliers of passive and active electronic components, component arrays and assemblies, and commercial and industrial electronic equipment and supplies.

- Electronic Industries Foundation (EIF)

  Helps young people develop critical science and technology skills vital to the electronic industries workplace through programs and partnerships with businesses, universities and nonprofit organizations.

- Government Electronics & Information Technology Association (GEIA)

  Represents the high-tech industry doing business with the U.S. government. Members are companies that provide the government with electronics and information technology solutions.

- Solid State Technology Association (JEDEC) (formerly, Joint Electron Device Engineering Council)

  The semiconductor engineering standardization body of the EIA.

- Telecommunications Industry Association (TIA)

  Represents providers of communications and information technology products and services for the global marketplace through standards development, market development, and trade promotion programs.

The EIA mission is to promote the market development and competitiveness of the U.S. high-tech industry through domestic and international policy efforts.

The EIA Technology Council is a body of member companies that explores how emerging technologies may affect segments of the electronics industry. EIA has an affiliate relationship with the Internet Security Alliance, a collaborative effort with the SEI's CERT Coordination Center (CERT/CC).

MODELS, STANDARDS, AND CERTIFICATION

The EIA does not address certification. However, two EIA standards have a broad and continuing influence on systems management:

ANSI/EIA-632 Processes for Engineering a System is the result of GEIA project SP3537, a joint activity with INCOSE to prepare a national process standard for engineering a system, which replaced MIL STD 499B. It is a high-level process standard that treats all stages of engineering a system, addressing all aspects of the engineering life cycle. It is applicable to both industry and government, it encourages tailoring to allow efficient application to any enterprise that performs engineering.

EIA/IS 731 Systems Engineering Capability Model (SECM) was a joint project of GEIA (G-47), EPIC, and INCOSE, to bring together the SE CMM (EPIC) and the SECAM (INCOSE) into a single capability model. The purpose was to minimize confusion within the industry and to relate the resulting capability model to the EIA-632.

SCOPE AND IMPACT

The EIA is comprised of more than 2,000 member companies, including many of the most dynamic and fastest growing companies in the world. Accredited by the American National Standards Institute (ANSI), EIA provides the forum for U.S. industry to develop standards and publications in the technical areas of electronic components, consumer electronics, electronic information, telecommunications, and Internet security.

The EIA's standards are widely accepted and its ANSI accreditation provides a means to impact ISO standards, as well. EIA

632 standard and ISO 15288 standard, while complimentary with different roles and details, have greatest impact when combined.

EIA-731 is one of the two major sources for the SEI CMMI Product Suite.

INSTITUTE OF ELECTRICAL AND ELECTRONICS ENGINEERS (IEEE)

Institute of Electrical and Electronics Engineers (IEEE) is a non-profit, technical professional association. It was formed in 1963 from a merger of the American Institute of Electrical Engineers with the Institute of Radio Engineers, two professional societies that had competed for membership since 1884. The IEEE (Eye-triple-E) helps advance global prosperity by promoting the engineering process of creating, developing, integrating, sharing, and applying knowledge about electrical and information technologies and sciences for the benefit of humanity and the profession.

MODELS, STANDARDS, AND CERTIFICATION

IEEE STD 1220–1994—Trial-Use Standard for Application and Management of the Systems Engineering Process defines the process and interdisciplinary tasks required throughout a system's life cycle to transform customer needs, requirements, and constraints into a solution.

IEEE/EIA 12207.0–1996—Industry implementation of International Standard ISO/IEC. The ISO/IEC12207 Standard for IT Software life cycle processes is a common framework for developing and managing software projects.

SCOPE AND IMPACT

IEEE membership is approaching one half-million members, at a 5 percent annual growth rate. It is predicted that only about half will be from the the United States by year 2010. Approximately 60 percent of the IEEE members come from industry, with smaller segments coming from government and academia. Over one half of its members are in computer/communications industries. Aerospace representation is about 2 percent.

The Institute is organized as 28 separate professional societies, each with its own publications and conferences. IEEE influence is significant due to sheer size of its membership and breadth of involvement in U.S. and international high-tech industries.

The IEEE Standards Association has an agreement with the Electronic Industries Alliance for joint development of a family of standards addressing project and product life cycles. While IEEE standards lack the impact of EIA or ISO, some organizations prefer IEEE's level of detail, as in the case of IEEE STD 1220 versus EIA 632 and/or ISO 15288.

INTERNATIONAL COUNCIL ON SYSTEMS ENGINEERING (INCOSE)

The International Council on Systems Engineering (INCOSE) is a not-for-profit membership organization founded in 1990 by 35 senior technical managers. Originally confined to the United States, and called National Council on Systems Engineering (NCOSE), the organization expanded to international scope and changed its name to INCOSE in 1995. INCOSE is an international authoritative body promoting the application of an interdisciplinary approach and means to enable the realization of successful systems.

As defined by INCOSE, its mission is "to foster the definition, understanding, and practice of world class systems engineering in industry, academia, and government." The major goal of the organization is to establish professional practice standards and encourage governmental and industrial support for research and educational programs. INCOSE encourages and sponsors conferences, seminars, and courses. It provides its members with necessary information in order to improve the dissemination of the systems engineering knowledge base. It also helps increase the funding of research and educational activities that enhance the practice of systems engineering.

MODELS, STANDARDS, AND CERTIFICATION

INCOSE is developing a certification program for system engineering practitioners. INCOSE does not publish its own standards. The organization's standards involvement is primarily participative rather than as a standards leader or owner.

INCOSE has a working group responsible for developing and maintaining its Systems Engineering Body of Knowledge (SE BOK). INCOSE has published a Systems Engineering Handbook that will be the knowledge baseline for their certification examination.

SCOPE AND IMPACT

INCOSE currently has over four thousand members and is growing about 10 percent annually. Members are from over 30 countries, and represent commercial companies, government organizations, educational institutions, and consulting firms. Its regions and chapters encompass Canada, Finland, Germany, The Netherlands, Norway, Sweden, the United Kingdom, and the United States.

INCOSE has been actively involved in several important standards activities in cooperation with the Electronic Industries Alliance (EIA), including: EIA-632, Processes for Engineering a System and EIA/IS-731 Systems Engineering Capability Model, a source standard for the SEI CMMI Product Suite, which is expected have major industry and government impact (refer to the Electronic Industries Alliance and Software Engineering Institute sections for further details).

INTERNATIONAL PROJECT MANAGEMENT ASSOCIATION (IPMA)

The International Project Management Association (IPMA) was formed in 1965 as an international project discussion group. IPMA is a nonprofit, Swiss-registered organization, based in the United Kingdom. Its function is to be the prime promoter of project management internationally, through its membership network of national project management associations around the world.

MODELS, STANDARDS, AND CERTIFICATION

IPMA has a four-level certification program and oversees certification programs of its national associations through that national association's designated certification body. The oversight includes validation by the IPMA on a regular basis. The IPMA certification model is based on four levels of tested knowledge and demonstrated competence, which includes experience and personal attitude:

A—Program or Projects Director
B—Project Manager
C—Project Management Professional
D—Project Management Practitioner

The certification process involves three stages:

1. Applications, self-assessment, and references.
2. Workshops, project reports, and an exam.
3. Interviews and exams.

SCOPE AND IMPACT

IPMA has approximately 20,000 members (primarily in Europe, but also in Africa and Asia), and consists of a number of national associations (member countries). IPMA National Associations average 500 to 1000 members, managed by a Board of Officers. IPMA offers different types of membership for individuals, higher education institutions, and corporate organizations.

Every two years, an IPMA World Congress on Project Management takes place in Europe. It draws around 1000 participants from all over the world and includes workshops, panels, exhibitors, and papers. The first Congress was held 1967 in Vienna with participants from 30 different countries.

The primary IPMA influence is through its certification program, on which the *asapm* program is based.

INTERNATIONAL ORGANIZATION FOR STANDARDIZATION (ISO)

The International Organization for Standardization (ISO) is a worldwide, nongovernmental federation of national standards bodies established in 1947. The mission of this international organization is to promote the development of standardization and related activities in the world with a view to facilitating the international exchange of goods and services, and to developing cooperation in the spheres of intellectual, scientific, technological and economic activity.

MODELS, STANDARDS, AND CERTIFICATION

ISO Certification or Registration (used interchangeably by ISO) means that a third party gives written assurance that a product, service, system, process, or material conforms to specific ISO requirements and standards. ISO does not control the certification bodies. It contributes to best practice and consistency in assessment activities through ISO/IEC Guide 62, which provides the general requirements for certification bodies carrying out assessment and certification/registration.

ISO standards that impact the practice of systems management include:

- ISO 15288 Systems Engineering—Systems Life Cycle processes (initiated in 1995). Stage: 40.20 DIS ballot initiated (approve/publish expected in 2002).
- ISO 12207 Software Engineering—Software Life Cycle processes (initiated 1995). Stage: 50.20 FDIS ballot initiated (earlier version published in 2001).
- ISO/IEC TR 15504—Software process assessment (published in 1998). A series of nine standards covering the capability model, performing assessments, assessor competency, and process improvement.

SCOPE AND IMPACT

ISO is a network of national standards institutes from 140 countries, one standards body from each country. The U.S. member in ISO is ANSI (American National Standards Institute). ISO consists of 187 technical committees, 552 subcommittees, 2,100 working groups, and 19 ad hoc study groups. ISO members have processed over 700,000 standards drafts, technical regulations and other standards-type documents from all over the world. 1,353 technical meetings are held annually in 29 countries.

ISO's work results in international agreements, which are published as International Standards. ISO has issued over 13,000 International Standards and standards-type documents. The current rate of release is about 1,000 per year.

PROJECT MANAGEMENT INSTITUTE (PMI®)

Project Management Institute (PMI®) was founded in 1969 to foster the profession of project management through education, certification, creation and promulgation of standards, and sponsorship of professional meetings. The PMI® is the largest not-for-profit project management professional association. It establishes project management standards, provides seminars, educational programs, and professional certification. PMI® members are individuals practicing and studying project management in many different industry areas, including aerospace, automotive, business management, construction, engineering, financial services, information technology, pharmaceuticals, and telecommunications.

MODELS, STANDARDS, AND CERTIFICATION

PMI® publishes the Project Management Body of Knowledge Guide (PMBOK® Guide), a globally recognized handbook for project management practices, approved as ANSI/PMI 99-001-200 standard. The stated purpose of the PMBOK® Guide is to identify and describe that subset of the general body of knowledge in project management that is generally accepted. PMI® also publishes specific practice standards such as the Practice Standard for Work Breakdown Structures.

The PMI® certifies individuals as a Project Management Professional (PMP®) through multiple-choice tests based on the PMBOK® Guide and project experience. PMP® certification is maintained by earning Professional Development Units (PDUs) through professional activities, academic courses, and/or training provided by PMI® Registered Training Providers. Nearly half of the PMI® members are certified as a PMP®.

SCOPE AND IMPACT

PMI® has over 80,000 members from 125 countries worldwide and has experienced strong growth since introducing the PMP® certification program. Over 70 percent of the PMI® members are in the United States, and slightly over 10 percent are in Canada. Over one-third of PMI® members come from computer industry, information technology, and telecommunications sectors.

PMI® cooperative agreements include the Construction Management Association of America and the Institute of Industrial Engineers.

Holding a PMI® certification is the de facto basis for judging an individual's knowledge about Project Management (especially in the United States). Many organizations encourage Project Managers to seek PMP® certification. In some companies, PMP® certification can be a condition for managing projects or for earning bonus pay.

The PMBOK® from PMI® with its nine process areas, is widely accepted in the PM vocabulary of many organizations.

SOFTWARE ENGINEERING INSTITUTE (SEI)

The Software Engineering Institute (SEI) was founded in 1984 as a federally funded research and development center sponsored by the U.S. Department of Defense and operated under contract to Carnegie Mellon University. The SEI mission is to provide leadership in advancing the state of the practice of software engineering to improve the quality of systems that depend on software. They accomplish this mission by promoting the evolution of software engineering from an ad hoc, labor-intensive activity to an orderly discipline that is well managed and supported by technology. The purpose is not only to advance the practice of software engineering, but also to make predictable the acquiring, developing, and sustaining of software-intensive systems, from design and through operation.

MODELS, STANDARDS, AND CERTIFICATION

One of the primary methods SEI has to carry out its mission is its capability maturity models, which include the SW-CMM,

People-CMM, and the CMMI Product Suite. The SW-CMM has been in use since 1987 and consists of five maturity levels and 18 Key Process Areas (such as Software Configuration Management and Software Quality Assurance). The CMMI Product Suite, introduced in August 2000 and referenced extensively in this dictionary, resulted from a major cooperative effort. Representatives of government and commercial organizations were involved in the development of the CMMI Product Suite, including the term definitions and the Standard CMMI Appraisal Method for Process Improvement (SCAMPI). The CMMI Product Suite covers both software and systems engineering disciplines and will eventually replace CMM and encompass other source standards.

The SEI authorizes Lead Appraisers, Lead Evaluators, Lead Assessors, and Evaluators to use the CMM Appraisal Framework and Appraisal Requirements for CMMI (ARC) through a program of training, mentoring, observation, and performance criteria. The authorized reviewers rate organizations as to their organizational maturity or process capability level. The appraisals are of three types:

1. Software Capability Evaluation (SCE) for external contract/acquisition, capability, and qualification purposes.
2. CMM-Based Appraisal for Internal Process Improvement (CBA-IPI) to accurately identify strengths and weaknesses.
3. Standard CMMI Appraisal Method for Process Improvement (SCAMPI), the CMMI-based method for both internal appraisals and external qualification.

SCOPE AND IMPACT

SEI offers training in some 24 areas, from consulting skills workshops to complete training programs for CMM/CMMI appraisers and evaluators. SEI courses include Risk Management, Defining Software Processes, Metrics/Measurements, and Software Acquisition.

The SEI technical program is executed by over two hundred members of the technical staff from government, industry, and academia with an average of 10+ years of experience in the field of software engineering.

SEI has evaluated thousands of organizations and tens of thousands of projects through its authorized appraisers. About two-thirds of the organizations were commercial, the others being government or government contractors. The reported gains in productivity range from 20 percent to 28 percent for organizations moving from CMM Level 1 to Level 3.

SYSTEMS ENGINEERING SOCIETY OF AUSTRALIA

The Systems Engineering Society of Australia (SESA) is a Technical Society of the Institution of Engineers, Australia. SESA is directly affiliated with the International Council on Systems Engineering, much like an INCOSE chapter, but operating independently.

SESA was formed in 1994 as a technically-oriented society for professional engineers and others associated with commercial infrastructure systems projects, major defense systems projects, and systems engineering education. Its stated mission is to foster the definition, understanding, practice, and advancement of systems engineering in Australian industry, academia, and government.

MODELS, STANDARDS, AND CERTIFICATION

These aspects of SESA are addressed by its affiliation with INCOSE.

SCOPE AND IMPACT

SESA membership is drawn from Australia, where it has its major impact. Members contribute to both national and international working groups through INCOSE.

4

THE REFERENCE PROJECT CYCLE

The purpose of this section is to describe the sample project cycle referenced by term definitions within this dictionary. This sample cycle is suitable as a template for tailoring and use on projects.

The Reference Project Cycle has three periods and ten phases as shown in Table 4.1. These periods and phases are each defined as separate terms in Part 5.

TAILORING THE PROJECT CYCLE

Depending on the type of project, the number and type of phases may vary. For example, a project cycle for design and construction of a major facility derived from the Reference Project Cycle has the following 10 phases:

1. User Requirements Definition Phase
2. Concept Definition Phase
3. System Specification Phase
4. Acquisition Preparation Phase
5. Source Selection Phase
6. Development Phase
7. Verification Phase
8. Deployment Phase

TABLE 4.1 Periods and Phases for the Reference Project Cycle

Phase	Period
1. User Requirements Definition 2. Concept Definition 3. System Specification 4. Acquisition Preparation	Study
5. Source Selection 6. Development 7. Verification	Implementation
8. Deployment 9. Operations and Maintenance 10. Deactivation	Operations

9. Operations and Maintenance Phase

10. Deactivation Phase.

CONTROL GATES

The most significant tailoring occurs in the number and type of control gates. While the concept and number (38) of control gates in our Reference Project Cycle may appear extensive, a home construction project offers a common basis for comparison. For constructing a custom residence in many areas, there are approximately 40 control gates requiring two official parties to formally agree to the outcome to proceed with the project. Examples are requirements definition, concept definition, planning department approval, building permit approval, and all of the in-process inspections with formal sign-off in the inspection log. In most geographical areas, owner occupancy cannot occur until the final building department approval confirms that all control gates have been completed satisfactorily.

Control Gate Content
The definition of each control gate should identify the:

> Purpose of the control gate.
> Host and chairperson.
> Attendees.
> Place.
> Agenda and how to be conducted.
> Evidence that is to be evaluated.
> Actions.
> Closure method.

At each control gate, the decision options are:

> Acceptable— Proceed with project.
> Acceptable with reservations—Proceed and respond to identified action items.
> Unacceptable—Do not proceed; repeat the control gate.
> Unsalvageable—Terminate the project.

Upon successful completion of a control gate, the appropriate agreements (usually in the form of a document) will be put under configuration management, requiring change authority approval to effect any changes.

For further details, see the Control Gate Example section that follows on page 70.

CONTROL GATES BY PHASE

The list that follows is in the sequential order that matches the preceding project cycle template. The last control gate in each phase must be completed satisfactorily to proceed to the next phase.

Unless noted otherwise, each control gate is defined as a separate term in the dictionary. Some control gates are part of a series that occur as needed at different intervals and/or at various levels of decomposition. In these cases, the title is plural and the term definition describes a series, rather than a single control gate. The name of the defining term for the series, if different from the control gate name, is shown in curly brackets.

User Requirements Definition Phase

Project Plans Review
System Requirements Review

Concept Definition Phase

System Concept Review

System Specification Phase

Interest/No Interest
Project Specification Review

Acquisition Preparation Phase

Acquisition Plan Review

Source Selection Phase

Pursue/No Pursue
Source Selection Initiation Review
Acquisition Review Board Review
Bid/No Bid
Final Proposal Review
Source Selection Authorization Review
Contract Acceptance Review

Development Phase

Project Implementation Review
Contract Implementation Review
Design Concept Review

Preliminary Design (Design-to) Review(s)
Critical Design (Build-to) Review(s)

Verification Phase

Components and Assemblies Test Readiness Reviews {Test Readiness Review}

Components and Assemblies Qualification Acceptance Reviews {Qualification Acceptance Review}

Components and Assemblies Acceptance Reviews {Acceptance Review}

Configuration Item Test Readiness Reviews

Configuration Item Qualification Acceptance Reviews {Qualification Acceptance Review}

Configuration Item Operation Acceptance Reviews {Configuration Item Acceptance Review}

System Test Readiness Review (seller's site)

System Qualification Acceptance Review (seller's site) {Qualification Acceptance Review}

System Acceptance Review (seller's site)

Deployment Readiness Review

Deployment Phase
System Test Readiness Review (staging/operational site)
System Acceptance Review (staging/operational site)
Operational Readiness Review

Operations and Maintenance Phase

User Readiness Review
User Acceptance Review
Production Readiness Review
Annual System Certification Review
Deactivation Approval Review

Deactivation Phase

Project Completion Review

CONTROL GATE EXAMPLE—SYSTEM CONCEPT REVIEW (SCR)

DESCRIPTION

A buyer Executive Control Gate to approve the recommended system concept and validation plan conceived to satisfy the requirements of the System Requirements Document. The SCR is the decision point to proceed with development of the System Specification for the selected concept.

Activities culminating in this review:
- Tradeoff of candidate system concepts
- Identification of risks and assessment of technical feasibility
- Selection of a system concept
- Development of the user's validation approach
- Development of the operational demonstration approach

Objectives: Approve System Concept, System Concept of Operations, and Validation Plan.

Host: Buyer executive management senior to the project champion.

Chairperson: Buyer executive responsible for success of the project.

Presenters: Buyer project champion, buyer systems engineer, user representative, and other key team members.

Reviewers: Buyer executive staff and objective peer evaluators.

Location: Buyer conference facility.

PROCESS

The Buyer project champion presents evidence of concept trade-off analysis leading to concept selection. Critical feasibility issues must have been be resolved and cost and schedule drivers must have been understood and provided for.

REQUIRED PRODUCTS

Primary Products

System Requirements Document:
- System Concept Document
- System Concept of Operations
- User Validation Plan with User approval

Supporting Products:
- System analysis and trades of alternate concepts
- Results of feasibility analysis and modeling
- Operational environment analysis
- Operational Demonstration Plan (ODP)
- Should-cost and should-take estimates
- Staffing and facility needs

CLOSURE

Executive management decides one of the following:

1. System Concept, System Concept Document, System Concept of Operations Document, and Validation Plan are approved and the project is authorized to proceed with System Specification Development.
2. Action Items are assigned that must be resolved before the SCR is considered complete.
3. SCR is unacceptable and must be repeated.
4. System Concept is too risky, expensive, or does not warrant the investment and the project is terminated.

CONSIDERATIONS

Alternate concepts

Concept selection criteria

Concept of operations

Context of implementation

Critical issues

Existing capability

Initial acquisition plan

Key personnel required

Key technology

Other potential users

Risk

Security

Should cost estimate

Should take estimate

Supporting organizations

User requirements

Validation plan

LESSONS LEARNED

SCR should baseline the System Concept, Validation Plan, and System Concept of Operations

SCR frequently ignores the Validation Plan

SCR frequently ignores the should-cost and should-take estimates

DELIVERABLE DOCUMENT EXAMPLE— CONOPS DOCUMENT

The following example outline is one of the primary products of the System Concept Review example control gate.

USER AND SYSTEM CONCEPT OF OPERATIONS DOCUMENT

Version X for (PROJECT NAME)

1. Scope
   1.1 Identification.
   1.2 Overview of User Needs (User ConOps).
   1.3 Overview of the Proposed System (System ConOps).

2. Referenced Documents

Part 1—User Concept of Operations

3. Overview of the Current System or Situation
   3.1 Description of the Current System.
   3.2 Operational Environment and Connectivity to Other Systems.
   3.3 Operational Policies and Constraints.
   3.4 Users and Potential Users of the Current System.
   3.5 Users and Potential Users of the Changed or New System.

4. Desired Changes
   4.1 Description of Desired Changes.
       a. Capability Changes—
       b. System Processing Changes—
       c. Technology Changes—
       d. Interface Changes—
       e. Personnel Changes—
       f. Environment Changes—

g. Operational Changes—

h. Support Changes—

i. Other Changes—

4.2 Priorities Among Desired Changes.

    a. Essential Features—

    b. Desirable Features—

    c. Optional Features—

4.3 Justification for Desired Changes.

4.4 Features Considered But Not Included.

4.5 Assumptions and Constraints.

Part 2—System Concept of Operations

5. The Proposed System

5.1 Operational Description of the Proposed System.

    5.1.1 Operational Features and Capabilities.

    5.1.2 Operational Environment of the Proposed System.

        5.1.2.1 Logical Environment.

        5.1.2.2 Physical Environment.

    5.1.3 Operational Policies and Constraints.

    5.1.4 Modes of Operation for the Proposed System.

    5.1.5 Users Classes for the Proposed System.

        5.1.5.1 User Profiles.

        5.1.5.2 Organizational Structure.

        5.1.5.3 Interactions among User Classes.

    5.1.6 Other Involved Personnel.

    5.1.7 Support Environment for the Proposed System.

5.2 Functional Description of the Proposed System.

    5.2.1 Major System Components.

    5.2.2 Inputs, Outputs, and Computational Flow.

    5.2.3 Desired Performance Characteristics.

    5.2.4 Desired Quality Attributes.

    5.2.5 Safety, Security, and Privacy Considerations.

    5.2.6 Continuity of Operations.

    5.2.7 Connectivity to Other Systems.

6. Operational Scenarios for the Proposed System

7. Summary of Impacts

    7.1 Operational Impacts.

    7.2 Organizational Impacts.

    7.3 Impacts During Development.

8. Analysis of the Proposed System

    8.1 Summary of Improvements.

        a. New capabilities—

        b. Enhanced capabilities——

        c. Deleted capabilities—

        d. Improved performance—

    8.2 Disadvantages and Limitations of the Proposed System.

    8.3 Alternatives and Trade-Offs Considered.

9. Notes

Appendixes

Glossary

5

TERMS AND DEFINITIONS

Terms that are related to a specific organization or based on another organization's glossary are identified in brackets at the end of the definition: [USG] for the U.S. government, [PMI®] for the Project Management Institute, and [SEI] for the Software Engineering Institute. More details are provided in the front matter (Using This Guide and Dictionary). The PMI® and SEI organizations are included in the term definitions.

Definitions that benefit from the context provided in Part 2 are designated as [VPM], referring to the Visual Process Model. Similarly, to provide project cycle context, we have designated relevant terms with [RPC], referring to the Reference Project Cycle in Part 4.

ability to perform

A common feature of CMMI model process areas with a staged representation that groups the generic practices related to ensuring that the project and/or organization has the resources it needs. [SEI]

abstraction

A selected system view to convey relevant properties while ignoring irrelevant details.

acceptable quality level   **AQL**

The allowable percentage of nonconforming items within a lot for the lot to be acceptable.

acceptability criteria

The boundary conditions for determining acceptance and rejection.

acceptance

The act of formally signifying satisfaction with the outcome based on verification evidence.

acceptance certificate

A document signifying acceptance when signed by the responsible parties.

acceptance criteria

Verification requirements that must be satisfied to achieve acceptance by an authorized entity.

acceptance number

The maximum number of defects in a sample that will permit acceptance of the entie lot.

Acceptance Plan

The overall approach to achieving acceptance. Includes the parties involved, the evidence required, and the approval process.

acceptance procedures

Detailed step-by-step instructions for achieving acceptance.

Acceptance Review   **AR**

The control gate held to ascertain and approve evidence of verification and acceptance. Acceptance Reviews are usually held for each system element to ensure readiness for integration into the next assembly sequence. The final Acceptance Review is for the total system following system verification. [RPC]

acceptance sampling

The testing of a portion of a lot to determine the defect rate for the purpose of accepting or rejecting the entire lot.

acceptance test   AT

Verification tests conducted in accordance with an approved verification plan and approved test procedures to provide evidence to support acceptance. Tests are best conducted by an independent organization and witnessed by a representative of the accepting entity for compliance with the test procedure and verification plan. Results of the tests may be audited at the Functional Configuration Audit (FCA), Physical Configuration Audit (PCA), and/or the Acceptance Review (AR). [RPC]

acceptance test procedure   ATP

Detailed step-by-step instructions for the set-up, operation, and evaluation of tests in accordance with the verification plan. The approach to sampling and statistical quality control is part of the ATP.

accident

An unexpected, unwanted, and undesirable event.

accountable

Answerable for success or failure. For example, persons responsible for a project or project tasks are held accountable for their actions in carrying out their responsibilities. The CEOs of major corporations have made the headlines as a result of being held accountable for the manner in which they fulfilled their responsibilities.

accountability/responsibility matrix

An arrangement of rows and columns that relates project items and tasks to those accountable/responsible.

accounting

Bookkeeping methods that record financial business events and results.

accounting period

A selected time period for the measurement and reporting of financial performance.

accounts payable

Debts not yet paid.

accounts receivable

Revenue due, but not yet received.

accreditation

Formal recognition of proving competency against a standard.

accrual accounting

An accounting method that recognizes and records financial events when work or a service has been performed, rather than when it has been paid for.

accuracy

The degree to which a measurement represents the actual value.

achievement profile

In the continuous representation of CMMI, a list of process areas and their corresponding capability levels that represent the organization's progress for each process area while advancing through the capability levels.
See also **target staging, capability level profile,** and **target profile.** [SEI]

acquirer

The organization that procures from others.

acquisition

The process of obtaining products or services, whether the products or services are already in existence or must be conceived, developed, demonstrated, or evaluated. It includes all aspects of contract administration and project management. Also called procurement.

acquisition decision memorandum

A U.S. Department of Defense document that records the decisions made at milestone reviews. [USG]

acquisition life cycle

See **Project Cycle.**

acquisition management

The orchestration of obtaining products or services.

Acquisition Period

See **Implementation Period.**

Acquisition Plan

The document that describes the project's approach to acquisition. It defines whether internal development, competitive, or sole source acquisition will be used. It contains the associated schedule, funding, manpower, facilities, risk, etc. Also called the system acquisition plan.

Acquisition Plan Review   **APR**

The control gate held to approve the acquisition plan. The APR is the decision point in the reference project cycle to initiate the project and commit funding, personnel, and other resources to the acquisition. [RPC]

Acquisition Preparation Phase

The fourth of ten phases of the Reference Project Cycle and the final phase of the Study Period. This is the phase in which preparations are made to select the best source to supply the system. The system acquisition plan and the bidders list are developed and approved in this phase. The phase ends with the Acquisition Plan Review. [RPC]

acquisition reform

The U.S. government initiative to simplify the acquisition and contracting processes and to improve the effectiveness of government management of contractors. It includes credit card use for small purchases, basic order agreements, performance based contracting, insight vs. oversight, team collaboration in day-to-day decisions, and other methods to streamline the acquisition, contracting, and management processes. An objective is to hold suppliers to required system performance rather than incremental delivery of elements of a system. [USG]

acquisition review board   **ARB**

A board that reviews contract actions estimated to exceed a predetermined value.

Acquisition Review Board Review

The pre-solicitation control gate held to ensure that proper judgment and preparation has been applied to the solicitation process. Approval by the board authorizes RFP release on receipt of project funding. [RPC]

acquisition strategy

The selection of supply sources, acquisition methods, contract and incentive types, and other provisions to manage the acquisition risk.

acquisition strategy report

A document that describes the acquisition strategy.

acquisition streamlining

Procurement innovations to improve the efficiency of acquisition. [USG]
See also **Federal Acquisition Streamlining Act.**

action plan

A compilation of tasks and accomplishments with assigned responsibilities and due dates.

activate

Enable something to function.

active listening

The receiver's repeating what has been said to ensure correctness of understanding.

activity

An operation or task that consumes time and or resources. An activity is the smallest unit of work within a project network and work breakdown structure (WBS).

activity based costing   **ABC**

Bottom up estimating and summation based on material and labor for required tasks.

activity based management

The achievement of strategic objectives and customer satisfaction by managing value added activities.

activity definition

A narrative description of the content and deliverables of an activity or task.

activity duration

The predicted time for an activity to be accomplished.

activity on arrow   **AOA**

A project network precedence diagramming technique in which tasks or activities are represented by lines and arrows. The lines and arrows are drawn between nodes, which are preceding and succeeding task junction identifiers.

activity on node   **AON**

A project network precedence diagramming technique in which circles, called nodes, represent the tasks or activities. Lines connect related nodes to depict precedence relationships.

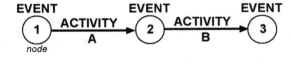

activity report

A report that covers project activity without regard to the plan. Not to be confused with status report.

activity sequencing

The dependency driven relationships of activities.

actual cost

Incurred costs to produce or buy a product or service.

actual cost of work performed   **ACWP**

Current factual expenses attributed to specified work. This phrase is known as ACWP and is used in the Earned Value Management System (EVMS).
See also **cost performance index (CPI).**

actual damages

The costs caused by an injurious act.

actual finish date

The time the activity was completed and accepted.

actuals

Cost and schedule data based on current facts. Past costs and schedule history, including prior commitments, but not including forecasted cost or schedule predictions.

actual start date

The time the activity was started.

adaptability

The capability to adjust to other circumstances.

adaptive control

Feedback in a control loop that adjusts to actual conditions.

adaptive control function

A parameter that adjusts to the actual conditions and is used in the control loop to modify the outcome.

Adjourning

The fifth and last stage of Tuckman and Jensen's team building model where the team disbands.

administrative change

A contract modification that only changes incidental management issues and does not change contract work effort.

administrative closure

The proper disposition of all project property, actions, and records in accordance with the controlling authority.

administrative contracting officer   ACO

The government contracting officer or representative assigned administrative responsibility for a contract to ensure the contractor delivers to the contract requirements. The procuring contracting officer (PCO) may delegate the ACO responsibilities to a government representative resident at the contractor's facility. [USG]

administrative expense

General business expenses that cannot be attributed to a specific project.

advanced development

Projects that convert theory and concepts into tangible hardware and software capable of being evaluated as to capability.

advanced development models

Hardware and software models that are used to prove an understanding of the problem, technical feasibility, and operational concepts.

advanced material release

The authorization of long lead material purchase prior to design approval.

affinity diagram

Pictorial clustering of entities or issues into like categories. Usually the items to be grouped are a result of brainstorming. The affinity diagram can be a catalyst for breakthrough ideas that emerge during the process.

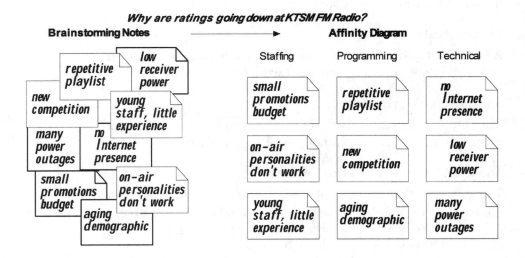

Why are ratings going down at KTSM FM Radio?

affordability

A measure of whether a customer has the resources to match the predicted cost.

after receipt of order   **ARO**

Days ARO indicates the number of days after receipt of a purchase order. Used for scheduling.

agenda

A list of things to be considered or done.

agreement

To concur as to facts or approach. Not to be confused with approval.

air force regulation   **AFR**

A U.S. Secretary of the Air Force document that implements policies and procedures. [USG]

alert

A warning signal or message.

algorithm

A step-by-step problem-solving sequence that is often computational.

allocated baseline

A U.S. government term that refers to the flow down of high-level requirements to the various configuration items of a system that are then placed under change control. [USG]

allocated configuration identification

The design-to specifications for the various configuration items.

allocated costs

Costs that are apportioned to a specific function.

allocated requirements

Requirements apportioned to the elements of a system by applying relevant knowledge and experience. Determination of allocated requirements is not as scientifically rigorous as determination of derived requirements.

allocation

A portion of a whole, distributed according to a plan, for example, the subdivision of a budget into individual groups or offices. Allocation is chiefly applied to money, material, authority, or responsibility.

allotment

To distribute and apportion to achieve an objective. Allotment may imply arbitrary distribution.

allowable cost

(1) Expenses legally allowed to be attributed to specified work within a contract for the purposes of determining reimbursement.
(2) Factors to be considered in determining whether a cost is allowable within government contracting are presented in the Federal Acquisition Regulations (FAR). [USG]

alphanumeric

Identifiers that combine letters, numbers, and other characters to represent information.

alpha test

The testing, evaluation, feedback, and correction of new products by the developers prior to release to beta test

alternative dispute resolution

Voluntary controversy settlement that eliminates the need for formal litigation such as mediation, arbitration, and negotiation.

alternative practice

A practice that is a substitute for one or more generic or specific practices contained in CMMI models that achieves an equivalent effect toward satisfying the generic or specific goal associated with model practices. Alternative practices are not necessarily one-for-one replacements for the generic or specific practices. [SEI]

alternatives

Different concepts of achieving an end result.

ambiguity

uncertainty in interpretation

amendment

Legal change to an approved baseline, usually a contract.

American Association of Cost Engineers   **AACE**

Professional organization of cost engineers.

American National Standards Institute   **ANSI**

A private, nonprofit organization dedicated to the propagation of standards. ANSI members, including government, education, and industry organizations, develop standards for a wide range of products. ANSI is the sole U.S. representative to the International Organization for Standardization (ISO).

American Society for the Advancement of Project Management   asapm

A not-for-profit professional society dedicated to advancing the project management profession, and providing leadership for professional growth of both members and the profession. The society focus includes standards, publications, education, certification, and research. Further information is available at http://www.asapm.org.

amortize

To account for an expenditure by prorating over a defined period.

analog

Capable of varying continuously rather than in discrete steps.

analog cost estimate

An estimate of costs, performance, and other factors, based on historical data too limited to allow statistical estimating, but which is more economical to prepare than a bottom-up estimate. Normally prepared by adjusting the historical data of a similar (analog) item by deducting for factors that are not comparable, and by adding estimated values for additional features.

analysis

(1)   The critical and careful evaluation of a situation or problem.
(2)   The separation of a whole into its constituent parts for individual study.

analytical hierarchy process   AHP

A decision process based on these steps:
(1)   pair-wise comparison of decision criteria
(2)   applying a mathematical process to calculate the relative importance of each criterion.
(3)   scoring the alternatives, again using pair-wise comparison, against those criteria to determine the best overall candidate.

anecdotal

Narrative hearsay rather than quantitative facts.

animation

Using motion pictures or active drawings to represent the behavior of a system, or to illustrate complex ideas.

annual operational performance report

A document that summarizes the project's operational performance on an annual basis. Includes operational history, problems and resolutions, cost savings recommendations, and potential upgrades.

Annual System Certification Review   ASCR

The control gate held to affirm that the system product continues to meet the users' requirements and the systems equirements document criteria, or recommend that improvements are required. [RPC]

anomaly

Deviation from the expected.

anticipatory breach

The anticipated breaking of a contract within the contract period.

Anti-Deficiency Act

The salient features of this U.S. government act include: prohibitions against authorizing or incurring obligations or expenditures in excess of amounts apportioned by the Office of Management and Budget (OMB) or in excess of amounts permitted by individual agency regulations; and establishment of procedures for determining the responsibility for violations and for reporting violations through OMB to the President and to the Congress. [USG]

apparent authority

The individual actually causing things to happen. This individual may or may not have been empowered with the authority of higher-level management.

applied rates

Rates used to manage by. Applied rates may be different than the bidding rates in order to provide contingency.

applied research

Effort to evolve laboratory theory into practical application.

apportioned task

A task that is dependent on or related to the performance of another task.

apportionment

(1) The U.S. government's Office of Management and Budget (OMB) action that limits obligations or expenditures usually over a specified time period. [USG]

(2) The distributed allocation of system requirements to lower level entities such as the distribution of the weight budget. Apportionment implies equitable or proportionate distribution.

appraisal findings

The conclusions of an appraisal that identify the most important issues, problems, or opportunities within the appraisal scope. Findings include, at a minimum, strengths and weaknesses based on valid observations. [SEI]

appraisal participants

Members of the organizational unit who participate in providing information during the appraisal. [SEI]

appraisal rating

As used in CMMI appraisal materials, the value assigned by an appraisal team to either (1) a CMMI goal or process area, (2) the capability level of a process area, or (3) the maturity level of an organizational unit. The rating is determined by enacting the defined rating process for the appraisal method being employed. [SEI]

appraisal reference model

As used in CMMI appraisal materials, the CMMI model to which an appraisal team correlates implemented process activities. [SEI]

Appraisal Requirements for CMMI   ARC

The specification and requirements for the CMMI classes of appraisal methods.

appraisal scope

The definition of the boundaries of the appraisal encompassing the organizational limits and the CMMI model limits. [SEI]

appraisal team leader

A person who leads the activities of an appraisal and has satisfied the qualification criteria for experience, knowledge, and skills defined by the appraisal method. [SEI]

appropriation

(1)   To set apart for a special use.
(2)   An act of the U.S. Congress to provide a specified amount of funds to be used for a purpose previously authorized by a Congressional act. [USG]

appropriation limitation

The funds limit of the U.S. Congressional appropriation. [USG]

approve

To confirm or ratify.

approved bidders list

A list of suppliers considered qualified to bid for a contract.

arbitration

Dispute resolution where the parties submit their differences to the judgment of an impartial person or group appointed by mutual consent or statutory provision.

arbitrator

The impartial person used by mutual consent in arbitration.

architectural design

The process of developing the system architecture and decomposition.

architecture

The framework and interrelationships of elements of a system. Typically illustrated by both a pictorial and a decomposition diagram depicting the segments and elements and their interfaces and interrelationships.

architecture and engineering   A&E

The type of organization normally employed to design and engineer major facility projects. May also be used to oversee or manage facility construction.

arrow diagramming method   ADR

Project schedule network diagramming technique that incorporates arrows to represent activities between nodes.
See also **activity on arrow.**

artificial

Not natural—simulated.

artificial intelligence

Computer science theory and associated computer systems that are able to reason, learn, and perform self-improvement.

as-built configuration

The final product, which includes design changes implemented for manufacturing improvements as well as integration and verification corrective actions.

as-built design documentation

The documentation that describes the ultimate as-built configuration to facilitate trouble analysis and to provide for future replication. It includes design changes implemented for manufacturing improvements and integration and verification corrective actions. The as-built baseline becomes the build-to baseline for new builds. In construction, as-built drawings are referred to as the "record" drawings.

as-coded documentation

The documentation that describes the final as-coded configuration. It includes design changes implemented for functionality improvements and alpha and beta test deficiency fixes.

assembly

A functional unit designed and managed as an entity. Examples include electronic boxes, mechanical assemblies, and software components. Level 2 in the example system decomposition hierarchy.

assess

To evaluate the significance of a condition, situation, or value.

assessment

The result of assessing a condition or situation. The findings.

assessment sponsor

The authorizer of the assessment.

asset

(1) Amounts on a balance sheet that represent the values of property, cash, accounts receivable, and investments.

(2) Intangible attributes such as skilled workforce, unique facilities and systems (whose value exceeds the component costs), and a good reputation.

assignable cause of process variation

In CMMI, the term *special cause of process variation* is used in place of *assignable cause of process variation* to ensure consistency. Both terms are defined identically.
See also **special cause of process variation.** [SEI]

assignment of contract

Transfer of obligations and rights of a contract to another party.

associate contractors

Two or more contractors, reporting directly to the same customer, that participate on the same project.

assumption

A best judgment supposition to approximate the missing information.

assurance

A declaration or promise intended to provide confidence.

asynchronous

Processes that are not simultaneous or contingent.

at-completion variance   **ACV**

Budget at completion minus the estimate at completion. (BAC-EAC)

attainable

Achievable, not impossible.

attribute

A measurable characteristic.

attribute sampling

The inspection of the attributes of a portion of a lot to statistically determine the quality of the entire lot.

attrition

The loss of a resource due to causes beyond the jurisdiction of the project manager such as the death or resignation of an employee, or spoilage, damage, or obsolescence of material.

audit

(1) The systematic examination of tangible evidence to determine adequacy, validity, and effectiveness of the subject under review. An audit may examine existence of and adherence to policies and procedures.

(2) In CMMI process-improvement work, an independent examination of a work product or set of work products to determine whether requirements are being met. [SEI]

authentication

A U.S. government term for approving a baseline. [USG]

authoritarian management style

A directive style as compared to consultative, counseling, or consensus.

authority

The power to exact obedience and to make the necessary decisions to fulfill specific obligations.

authority to proceed

Contractual authorization to proceed with work.

authorization

(1) Permission.

(2) An act of the U.S. Congress that authorizes federal programs, obligations, or expenditures. [USG]

authorized unpriced work   AUW

Any work authorized to start under a contract change but for which estimated costs have not yet been negotiated to settlement.

authorized work

Work tasks that have been approved by management. A project work authorizing agreement (PWAA) or substitute is used to authorize in-house work; contracts and subcontracts are used to authorize work with external organizations.

automated data processing   ADP

The application of electronic equipment, especially computers, to manage, manipulate, display, and store data.

automated data processing equipment   ADPE

Electronic equipment, especially computers, used to manage, manipulate, display, and store data.

automated information system   AIS

A computer-based information retrieval system.

automatic self test

The ability of equipment to diagnose the cause of internal anomalies.

automatic test equipment   ATE

Equipment built to perform a test or sequence of tests. ATE ranges from simple devices to verify mechanical or electrical continuity to sophisticated computerized systems with automatic sequencing, data processing, and readout. Automatic test equipment may be stand alone test units or may be built into the operational equipment. If built-in, it is referred to as BITE (built in test equipment).

auxiliary ground equipment   AGE

System support equipment that provides power or environment normally provided by internal systems.

availability

The proportion of operational time that a system is not impaired by malfunction or maintenance. The availability factor is a major issue in emergency support systems, and other systems that must always be on line, to reduce risk to an acceptable level. For instance fire alarm systems must always be available hence the provision of backup batteries to provide capability during power outages.

avoidance

Elimination of risk by eliminating the cause.

award

Notification that a contract will be negotiated between a buyer and a seller.

award fee   AF

A contract fee provision used to motivate a contractor to respond to issues that are assigned and measured periodically and subjectively. The contract specifies award fee periods, usually six to nine months long. The award fee criteria are negotiated prior to the start of each award fee period, providing the buyer flexibility to change the incentive emphasis as the project evolves. The determination is made unilaterally by the buyer and is not subject to the legal disputes clause provisions.

award fee determination official

The executive responsible for approving the contractor's award fee for an evaluation period. The buyer's project team usually sets the criteria for fee award and also rates the seller on the performance relative to the fee criteria. The award fee determination official reviews and approves the recommended award.

award without discussion

Contractor selection based solely on proposal content as opposed to requesting discussions for clarification and corrections possibly followed by a best and final offer based on any adjustments to the proposals.

back charge

Buyer costs for corrective action of defects that are billed back to the supplier.

backward pass

Calculations of the latest acceptable finish and start dates for un-completed work by working backwards through the network from the delivery date.

balance sheet

A financial report that itemizes assets, liabilities, and net worth.

bar chart

Graphical bars where bar lengths represent relative values of se-lected parameters. Bars may be horizontal or vertical and when vertical are called columns.
See also **Gantt chart.**

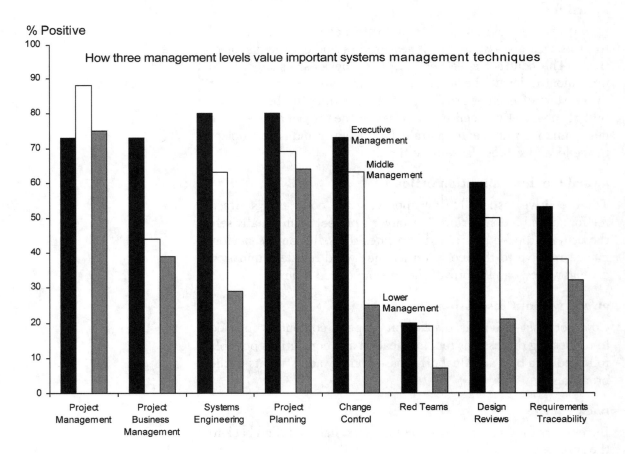

base

(1)   A reference level or starting point.
(2)   Resources needed to operate and maintain throughout the budget year capabilities that exist at the beginning of the fiscal year.

base fee

A minimum fixed dollar amount of fee to be awarded under a fee-based contract regardless of the seller's performance.

baseline

(1)   The gate-controlled step-by-step elaboration of business, budget, functional, performance, and physical characteristics, mutually agreed-to by buyer and seller, and under formal change control. Baselines can be modified between formal control gates by mutual consent through the change control process. Typical baselines are contractual baseline, budget baseline, schedule baseline, user requirements baseline, concept baseline, system specification baseline, design-to baseline, build-to baseline, as-built baseline, as-tested baseline, and as-fielded baseline.
(2)   A reference from which changes are measured.

baseline—budget

The buyer/seller agreed-to budget and budget management approach that is under formal change control. Can include the funding source, time-phased budget, total funding, time-phased funding profile, management reserve and method for handling funding needs beyond the funding limit.

baseline—business

The buyer/seller agreed-to business requirements and business approach that are under formal change control. Can include the acquisition plan, contract, subcontracts, project master schedule, implementation plan, systems engineering management plan, contract deliverable(s) list, and the contract documentation requirements list.

baseline—technical

The buyer/seller agreed-to technical requirements and technical approach that are under formal change control. Can include the user requirements document, user concept of operations document, system requirements document, concept definition document, system concept of operations document, system specifications, design-to specifications, build-to documents, and as-built, as-tested, as-accepted, and as-operated configurations.

baseline configuration management

See **configuration management.**

baseline control

Formal change authority approval and management of the evolving baseline. Changes to the baseline require change authority approval. Part of configuration management.

baseline cost estimate   BCE

The estimated cost to perform all work contained in the project baseline in accordance with the prescribed conditions, for example, without overtime.

baseline management

The gated review and approval of the evolving baseline at prescribed control gates and the formal review and approval of changes to the approved baseline.

base measure

A distinct property or characteristic of an entity and the method for quantifying it.
See also **derived measures.** [SEI]

base practices

In the continuous representation, all the specific practices with a capability level of 1. [SEI]

base program

The program described in the future years defense program (FYDP) base file, updated to conform to the budget presented to the U.S. Congress. It constitutes the base from which all current year program changes are considered. [USG]

base year   **BY (1)**

A reference period that determines a fixed-price level for comparison in economic escalation calculations and cost estimates. The price level index for the Base Year is 1.000.

basic ordering agreement   **BOA**

An instrument of understanding (not a contract) executed between a procuring organization and a contractor that sets forth negotiated contract clauses that will be applicable to future procurements entered into between the parties during the term of the agreement. It includes as specific a description as possible of the supplies or services and a description of the method for determining pricing, issuing, and delivery of future orders. Typically used when quantities, prices, and delivery dates are not known but substantial quantities are anticipated.

basic reliability

The duration or probability of failure-free performance under stated conditions.

basic research

Scientific investigation undertaken to increase knowledge.

basis of estimate   **BOE**

The rationale for arriving at a particular cost or schedule estimate. This can include the estimating methods, approach taken, historical experience, prices used, etc. The basis of estimate section of a proposal that includes a justification of the cost estimate.

bathtub curve

A horizontal line graph that looks like a bathtub in that it descends vertically at the left end and then remains flat until it increases vertically at the right end. It is the typical shape of defect discovery at the beginning of system life, characteristic performance through midlife and then increasing incidents of defects from wear out toward the end of system life.

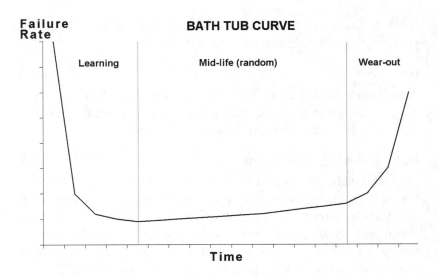

behavior

The inherent actions, reactions, and the responses to external events that describe the dynamics of a system.

behavior diagram

A system logic diagram or model using symbols to depict the elements of a system and lines to represent the functional

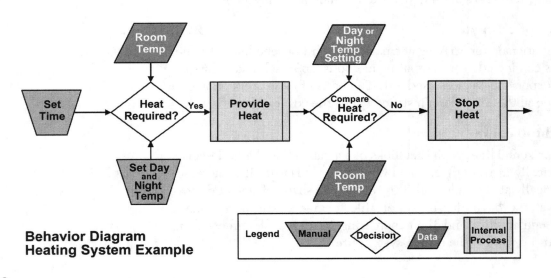

**Behavior Diagram
Heating System Example**

interactions. Some models are functional and provide for what-if experimentation.

behavioral analysis

The interactive evaluation of a system's functional representation (typically described by a behavior diagram). Also called functional analysis.

benchmark

A quantitative or qualitative reference against which to make comparisons.

benchmarking

(1) A review of what experts are doing to achieve their level of superior performance for the purposes of replication.
(2) The comparison of performance of new designs or implementations to an existing component or system with known performance as the benchmark.

benefit-cost ratio

A metric to compare the value of projects and project approaches. Value equals benefit divided by cost

benign failure

A failure that does not impair or preclude normal system operations.

best and final offer   BAFO

An offeror's revision to a proposal in response to Request For Proposal (RFP) modifications, clarifications, or discussions.

best effort contract

A contract, usually cost reimbursement research or development, to commit the contractor to do the best job possible under conditions of significant risk with no legal obligation to complete.

best practices

Processes, procedures, and techniques that have consistently demonstrated achievement of expectations and that are documented for the purposes of sharing, repetition, and refinement.

See also **competency-based asset** and **competency-based process.**

best value

The most advantageous selection in a competitive acquisition resulting from a value vs. cost and schedule analysis. Sometimes called the trade-off process.

beta test

The testing, evaluation, and constructive feedback to the developers of a new product by a select group of potential users prior to product release.

beta version

A distribution of software for user trial and comment before final release. Usually follows internal alpha testing by the developing organization.

bid

A company's written response to an invitation for bid (IFB).

bid and proposal funds   B&P

Contractor funds used to pay for proposal preparation, fact-finding, and negotiations. (In the U.S. government contracting environment, allowable B&P funds are part of the contractor's general and administrative (G&A) expenses.)

bidders conference

A meeting hosted by the buyer's contracting organization to assist prospective bidders in understanding the request for proposal (RFP). The questions asked and the answers provided are usually formally sent to all prospective bidders following the conference.

bidders list

A list of companies or suppliers judged capable by the procuring organization from which bids, proposals, or quotations may be solicited.

Bid/No Bid   BNB

The seller control gate held to approve developing a proposal in response to an official request for proposal. [RPC]

bid opening

The officially opening of bids submitted in response to a competitive solicitation.

bid protest

An action by an unsuccessful bidder to halt a procurement based on an unfair competition or unjustified award.

bill

A list of particulars often including charges.

bill of material   BOM

A listing of all the subassemblies, parts, and raw materials required in making an assembly or a system.

binary digit

One or zero, the digits of the binary numbering system.

binding arbitration

A decision process by a third party arbitrator in which all parties are bound to the outcome.

black box

A functional entity with known inputs, outputs, and behavior but whose internal content and functions are unknown.

black box testing

Verification of entity inputs and outputs only.
See also **white box testing.**

blanket purchase agreement   BPA

A method of purchasing repetitive items where price is negotiated but quantities are determined as needed.

block diagram

A graphical representation of a system that depicts objects of decomposition or functional groups as interconnected geometric figures (usually rectangles and triangles). Provides an easy to understand overview of the make-up and interconnections of a system.

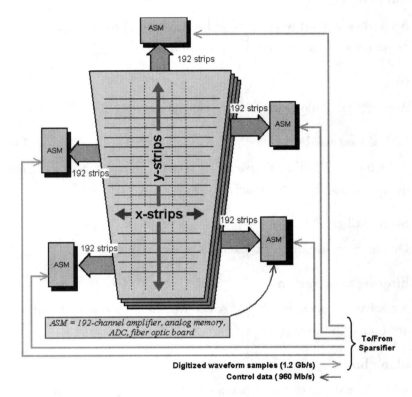

ASM = 192-channel amplifier, analog memory, ADC, fiber optic board

To/From Sparsifier

Digitized waveform samples (1.2 Gb/s) →
Control data (960 Mb/s) ←

blue ribbon committee

A committee of experts that examines evidence to determine that a high-risk project has been properly planned, is being properly managed, and the probability of success is sufficient that the project should be permitted to proceed.

boiler plate

Essential contract terminology and clauses that are not subject to frequent change. This use of this term is dangerous because it may lull the project team into insufficient attention to the binding clauses.

bond

A written agreement by a contractor or a second party to ensure fulfillment of the contractor's obligations to a third party. If the contractor fails to perform, the third party is protected to the limits defined by the bond.

bonus

Money paid or other benefit provided in addition to the expected.

bottom up

Viewing integration, cost estimating, and other activities from the lowest level of decomposition and moving up to the system level.

bottom-up cost estimate

A cost estimate derived by summing detailed cost estimates of individual work packages (labor and materials) from the bottom up and applying appropriate cost burdens. A bottom-up schedule estimate is usually created at the same time.

brainstorming

A group technique that attempts to uncover all possible approaches to an issue in which ideas are encouraged and discussed, no matter how abstract they seem or how removed from practical realization.

brassboard

An experimental technical demonstration model developed in a laboratory environment to demonstrate the application of a scientific or engineering principle, or to test design concepts and technical feasibility where certain dimensions are critical as in RF devices. The data accumulated primarily relate to the electromechanical or critical physical design aspects within geometric constraints, but without attempt to meet final shape or weight specifications. Also called brassboard model.

PROPYLENE HEAT PIPE

-80°C STIRLING COOLER

VACUUM PANEL INSULATION

STIRLING R/F

NASA Space Refrigerator Brassboard

breach

Failure to satisfactorily complete a contract obligation.

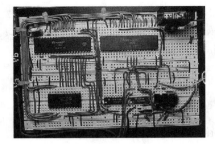

breadboard

An experimental technical demonstration model developed in a laboratory environment to demonstrate the application of a scientific or engineering principle, or to test design concepts and technical feasibility. The data accumulated primarily relate to the electronic or circuit design aspects without emphasis or attempt to meet overall size, shape, or weight specifications. Also called breadboard model.

break even point

The time when the profit earned is equal to the investment that was made to achieve the profit.

bribe

A payment to change a normal course of action to benefit the payor. A gift or favor bestowed or promised with a view to distort the judgment or corrupt the conduct of someone.

broad agency announcement   BAA

An announcement by a procuring agency of the U.S. government seeking responses in specific areas of research. BAAs should (1) describe the agency's research interest, (2) describe the criteria for selecting the proposals, the relative importance, and the method of evaluation, (3) specify the period of time within which the proposals must be submitted, and (4) provide instructions for the preparation and submission of the proposals. [USG]

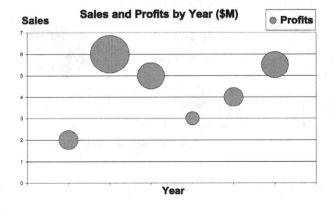

bubble chart

An entity and relationship diagram where circles represent the entities and lines depict the relationships between the entities.

budget

A time-phased expenditure plan usually expressed in dollars or labor units. Can also refer to technical parameters (e.g. weight budget) or an allowance for technical uncertainty, as in error budget.

Budget Aspect of the Project Cycle

The portion of the baseline Project Cycle dedicated to the acquisition and spending of the funding for work or materiel necessary to meet the objectives of the project. It includes developing the Study Period should-cost estimates, the most probable cost estimates, the estimates at completion (EACs) and the estimates to complete (ETCs), and the on-going budget cycle management necessary to keep the project funded to the level required for effective management. [VPM]

budget at completion   BAC

The planned budget for a task or project, excluding management reserve. The BAC plus management reserve (MR) equals the target cost. Also called budgeted cost at completion.
See illustration under **performance measurement system.**

budgeted cost at completion

See **budget at completion.**

budgeted cost of work performed   BCWP

A performance measurement term representing work accomplished, which is equal to the planned cost of achieving specified milestones. When a task is completed, the budgeted cost of work performed (BCWP) is the earned value for that task. Also when a task is completed the BCWP is exactly equal to budgeted cost of the work scheduled (BCWS). The most common methods for calculating BCWP are: 0–100; 50–50; percent complete; and level of effort.
See illustration under **performance measurement system.**

budgeted cost of work scheduled   BCWS

A performance measurement term representing the planned time-phased cost (budget) for project tasks and the entire project.
See illustration under **performance measurement system.**

budget estimate

A prediction of the expected costs and schedule to achieve an objective. Can also refer to technical parameters (e.g., weight budget estimate) or an allowance for technical uncertainty, as in error budget estimate.

budget execution year

The third year of the three-year U.S. government budget cycle where the appropriated funds are approved by Congress and are spent for products and services. [USG]

budget formulation year

The first year of the three-year U.S. government budget cycle where estimates are prepared for Congressional approval for the work to be done two years later. [USG]

budget review year

The second year of the three-year U.S. government budget cycle where Congress reviews estimates for the work to be done one year later. [USG]

budget unit

The metric used for management. Can be dollars, hours, pounds, etc.

budget year   **BY (2)**

The fiscal year defined for a project.

build

To develop according to a plan or process.

build-to documentation

Documents that define the build and coding details that will be used by the producers to create the product satisfying the design-to specifications. May include material and process specifications.

built in test   **BIT**

Designed-in hardware and software capability to detect failures and/or perform self diagnosis of anomalies.

built-in test equipment   **BITE**

Test capability that is built internal to systems for fault detection and/or diagnosis.

burden

General costs that cannot be assigned to direct project tasks such as management salaries, rent, insurance, benefits, etc. Referred to as burden rate when expressed as a percentage of direct costs.
See also **general and administrative** and **overhead.**

burn-in

Operating an item, sometimes under stress, to stabilize its characteristics.

burn rate

The rate at which funds are expended as in total dollars per day or total dollars per week.

business aspect

The nontechnical aspects of managing the project such as contractual, legal, scheduling, money management, resource management, subcontractor management, supplier management, leadership, human factors, etc.

Business Aspect of the Project Cycle

The portion of the baseline Project Cycle dedicated to the justification and selling of the project based on its merits and the on-going running of the project as a business. Typically includes the business case development and the study results that confirm the validity of the business case. In commercial projects, this includes test marketing. The business case must be revisited and reconfirmed throughout the Project Cycle or the project may become obsolete before delivery. Also includes contracting and subcontracting and the management of all resources to the predictions. [VPM]

business case

The end use scenario that describes the justification for the project in economic terms. Usually includes the opportunity, market, competition, market penetration expected, cost and time to break-even, profit expectations, follow-on opportunities, etc.

business manager

The person responsible for managing the project's business functions such as contracting, subcontracting, planning, scheduling, budgeting, data management, human resources, legal, etc.

business objectives

Organization's strategic goals to enhance market position, profitability, customer satisfaction, product life, and other enterprise health issues.

business process model

A network of activities that consistently and routinely produces a planned result.

business process reengineering

The critical examination of business processes and the revisions needed to improve the value added of the required steps and to improve the outcome.

business risk

A potential event or factor that could prevent the desired business outcome from being achieved, often expressed as a probability.

buyer

The procuring organization. For an internal project, the buyer could be the marketing department or any other organization requiring a service.
See also **seller.**

buy-in

The deliberate submission of a price or target cost substantially below estimated cost in order to win a competition or to establish a project.

calendar

A system for displaying the beginning, end, and divisions of a year. Projects frequently use specialized forms, such as a manufacturing calendar which numbers work days sequentially through the year from 1 to approximately 250.

calendar year   CY

January 1 through December 31.

calibration

To compare and align to a standard.

candidate concepts

Alternative solutions conceived to solve a problem. The best is selected by using a formal or informal process based on intuition, judgment, group consensus, or an analytical decision process.

capable process

A process that can satisfy its specified product quality, service quality, and process performance objectives.
See also **stable process, standard process,** and **statistically managed process.** [SEI]

capability

The ability to perform as expected.

capability certification

A certified summary of the proven range of performance of an entity.

capability evaluation

(1) A process assessment by a certified team.
(2) An appraisal by a trained team of professionals used as a discriminator to select suppliers, for contract monitoring, or for incentives. Evaluations are used to help decision makers make better acquisition decisions, improve subcontractor performance, and provide insight to a purchasing organization. [SEI]

capability level

Achievement of process competency within an individual process area. A capability level is defined by the appropriate specific and generic practices for a process area.
See also **maturity level, process area, generic practice,** and **generic goal.** [SEI]

capability level profile

In the continuous representation, a list of process areas and their corresponding capability levels.
See also **target staging, capability level profile, achievement profile**, and **target profile.**

The profile may be an **achievement profile** when it represents the organization's progress for each process area while advancing through the capability levels. Or, the profile may be a target profile when it represents an objective for process improvement. [SEI]

Capability Maturity Model   CMM

A Capability Maturity Model (CMM) contains the essential elements of effective processes for one or more disciplines. It also describes an evolutionary improvement path from ad hoc, immature processes to disciplined, mature processes with improved quality and effectiveness.

See also **Software Engineering Institute** and **Capability Maturity Model Integration.** [SEI]

Capability Maturity Model Integration   CMMI

The purpose of CMMI is to provide guidance for improving an organization's processes and its ability to manage the development, acquisition, and maintenance of products and services. CMM Integration places proven practices into a structure that helps an organization assess its organizational maturity and process area capability, establish priorities for improvement, and guide the implementation of these improvements. [SEI]

Provides pre-defined roadmap for *organizational improvement*, based on proven grouping of processes and associated organizational relationships.

STAGED (by Maturity Level)

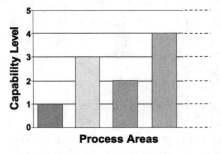

Provides flexibility for organizations to choose *which* processes to emphasize for improvement, as well as *how much* to improve each process.

CONTINUOUS (by Process Areas)

CMMI Model – Two Representations

capability survey

A survey of a producer's capability without specific regard to any project.

capital

Money or property used in the conduct of business.

capital assets

Tangible property that includes buildings, land, equipment, and durable goods.

capital investment

The amount of money invested in capital assets used on the project.

capitalization

The recording of asset expenditures as capital investment as opposed to an expense of running the project.

cards on the wall planning   COW

A planning technique in which team members interact to create a project strategy, tactical approach, and resulting network by positioning and interconnecting task cards using walls as the work

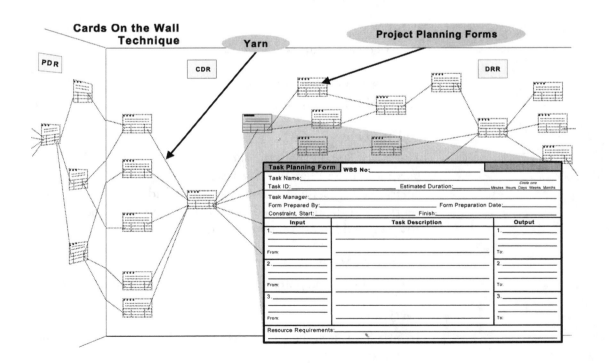

space. The wall data are transferred into a computer for scheduling, critical path analysis, and iteration.

CASE tool

(1) Computer Aided Software Engineering tool to support software development from design through test.

(2) Computer Aided Systems Engineering tool to support the requirements definition and decomposition process, traceability, documentation of the verification plans, graphical depiction of the system logic flow, and for some CASE tools, to provide an executable display of the system logic.

cash flow

The on-going relationship of incoming to outgoing cash and the resulting availability of cash.

casual analysis

The determination of the source of defects.

catalyst

One who causes an event or event series.

cause and effect diagram

See **Ishikawa Diagram.**

ceiling price

The price established by the contractual parties that is the maximum price that the buyer will pay regardless of the cost of performance. Ceiling price is usually included in fixed price incentive and fixed price redetermination contracts, and occasionally included in cost reimbursement contacts.

central processing unit   **CPU**

The heart of a computer system where data manipulation occurs.

certification

To attest by a signed certificate or other proof to meeting a standard.

certification authority

The person or organization with the power to certify.

certified public accountant   CPA

A person holding an official certificate as an accountant, having fulfilled all legal requirements.

chain

A series of linked things or events

champion

The individual that supports and promotes an idea into a fully supported project.

change

To cause to be different. (Usually from the approved baseline.)

change control

The process of considering and approving or disapproving changes to any change controlled baseline.

change control authority   CCA

The person or group responsible for the integrity of a baseline and with the power to approve changes to the baseline.
See also **change control board, configuration control board**, and **project control board.**

change control board   CCB (1)

A body having authority similar to the configuration control board, but the scope includes all technical and programmatic changes to the project baselines.
See also **configuration control board**, and **project control board.**

change control procedure

The process for initiating baseline changes, analyzing the impact of the changes, approving or denying the changes, and updating the baseline if approved.

change management

The comprehensive evaluation and approval or disapproval of a change that takes into consideration all effects of the change.

change order   CO (1)

A written order directing that changes be made to a contractual effort. It may include a negotiated equitable adjustment to the cost and schedule baseline.

characteristic

A feature that helps to describe and distinguish.

chart

A pictorial diagram that represents data patterns.

charter

The (oral or written) authority given by executive management to the project manager and all supporting organizations to manage the project.

checklist

A list of steps to be performed to accomplish a result.

chief executive officer   CEO

The employee with the highest authority, responsible and accountable for a company's performance.

chief systems engineer   CSE

The senior technical authority for a project. Ensures system integrity and certifies technical performance to management and the customer.

claim

A written assertion by one of the contracting parties seeking the payment of money or adjustment in contract terms as a result of either party's behavior.

clarification

As a contractual term, refers to communication between a buyer and a seller to eliminate minor irregularities, ambiguities, or apparent clerical errors in a proposal.

class 1 change

A change that affects the contract requirements or the form, fit, or function of the customer-approved baseline.

class 2 change

A change that is internal to the project and does not affect the contract requirements or the form, fit, or function of the customer-approved baseline.

classification of defects

Defects grouped and ranked according to seriousness.

clearance number

The number of successively inspected units which must be found free of defects before a change to the inspection procedure and sampling rates can be justified.

client

A customer or patron.

client-server architecture

System structure that distinguishes between multiple users/requestors (clients) and a source/provider (server).

CMMI appraisal tailoring

Selection of options within the appraisal method for use in a specific instance. The intent of appraisal tailoring is to assist an organization in aligning application of the method with its business objectives. [SEI]

CMMI model component

Any of the main architectural elements that compose a CMMI model. Some of the main elements of a CMMI model include specific practices, generic practices, specific goals, generic goals, process areas, capability levels, and maturity levels. [SEI]

CMMI model tailoring

The use of a subset of a CMMI model for the purpose of making it suitable for a specific application. The intent of model tailoring is to assist an organization in aligning application of a model with its business objectives. [SEI]

coaching

The use of a mentor to advise and/or assist in training another individual.

code

A system of symbols used to represent information, such as a computer programming language or cipher.

code of conduct

The team's adopted rules relating to team behavior in the conduct of the project. It includes work habits and ethics, communication rules, problem escalation methods, business issues, and any other potential points of conflict.

code review

Peer or expert review and critique of software.

coding

The process of converting software designs into machine readable instructions.

coding and computer software unit testing

A software development activity during which computer software units (CSUs) are coded and tested as stand-alone entities.

cohesion

The degree of interactivity and interdependence among solution elements.

collaborate

To work together

collaborate to consensus   CTC (1)

A decision process that requires the parties to interact and challenge each other until they have achieved consensus on the outcome.

collaboration

To cooperate with others toward a mutual goal.

collocated matrix

A matrix organization where all borrowed personnel reside at the project work site.

Commerce Business Daily   CBD

A paper published daily by the U.S. government Printing Office (GPO), and uploaded to the Web by Community of Science, that lists notices of proposed government procurement actions, contract awards, sales of government property, and other procurement information. Each edition contains approximately 500 to 1,000 notices and each notice appears only once. [USG]

commercial item

Entities and services that are or will be available to the public for other than government purposes, and that can be purchased, leased, or licensed at the time of need. The Federal Acquisition Streamlining Act of 1994 contains detailed provisions stating a preference for commercial items and establishing acquisition policies for commercial items more closely resembling those of the commercial marketplace. These polices are now a part of the U.S. Federal Acquisition Regulations. [USG]

commercial item description   CID

Specifications and other documentation that describe the capability and performance of commercial products or services.

commercial off-the-shelf   COTS

Hardware, software, or services readily available commercially.

commitment

(1)   A pledge to perform.
(2)   An allocation of buyer funds to satisfy commitments made for goods or services.

commitment to perform

A common feature of CMMI model process areas with a staged representation that groups the generic practices related to creating policies and securing sponsorship. [SEI]

committed work

An agreement concerning the scope of work to be performed and the work products or services to be produced.

common cause

Failure that bypasses redundancy, i.e., a failure that causes the simultaneous loss of several related items.

common cause of process variation

(1) Normal variations of a process because of expected interactions within the process.
(2) The variation of a process that exists because of normal and expected interactions among the components of a process.

See also **special cause of process variation.** [SEI]

Communication

The first Project Management Essential. The language and the techniques used by a particular person or group to achieve understanding. In project management, the Essential that enables team members interact effectively and function as a team. Communication encompasses vocabulary, which previous versions of the Visual Process Model identified as the first Project Management Essential. [VPM]

communications

The exchange of thoughts, messages, or information, as by speech, signals, writing, or behavior.

compatibility

(1) The extent to which two or more entities or systems can function together without difficulty.
(2) The extent to which a system or entity can function within its operational environment without difficulty.

compensable delay

A buyer-caused delay incurred by a seller in contract performance for which the buyer must give compensation.

compensation

A payment of something of value for a service or a loss.

compensation strategy

An organization's approach to employee compensation.

competency

The knowledge and skills capability of an individual or organization.

competency assessment

An independent evaluation of an organization's capability when compared to a commonly accepted standard such as the Software Engineering Institute's capability maturity models.

competency-based asset

An organization's documented collection of processes, practices, and lessons learned to be used by the organization to achieve standards of performance.
See also **competency-based process** and **best practices.**

competency-based process

Descriptions of how the workforce is expected to perform work in specific disciplines such as sales, software development, testing, and the like.
See also **competency-based asset** and **best practices.**

competency community

Those who share common work practices and skills.

competency development plan

A description of how the organization will improve competency.

competency information

A comparison of an individual's capability against a competency description.

competency management

The approach and effort to improve the team's ability to perform their assigned responsibilities.

competition

An acquisition strategy where more than one qualified supplier is solicited to bid on performing a service or function.

competition advocate

The individual responsible to encourage and foster full and open competition.

Competition In Contracting Act of 1984　　　　CICA

An act of the U.S. Congress mandating policy regarding the awarding of Federal contracts through the competitive process, as opposed to sole source procurement. The Competition in Contracting Act was passed in 1984 (Public Law 98-369,98 Stat. 1175-1230). [USG]

competitive range

Proposals that are responsive to the RFP, and that have a reasonable chance of being selected for award, are considered in the competitive range and are candidates to proceed to written or oral discussions.

complexity

A measure of the difficulty of a project. Includes how elaborate, sophisticated, intricate, and involved the project solution is. The more complex the project the higher the need for expert techniques and tools. Complexity rather than size or dollar value is the most important driver for sophisticated management techniques.

complexity assessment

Numerical estimation of project factors for comparing project complexity.

compliance

Fulfilling expectations and/or conforming to standards.

component

A constituent element of a system.

component integration and test　　　　CIT

Assembling units into the next higher assembly and testing the integrated element.

computer aided design   **CAD**

The application of computers to facilitate design, including methods, forms, functions, algorithms, virtual mock-ups, and object integration.

computer aided document management   **CADM**

The application of computers to manage documents, including configuration control, identification, format, distribution, and related fields.

computer aided manufacturing   **CAM (1)**

The application of computers to facilitate manufacturing in the areas of numerically controlled machine operations, robotic production lines, just-in-time supply systems, inventory control, and configuration management.

computer aided software engineering   **CASE (1)**

The application of computers to facilitate the development of software. CASE tools usually include libraries of reusable code (modules of software that can be easily modified for specific tasks), programmer productivity tools, and testing utilities. CASE tools also provide requirements management, system simulation, test management, etc.

computer aided systems engineering   **CASE (2)**

The application of computers to facilitate requirements management, requirements flowdown, behavior simulations, system modeling and system trades, verification planning, change control, and baseline management.

computer aided testing   **CAT**

The application of computers to facilitate testing hardware, software, and systems, including softwarethat simulate inputs and environments.

computer hardware

Physical devices capable of accepting and storing digital data, executing a systematic sequence of operations on that data, and producing outputs. Such devices can perform substantial interpretation, computation, communication, control, or other logical functions. They include peripheral equipment such as storage devices.

computer program

A set of statements and instructions that is designed to solve a particular function, task, or problem and that conforms to the rules of a programming language.

computer program component   CPC

A computer software module forming a portion of a computer software configuration item (CSCI). CPC is now called computer software component (CSC).

computer program configuration item   CPCI

A term denoting a software component of a system, which is designated for configuration management to ensure configuration integrity. It may exist at any level in the hierarchy where interchangeability is required. CPCI is now called computer software configuration item (CSCI).

computer resource

Data processing system elements configured for a specific purpose.

computer resources working group   CRWG

Advisors that review the adequacy of the development environment and recommend improvements.

computer science

The professional discipline dedicated to computers and applications of computers.

computer software

A sequence of instructions and/or computer programs suitable for processing and execution by a computer. Software may reside in various types of media and computer memory.

computer software component   CSC

An element of a computer software configuration item (CSCI). CSCs may be further decomposed into computer software units (CSUs).

computer software configuration item   **CSCI**

A software component of a system that may exist at any level in the hierarchy and that is designated for configuration management to ensure configuration integrity. Configuration integrity is particularly important where interchangeability is required. See also **configuration item.**

computer software documentation

Technical data, including computer listings and printouts, which document the requirements, design, and/or coding details of computer software, explain the capabilities and limitations of the software, and/or provide operating instructions for using or supporting computer software during the software's operational life.

computer software unit   **CSU**

The lowest group of software code created to perform a specified function or functions. An element of a computer software component (CSC) that is separately testable.

computer system operators manual   **CSOM**

The manual that provides information and detailed procedures for initiating, operating, monitoring, and shutting down a computer system and for identifying/isolating a malfunction in a computer system.

concept

A general idea of a problem solution.

concept definition document   **CDD**

A document describing the concept selected for development and the results of investigating alternative system concepts. It is used to derive the system concept of operations document, system specifications, and the statement of work. Also known as system concept document.

Concept Definition Phase

The second of ten phases of the Reference Project Cycle and the second phase of the Study Period. In this phase, alternative concepts are evaluated and one is selected for approval at the System

Concept Review control gate. The system concept document, system concept of operations document, user validation plan, and updated should-cost and should-take estimates are produced in this phase. [RPC]

concept evaluation criteria

The musts, wants, and weights used to judge alternative concepts.

concept of operations   **CONOPS (1)**

See **user concept of operations** and **system concept of operations.**

Concept Phase

See **Concept Definition Phase.**

conceptual model

A representation of the concept under consideration.

conceptual system design

See **concept.**

concise

Clear and succinct. No extraneous information.

concurrency

Part of an acquisition or development strategy that combines or overlaps life cycle phases (such as engineering and manufacturing development, and production), or activities (such as design and operational testing).

concurrent engineering

The early consideration of all aspects of the product's life cycle to ensure completeness of design, optimum manufacturing or coding, efficient verification, ease of operations, minimum maintenance, and ease of disposal. Includes integrated development of both the product and the processes need to produce and field the product. Provides for early consideration of such disciplines as human factors, quality engineering, producibility, reliability, inspectability.

configuration

An arrangement of parts and elements.

configuration audit

An examination of the produced item against its standard.

configuration baseline

The description that is under change control.

configuration control

The requirement for formal change approval of changes to an approved baseline. The baseline may be business, budget, or technical and often is all three. Change approval is required from those accountable for managing and approving the baseline. The technical baseline often relates to the form, fit, and function of a baselined design.

configuration control board   CCB (2)

The body with the authority to approve proposed changes to a baseline.

See also **change control board** and **project control board**

configuration documentation

The documentation that represents the business, budget, or technical baseline under change control.

configuration identification

(1)   The identifier for the baseline under change control.
(2)   The use of alphanumeric codes to identify configuration items and lot date codes. Facilitates the management and potential recall of specific lots of products.

configuration item   CI (1)

A hardware, software, or composite item at any level in the system hierarchy designated for configuration management.

CIs have four common characteristics:
(1)   Defined functionality,
(2)   Replaceable as an entity,
(3)   Unique specification,
(4)   Formal control of form, fit and functionality.

Each CI should have an identified manager and may have CI-unique design reviews, qualification certification, Acceptance Reviews, and operator and maintenance manuals.

configuration item acceptance

The approval of a CI to be further integrated into the system for succeeding verification and system acceptance.

Configuration Item Acceptance Review   CIAR

A control gate of the Reference Project Cycle held to confirm that the configuration item (CI) has passed all verification or qualification requirements.

There are two types of CI Acceptance Reviews
(1)   Operational acceptance—proof of quality
(2)   Qualification acceptance—proof of design margin [RPC]
See also **Acceptance Review.**

Configuration Item Test Readiness Review   CITRR

A control gate of the Reference Project Cycle held to review readiness to initiate CI verification in accordance with the CI verification procedure. [RPC]

configuration item verification

Proving compliance with the CI design-to specification using test, inspection, demonstration, and analysis techniques.

configuration item verification procedures

Detailed step-by-step instructions for the set-up, operation, and evaluation of tests, inspections, demonstrations, or analyses to be used for CI verification.

configuration management   CM

The process to:
- Define and approve the evolving technical, budget, and business baselines of the project
- Control changes to the approved baselines
- Record and communicate the change and change status
- Audit actual performance to verify conformance to baselines.

configuration management officer   CMO

The individual responsible for managing the configuration management process including documentation and change notification. The CMO provides administrative support to the change control board.

configuration management plan

The document that describes configuration management process.

configuration status accounting

Recorded history of a configuration and the changes over time to the configuration.

conflict

(1)   Disharmony among participants.
(2)   Interference between system components (hardware and/or software).

conflict management

The approach to resolving disagreements among team members and other stakeholders.

conflict of interest

The condition when business and personal or organizational objectives are incompatible and not in the best interests of the business. The term is often used in regard to public officials and their relationship to matters of private interest or personal gain. It is also used in regard to persons who have left the government employment and seek employment in the private sector with contractors that they formerly had a business relationship with.

conflict resolution

The solving of conflict. Can include 1. Working together to reach a resolution, 2. Compromising, 3. Forcing, 4. Smoothing, and 5. Withdrawing.

conformance

Agreement between actual and expected.
See also **compliance.**

confrontation

Resolving issues by directly addressing them face to face.

congressional authorization

An act of the U.S. Congress that authorizes Federal programs, obligations, and expenditures. Congressional appropriation must follow to provide the necessary funds. [USG]

congressional budget justification   CBJ

Documents prepared by each U.S. government agency to justify future budgets to Congress. [USG]

Congressional Budget Justification Review   CBJR

U.S. government agency executive control gate held to approve the U.S. Congressional Budget Justification Package. [USG]

congruence

The quality of a set in which the members are consistent — in conformance or correspondence. A state of agreement.

consensus

A group decision rooted on open and thorough discussion until all parties agree that they can live with and actively support the outcome.

consensus decision process

Group decisions resulting from members engaging in full and open discussion and then reaching consensus to accept and openly support the resulting decision.

consent

To agree.

consent-to meeting

A meeting, with all parties directly involved in a decision, held to critically examine readiness to proceed. Typically used for consent to ship, deploy, machine, print, test, and so forth. Not all consent-to meetings are control gates, but all control gates are consent-to meetings.

See **control gate.**

consent-to ship certificate

A document signifying readiness to ship. Approval allows product transfer to the shipping organization.

consistent

Requirements that do not conflict.

constant year dollars

A method of relating dollars in several years by removing the effects of inflation or deflation and showing all dollars at the value they would have in a selected base year.

constraint

Restriction within defined bounds. Projects often have technical, cost, and schedule constraints.

Construction Performance Verification Review   CPVR

A review held to assure compliance of construction to the specification and other construction documentation.

constructive challenge

Informed interrogation and discussion of proposed concepts/solutions by peers and experts to ensure that the concepts/solutions are well-founded and justified.

constructive change

Change caused by new and different work from the contract as a result of an overt action by the buyer or by the buyer's failure to act. Based on case law, the seller can submit a constructive change order to formally pursue compensatory adjustments to the contract.

Constructive Cost Model   COCOMO

A nonproprietary software cost and schedule estimating method originally developed by Dr. Barry Boehm (Software Engineering Economics, 1981). Produces an estimate of the number of person-months required to develop common software products at three levels of complexity: basic, intermediate, and detailed.

consumables

Expendables that are depleted and must be replaced like fuel.

context

The environment and external interfaces that can affect the solution.

context of implementation

The problem space, interfaces, and environment that any solution must operate in.

contingency

A possibility that must be anticipated, which typically includes cost and schedule issues.

contingency reserve

Schedule and/or financial resources set aside to be used for unforeseen but reasonably anticipated surprises.

continuing resolution

The U.S. government process to provide budget authority for specific on-going activities where the regular fiscal year appropriation has not been enacted by the beginning of the fiscal year. The Continuing Resolution usually specifies a designated period and a maximum rate at which government agencies may incur obligations based on the rate of the prior year, the President's budget request, or an appropriation bill passed by either or both Houses of Congress. Normally new programs cannot be started under a Continuing Resolution. [USG]

continuous improvement   CI (2)

The on-going effort to improve quality by eliminating causes of defects or substandard results as a continuing process.

continuous process improvement   CPI (1)

The on-going efforts to improve the effectiveness of processes by examining each step for value-added and adjusting the steps and/or sequence to improve the results.

continuous quality improvement   CQI

The on-going effort to improve quality by eliminating causes of defects as a continuing process.

continuous representation

A capability maturity model structure wherein capability levels provide a recommended order for approaching process improvement within each specified process area.

See also **staged representation, capability level,** and **process area.** [SEI]

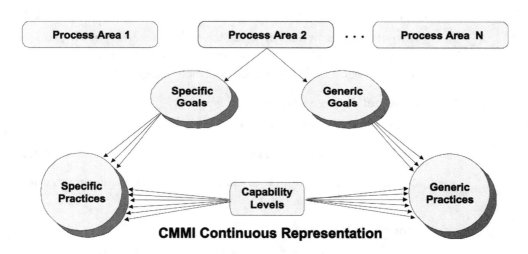

CMMI Continuous Representation

contract

A mutually binding legal relationship obligating the seller to furnish products or services and the buyer to pay for them.

Contract Acceptance Review   **CAR**

The control gate of the Reference Project Cycle held for the buyer and seller to ratify their contractual agreement. [RPC]

contract action

An action to change a contract.

contract administration

Contract management actions to ensure compliance with the contract and to keep the contract baseline current.

contract administrator   **CA**

An official, who has the authority to negotiate, enter into, modify, and administer contracts.

contract award

The act of negotiating and signing a contractual agreement.

contract budget baseline

The negotiated contract cost and the estimated cost of changes authorized but not yet negotiated.

contract change notice   **CCN**

A written buyer notice directing the seller to make specific changes to the contractual effort. Cost and schedule impacts of the change must be negotiated. Also called contract change order (CCO).

contract change order   **CCO**

See **contract change notice.**

contract change proposal   **CCP**

A formal priced proposal to change a contract. Sometimes called task change proposal (TCP).

contract changes

Modifications to the general scope of the agreed-to contract. If such change causes an increase or decrease in the cost or time required or otherwise affects any other terms or conditions of the contract, the buyer is expected to make an equitable adjustment.

contract close-out

Final contract settlement including resolution of all outstanding items and payments.

Contract Data Classification Guide   **CDCG**

A U.S. government document providing rules for classifying project data. [USG]

contract data requirements list   **CDRL (1)**

A listing of documentation, required by contract, with quantities and delivery dates. documentation requirements descriptions (DRDs) define the required content of each CDRL item.
See also **contract documentation requirements list.**

contract documentation requirements list   CDRL (2)

A listing of documentation required by contract, with quantities and delivery dates. Documentation Requirements Descriptions (DRDs) define the required content of each CDRL item.
See also **contract data requirements list.**

contracted advisory and assistance services   CAAS

Those services acquired directly by the U.S. Department of Defense from nongovernmental sources to support or improve policy development or decision-making, or to support or improve the management of organizations or the operation of weapon systems, equipment, and components. [USG]

contract funds status report   CFSR

A report normally required on cost or incentive type contracts to inform the buyer of funds used and status of remaining funds.

Contract Implementation Review   CIR (1)

The control gate of the Reference Project Cycle held for the buyer to approve the seller's Implementation Plan. Also called **Start-Up Review, Initial Design Review**, or **Project Initiation Review.** [PRC]

contract information file

A database that includes contracts, contractor performance, and contractor payments.

contracting officer   CO (2)

The official with the warranted authority to enter into, administer, and/or terminate contracts. Only the CO can obligate the government to pay for contractor or supplier-provided goods or services.

contracting officer's representative   COR

An individual empowered by the contracting officer (CO) to act on behalf of the CO in defined contract areas. Typically the individual responsible for contractor technical or administrative performance within the bounds of the contract. The COR cannot obligate the government to pay for goods or services.

contracting officer's technical representative   **COTR**

An individual empowered to act on behalf of the contracting officer in defined contract areas. Typically the individual responsible for contractor performance within the bounds of the contract. The COTR cannot obligate the government to pay for goods or services.

contract inspection report   **CIR (2)**

A buyer's assessment of contractor performance.

contract line item numbers   **CLIN**

An identifier used in request for proposals (RFPs) and the subsequent contract to describe deliverables under the contract.

contract manager

The manager responsible for overseeing all aspects of contract preparation and administration.

contract modification

Any unilateral or bilateral written alteration of the specification, delivery point, rate or delivery, contract period, price, quantity, or other provision of an existing contract, accomplished in accordance with a contract clause (for example, change order, notice of termination, supplemental agreement, or exercise of a contract option).

contract negotiations

The process of buyer and seller discussion and position modification through offers and counter-offers in order to reach mutual agreement on contract content.

contractor

An individual or organization that enters into contract with a buyer.

contractor furnished equipment   **CFE**

Contractor equipment that is committed for use to satisfy a contract.

contractor management systems evaluation program   **CMSEP**

Buyer evaluation of the contractor's internal systems for managing cost and schedule.

contract project office   CPO

The contractor's project manager and associated immediate staff.

contract proposal

A document submitted in response to a request for proposal (RFP).

contract quality requirements

Verification requirements imposed on the seller to ensure achievement of required quality.

contract system status report   CSSR

A report of the U.S. government's audit of a contractor' compliance with required practices and procedures. [USG]

contract target cost   CTC (2)

The negotiated target cost for the original contract plus all contractual changes that have been defined, but excluding the estimated cost of any authorized, unpriced changes.

contract target price   CTP

The negotiated estimated cost (contract target cost) plus profit or fee.

contract type

Specific pricing (or compensation) arrangements, expressed as contract types, include firm-fixed-price, fixed-price-incentive, cost-plus-fixed-fee, cost-plus-incentive-fee, cost-plus-award-fee, and several others. Among special arrangements that use fixed-price or cost-reimbursement pricing provisions are indefinite delivery contracts, basic ordering agreements, letter contracts, and others.

contract work breakdown structure   CWBS

The hierarchical decomposition of the system under contract into components, services, and associated work tasks to satisfy the contract statement of work.

control

Means to manage people and/or regulate processes and events.

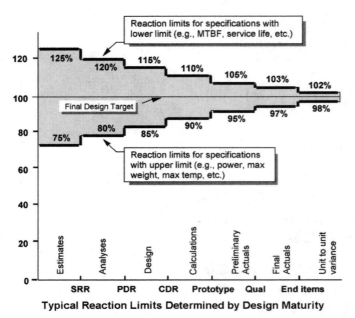

Typical Reaction Limits Determined by Design Maturity

control chart
The display of process results over time with control limits to reveal whether the process is in control or whether corrective action is required.

control gate
A preplanned event to demonstrate accomplishments, approve and baseline the results, and approve the approach for continuing the project.

Cooperative Research and Development Agreement CRADA
An agreement entered into by the U.S. government with any of the following organizations to pursue research and development: industry, university, not-for-profit, as well as a state or local government. Under a CRADA arrangement, a government laboratory may contribute people, equipment and facilities but no money. The collaborating party may contribute the same and may provide money to the laboratory for manpower reimbursement or other things if required. [USG]

coordination
The orchestration of project activities to achieve a defined result.

core competency
Knowledge and skills essential to the competitive position of the organization.

Corrective Action

One of ten Project Management Elements.

Includes reactive actions taken (1) to return the project to plan and (2) to ensure that identified variances or anomalies will never recur.

cost account

An accounting system identifier used by project participants to charge time and other allowable charges to a project. In performance measurement systems, the cost account usually comprises work packages and is the lowest summation level in the work breakdown structure (WBS).

cost accounting standards   CAS

The U.S. government's guidelines for contractor accounting practices. [USG]

cost account manager   CAM (2)

The individual responsible for managing a cost account or task. Also called a task manager.

cost analysis

The analysis of the cost elements of a proposal or on-going work. It includes verification of cost data, evaluation of all elements of costs, and projection of these data to determine the effect on price.

cost as an independent variable   CAIV

A strategy that entails setting aggressive, yet realistic, cost objectives when defining system operational requirements and managing acquisition to these objectives. Cost objectives must balance customer needs with projected future resources, taking into account existing technology, maturation of new technologies, and anticipated process improvements. As system performance and cost objectives are decided (on the basis of cost-performance trade-offs), the acquisition processes will make cost more of a constraint, and less of a variable, while nonetheless obtaining the needed capability of the system.

cost at completion   CAC

The summation of all project costs incurred throughout the project.

cost center

(1) An organization responsible for the total costs of a specified function like design, or some element or group of elements of the system.
(2) An organization that represents a cost of doing business or executing a project task as opposed to generating income.

cost codes

Alphanumeric identifiers assigned to project elements and work tasks that are used in cost and schedule planning and recording.

cost effectiveness

The perceived value of a decision where value is benefit divided by cost.

cost estimating

Predicting future costs based on past experience and/or accepted models.

cost estimating methodologies

Approaches to predicting costs of a project such as top down, bottom up with detailed bases of estimates, computerized cost models, and historically based empirical guidelines.

cost estimating relationship

A ratio used in costing such as dollars per pound, dollars per hour, dollars per function point, etc. Estimators predict the amount of resources to be applied and cost analysts apply the cost estimating relationship to convert to dollars. If the estimate is required in then-year dollars, formulas for predicted inflation and cost of money are applied.

cost evaluation team   CET

The team formed to evaluate cost proposals and basis of estimates.

cost growth

Increase in projected cost due to increases in scope. Not to be confused with cost overrun that is spending more than predicted for the same work.

cost model

A cost estimating algorithm used to estimate future cost such as dollars per square foot for building construction.

cost of capital

The commonly accepted rate of return for capital if invested at a similar risk to the project.

cost of money

Normal charges for the loan or use of money. Usually relates to the U.S. Treasury interest rate.

cost of quality

Costs attributed to the achievement of quality including the cost of handling nonconformance and the associated rework or scrap. If hardware and software development and production processes are thoughtfully documented and carefully followed, rework and scrap rates can be dramatically reduced and customer satisfaction dramatically increased. Hence the expression, "Quality is free."

cost overrun

The amount over (or under) the contract target price (for fixed price incentive type contracts), estimated target cost (for cost reimbursement type contracts), or redeterminable price (for fixed price redeterminable type contracts). Also, the comparison of the final cost against the predicted cost.
See also **cost underrun.**

cost performance index   CPI (2)

A performance measurement system factor that is the budgeted cost of work performed (earned value) divided by the actual cost of work performed (ACWP). If ACWP is twice BCWP then the CPI or financial efficiency is 0.5, which predicts a significant project cost overrun.

cost performance measurement baseline

The cost and schedule plan against which the project's performance is measured.

cost performance report   CPR

A set of five performance status reports associated with cost/schedule control system criteria (C/SCSC) performance measurement. The first four reports present project budget and actuals as a function of the work breakdown structure, functional organization, baseline, and personnel. The fifth report is variance analysis.

cost plus award fee   CPAF

A cost-reimbursement contract with award fee provisions to motivate and reward contractors to meet standards such as quality, timeliness, efficiency, and cost effectiveness. The amount of award fee is determined by the buyer's subjective evaluation of the contractor's performance.
See also **award fee** and **fixed price award fee.**

cost plus fixed fee   CPFF

A cost-reimbursement contract that provides a fixed fee to the contractor. The fixed fee, once negotiated, does not vary even though the costs may exceed the original estimate. It may be adjusted however, as a result of approved contract changes.

cost plus incentive fee   CPIF

A cost-reimbursement contract that provides predetermined incentive targets to motivate the contractor to achieve specified performance. The incentive fee criteria are established during contract negotiation and cannot be changed without renegotiation (unlike award fee).

cost plus incentive fee with ceiling price

Like cost plus incentive fee except that when the project reaches the ceiling price, the seller assumes full financial responsibility. Since the contract is a "best effort" contract and there is no contractual requirement to continue, the contractor usually continues to honor the informal promises made to the buyer.

cost plus no fee   CPNF

A cost-reimbursement contract that provides payment for allowable costs but with no fee.

cost pool

When costs for services or equipment cannot be associated with a specific project, but are used by several projects (for example, a software rapid prototyping facility), the costs are pooled and allocated to each project in proportion to the level of use. If the services are broadly used throughout a company or major division, the cost pool is commonly called overhead.

cost realism analysis

An evaluation of the predicted cost of a project developed by knowledgeable, unbiased personnel. In the acquisition process the objective is to determine if the estimated proposed cost elements are realistic for the work to be performed; reflect a clear understanding the requirements; and are consistent with the unique methods of performance and materials described in the offeror's technical proposal. Cost realism analysis is required on cost reimbursement contracts to determine the most probable cost which is an evaluation factor in selecting the winning contractor. Cost realism analysis may also be required on sole-source or single-bidder fixed price contracts to determine if the contractor understands the work and/or is a responsible contractor.

cost-reimbursement contract

A "best effort" contract that provides payment for allowable costs and fees as prescribed by the contract.

Cost/Schedule Control System Criteria   C/SCSC

A performance measurement system for project status that provides for cost performance reports (CPR) or cost/schedule status reports (C/SSR), and contract funds status reports (CFSR).

cost/schedule status report   C/SSR

A reduced cost/schedule control system criteria (C/SCSC) performance report. It requires two status reports: cumulative budgets and actuals by work breakdown structure (CSSR) and a variance analysis report.

cost-sharing contract

A contract that provides payment for only a share of allowable costs. Cost sharing contracts are often awarded to motivate development of new technologies.

cost to complete   CTC (3)

The projected cost to complete the project from its present state.

cost variance CV

A performance measurement value obtained by subtracting actual cost of work performed (ACWP) from budgeted cost of work performed (BCWP).

crashing

The adding of personnel and daily work hours to shorten the schedule.

critical activity

Tasks on the critical path.

Critical Chain Method

Eli Goldratt's theory of constraints (TOC) based planning approach that moves most individual task contingencies to the end of the critical path and applies resource availability as a driving factor in schedule achievement and critical path determination. The process surfaces resource constraints that must be addressed to perform to schedule.

critical competency-based processes

Processes within the core competencies of an organization that are essential to achieving the organization's business objectives.

critical component

A component essential to the accomplishment of the primary mission.

Critical Design Review CDR

The series of control gates of the Reference Project Cycle held to approve the build-to and code-to documentation, associated draft verification procedures, and readiness and capability of fabricators and coders to carry out the implementation. All hardware, software, support equipment, and tooling should be reviewed in ascending order of unit to system. More appropriately called Production Guarantee Review since proof is required that the fabrication and coding called for can actually be carried out and that it will yield results that meet the design-to specifications. The evidence provided is typically samples of the critical processes to demonstrate credibility and repeatability. [RPC]

critical item

An entity essential to the accomplishment of the primary mission.

criticality

The measure of importance, usually in failure modes and effects.

critical path

The longest sequence of activities with minimum or zero slack that paces the project schedule. Often referred to as the long pole in the tent.

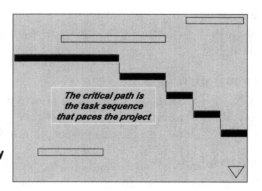

Pack clothes
Prepare boat
Have car fixed
Pick up supplies
Install hitch
Pick up boat
Pick up friends
Arrange house security
Cancel newspaper

The critical path is the task sequence that paces the project

Critical Path - Vacation Preparation Example

Critical Path Method   CPM

A project network and schedule development approach that analyzes the network and determines the project's critical path. A single estimate is made for the duration of each task in the network. This distinguishes CPM from PERT, which uses three estimates for the duration of each task: earliest, nominal, and latest finish.
See also **Project Evaluation Review Technique.**

critical positions

Positions essential to the success of the organization such as chief systems engineer.

critical skills

Skills essential to the success of the organization such as particular design and software skills.

critical task

A task essential to an organization's or individual's performance objectives.

critical workforce competency

Competencies most essential to an organization's ability to succeed and prosper. These competencies should be continuously measured and improved.

culture

Socially transmitted behavior patterns, beliefs, work habits, and thoughts.

cure notice

A buyer notification informing a contractor of failure to perform, and that, if improvement does not take place within a stipulated period of time, the buyer may terminate the contract.

customer

The individual or group that receives project deliverables. The customer usually determines acceptance and controls the resources for acquiring the solution. The customer is not necessarily a user of the solution.

customer requirements

The business and technical musts, wants, and operational context that are to be satisfied.

cutover

The transition from one system to a successor system.

damages

Money ordered to be paid as compensation for injury or loss.

data

The raw materials from which a user extracts information and knowledge.

data analysis

The evaluation of information considering various aspects or points of view.

data bank

Information organized by type and subject for accessibility.

database

A repository of data that can be queried. Two common database structures are hierarchical and relational.

data dictionary

A specialized type of database containing meta-data, which is managed by a data dictionary system; a repository of information describing the characteristics of data used to design, monitor, document, protect, and control data in information systems and databases; an application of data dictionary systems.

data flow diagram

An illustration of the inputs, outputs, interfaces, and data paths of a system, used to communicate the routing of data.

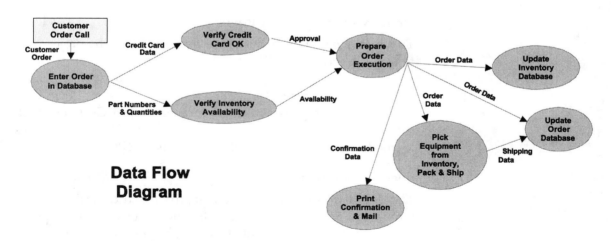

**Data Flow
Diagram**

data item description   DID

The content outline of a required document. An alternate term for documentation requirements description (DRD).

data management

Systems and processes for the manipulation, storage, control, and sharing of data.

data management officer

See **documentation management officer.**

data model

Properties, characteristics, and relationships among a set of data. See also **schema.**

data processing   DP

The manipulation of data to achieve an objective such as statistical analysis or arithmetic operations.

DD 250   DD 250

Material Inspection Receiving Report (DD250) is one of the most widely used U.S. government DoD forms. It provides evidence of government acceptance, receipt, inventory, and status control. Contractors may use the DD Form 250 as an invoice, packing list, and as shipment notice to aid the government in its inventory control.

Deactivation Approval Review   DAR

The control gate held to authorize termination of the project and to begin deactivation. [RPC]

Deactivation Phase

The tenth of ten phases in the Reference Project Cycle in which the system is deactivated and disposed of. The final lessons learned document is prepared in this phase. [RPC]

deactivation plan

The document that describes the approach and critical processes required to convert the project to the safe, deactivated, or disposed state. It includes methods of shutdown, disposition of records and hardware, security issues, and transition to new or follow-on systems. The plan may include lessons learned, disposition of items of historical interest, environmentally sensitive and hazardous materials issues.

deactivation procedures

Step-by-step instructions to safely deactivate and dispose of a system.

debriefing

Summarization of the circumstances of an event after the event. In acquisition, a formal explanation of why an offeror won or did not win a competition for a negotiated contract. Offerors excluded from the competitive range or otherwise excluded from the competition before award may request a debriefing.

The debriefing for those excluded must include: (1) the evaluation of significant elements in the offeror's proposal; (2) a summary of the rationale for elimination from the competition; and (3) reasonable responses to relevant questions about whether source selection procedures contained in the solicitation, applicable regulations, and other applicable authorities were followed.

For post award debriefings the debriefing must include: (1) the evaluation of the significant weaknesses or deficiencies in the offeror's proposal; (2) the overall evaluated cost or price and technical ratings of successful and debriefed offerors; (4) a summary of the rationale for award; (5) for acquisitions of commercial end items, the make and model of the selected item; and (6) reasonable responses to relevant questions about whether source selection procedures contained in the solicitation, applicable regulations, and other applicable authorities were followed.

decision

The selection of one course of action from two or more alternatives.

decision coordinating papers

A DoD document describing the government's intention to acquire a system. [USG]

decision support data

Data that supports trade study decisions. Includes analysis, trade study results, test results, data from model and simulation studies, engineering data and customer inputs.

decision tree

A decision analysis technique consisting of a diagram showing the sequence of alternatives considered and those selected.

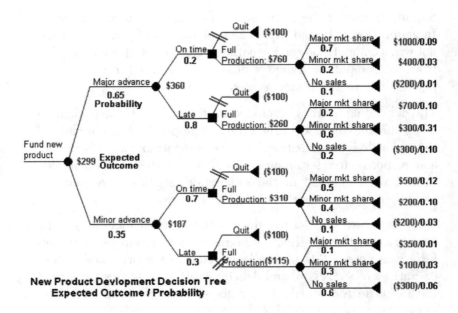

New Product Deviopment Decision Tree
Expected Outcome / Probability

decomposition

The hierarchical functional and physical system partitioning into hardware assemblies, software components, and operator activities that can be scheduled, budgeted, and assigned to a responsible individual.

Decomposition Analysis and Resolution   DA&R

The business- and technically-driven decision process at each level of system decomposition to select the best of alternative solutions at that level. [VPM]

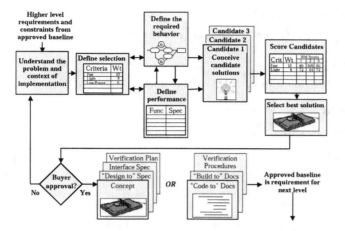

decomposition and definition

The hierarchical functional and physical system partitioning into hardware assemblies, software components, and operator activities that can be scheduled, budgeted, and assigned to a responsible individual and the development of the associated design-to, build-to, and verification documentation.

decomposition diagram

The noun levels of the work breakdown structure that represent the structured decomposition and integration of a system.

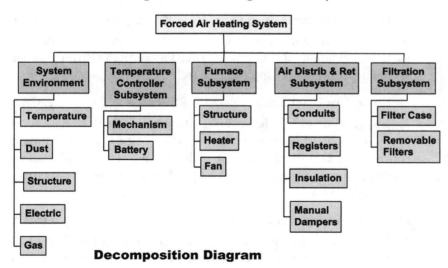

Decomposition Diagram

decomposition hierarchy
See **system decomposition hierarchy.**

decoupling
The minimization of interactions between elements.

default
Failure to fulfill the terms of a contract.

defect
A substandard condition.

defect density
Number of defects per sampled population.

defective pricing
Seller submitted cost or pricing data that was know by the seller to be inaccurate, incomplete, or not current.

defect rate
Defect density normalized to a base, such as defects per hundred units.

defects per hundred units
Defect rate normalized to a base of 100 units.

Defense Advanced Research Projects Agency   DARPA
A U.S. government Department of Defense agency responsible for new technology development. DARPA contracts through other agencies for basic and applied research. [USG]

Defense Contract Administration Service   DCAS
A U.S. government Defense Logistics Agency unit charged with providing contract administrative services in or near government contractor's facilities. Services include contract administration, quality assurance, engineering and production, materials, security and transportation. [USG]

Defense Contract Audit Agency   DCAA
A U.S. government agency charged with oversight and audit of contractor's accounting system and cost records. DCAA works closely with DCAS in managing contractors. [USG]

Defense Logistics Agency   DLA

A U.S. government Department of Defense agency charged with logistics support (warehousing, transportation, maintenance, and contract services) to military services. [USG]

Defense Plant Representative Office   DPRO

An on-site U.S. government DCAS team to provide administrative, security, logistics, or quality assistance to the contractor at the direction of the contracting officer.

Defense Priorities And Allocation System   DPAS

A U.S. government Department of Commerce Regulation that rates orders for goods and services procured in the national interest and they must be provided preferential treatment with respect to delivery and performance. Priorities from highest to lowest are DX, DO, and unrated.

Defense Systems Management College   DSMC

A U.S. government DoD college dedicated to teaching the **DoD** acquisition process and to conducting research to improve acquisition program management.

deficiency

(1)   Substandard.
(2)   A part of a proposal that fails to meet the requirements.

defined process

A managed process, tailored to the organization's objectives and tailoring guidelines, that has a maintained process description, and that contributes work products, measures, and other process improvement information to the organization's process assets.

definitization

Formal incorporation of negotiation results into the contract. Usually a conversion of the negotiating team's minutes into appropriate contract language by the contacting official.

deflect

Transfer risk to others usually by insurance, warrantee, or other means.

deliverable

An item produced for a project. May be an internal deliverable like handling equipment or a customer deliverable to satisfy the contract.

delivery

Release of a system or component to its customer or intended user.

delivery strategy

The selection of single or multiple deliveries regardless of whether incremental or evolutionary development strategy is adopted.

Delphi Technique

A consensus process that uses experts to help reach a common result. The Delphi Technique was originally conceived as a way to obtain the opinion of experts without necessarily bringing them together face to face. {http://instruction.bus.wisc.edu/obdemo/readings/delphi.htm}

demonstration

Verification by witnessing an actual operation in the expected or simulated environment, without need for measurement data or post-demonstration analysis.

de-obligate

To cancel a current commitment so that there is no obligation to perform.

dependability

The degree of being capable of performing required functions at any time.

dependency

The relationship between adjacent tasks in a task network.

deployment

Placing into use.

Deployment Readiness Review   **DRR**

The control gate held to approve readiness for deployment into the staging or operational environment. [RPC]

depot maintenance
Maintenance that must be performed at a distribution/maintenance center as opposed to being performed at the operational site.

depreciation
The periodic devaluation of an asset to account for aging and use.

derived measures
Data resulting from the mathematical function of two or more base measures.
See also **base measure.** [SEI]

derived requirement
A requirement determined by quantitative analyses, testing, calculations, simulations, and/or inference.

design
The process of developing and documenting a solution to a problem using technology, experts, and tools.

design-bid-build
The term used when different contractors will be used for the design and build phases of facility development and bids will be solicited for the build portion.
See also **design-build.**

design-build
The term used when a single contractor will be used both to design and to build a facility.
See also **design-bid-build.**

design concept description document
Identification and description of the system's architecture, decomposition, and hardware configuration items (HWCIs), computer software configuration items (CSCIs), and manual operations.

Design Concept Review   DCR
A control gate held to review and approve the top-level solution concept and expected decomposition into identified hardware, software, and operator configuration items. [RPC]
See also **System Design Review** (SDR).

design constraint

A limitation to the design trade space.

design description

A narrative description of the design approach and design of an entity or system

design, development, test, and evaluation   **DDT&E**

A name sometimes applied to the System Implementation and Verification Phases of the Reference Project Cycle. [RPC]

design independent

Requirements that are free of design constraints.

design load

The most stressful condition that the design should accommodate.

design margin

Built-in capability beyond that operationally specified to provide robustness or to provide for future add-on capability.
See **qualification** and **pre-planned product improvement.**

design process

Development of the concept, design-to specification, build-to and code-to documentation, and user documentation, as needed to define the solution. The process includes creation of evidence that the design, if implemented, will meet the requirements.

design producibility

The ability of the design to be produced using state of the art processes.

design release status

A metric associated with the engineering organization's schedule performance that compares actual and planned engineering release (approval) of specifications, drawings, design documents, etc.

design requirement
See **design-to specifications.**

design review

Systematic examination of a design to ensure that it will satisfy the specifications when produced.

design-to-cost   DTC

A process that constrains concept and design options to a fixed cost limit. The cost limit is usually what the buyer will pay or what satisfies the market opportunity.

design-to-schedule   DTS

A process that constrains design options to a fixed schedule limit. The schedule limit is usually what the buyer can accept or what satisfies the market window of opportunity.

design-to specifications

Documents that specify the design-to requirements for a system or the elements of a system. May include functionality, performance, interfaces, constraints, effectiveness, and verification.

detailed design

The conversion of concepts and their design-to specifications into associated build-to and code-to documentation and verification procedures. Includes development items such as platform and language, producibility documentation, and material and process specifications.

developer

The organization or individual responsible for development.

development

The process of bringing something into being.
See also **development cycle.**

development baseline

The baselined specifications, under change control, that are driving the development.

development cycle

In the Reference Project Cycle of three periods, it is the Study and Acquisition periods and does not include the Operations period. [RPC]

development life cycle
See **Project Cycle.**

development method
The selection of the Waterfall, Spiral, or Vee method as the approach to managing the development process. Selection depends on the approach to risk management and other factors.

Development Phase
The sixth of ten phases of the Reference Project Cycle in which the designs of all levels of the system are defined, subcontractors and vendors are selected, and the system is developed. This second phase of the Implementation Period is preceded by the Source Selection Phase and followed by the Verification Phase. All of the design-to, build-to and code-to documents and associated verification plans and procedures are prepared in this phase. [RPC]

development specifications
See **design-to specifications.**

development strategy
The selection of planned incremental or evolutionary development as the baseline approach for the project.

development test and evaluation   DT&E
Test and analysis to demonstrate that engineering design and development is complete; that design risks have been minimized; that the system will meet specifications; and the system has utility when deployed.

development testing
Informal and formal testing of models to prove technical feasibility and the validity of design concepts.

deviation
A written buyer authorization permitting a provider to not satisfy a specified requirement for a limited number of items or time. A deviation usually includes financial consideration to compensate for reduced performance.

direct cost

An allowable cost directly attributable to the project. It may include labor, material, subcontractors, computer hours, and other expenses.

discrepancy report   DR

A document that identifies discrepant conditions and requires corrective action.

discrete task

A measurable activity with an output.

discussion

Any written or oral communications between the contracting officer and the offeror to determine acceptability of a proposal. [USG]

dispersion ratio

The ratio of total equivalent headcount charging to a project for a specific period divided by the number of different individuals charging in the same period. An important metric to reveal the extent of part time individuals working on a project. A value of one would indicate no part time personnel while a value of 0.5 would indicate that, on average, a person is only working half time on the project.

disposal

The process of removing a system or component, ensuring proper handling of any environmentally sensitive materials, and sending the remainder to surplus storage or sale.
See also **Deactivation Phase.**

disposition

A settlement of an issue.

disposition of nonconformity

Actions to resolve nonconformity that can range from use-as-is, to rework, to scrap.

dispute

Disagreement between a buyer and a contractor about contract provisions.

distributed architecture

Solution structure that uses two or more networked processing elements.

doability

Achievability.

document

A type of project deliverable or any text or pictorial information to describe project deliverables. Also referred to as documentation.

documentation change notice   DCN

A notification of change to holders of controlled documentation.

documentation management officer   DMO

The individual responsible for management of all project document baselines especially those of the Contract and subcontract documentation requirements lists.

documentation requirements description   DRD

The content outline of a required document. An alternate term to data item description.

documentation tree

The hierarchical relationship diagram for all project documents.

Documentation Verification Review   DVR

Review to ensure documentation compliance with documentation standards.

down select

The acquisition process of reducing the number of competitors based on demonstrated performance in a sequence of competitive events, which may include studies, concept definition, or delivery of a model. Also, a two step procurement technique: (1) the number of competitors are reduced by preliminary screening; (2) a best value procurement is conducted between the remaining competitors.

draft RFP

The preliminary request for proposal sent to candidate bidders for evaluation and voluntary comments.

drawing

A likeness or representation for the purpose of specifying.

dual source

A secondary supplier for a product or service as a hedge against risk.

dummy activity

A zero duration activity to show logical dependency in an activity on arrow network.

dynamic analysis

Evaluation of behavior in response to variable inputs.

earned value   EV

The budgeted cost of work performed (BCWP). A performance measurement term representing work accomplished, which is equal to the planned cost of achieving specified results. Earned value is also the official name for the U.S. government's performance measurement system formerly called Cost/Schedule Control System Criteria.

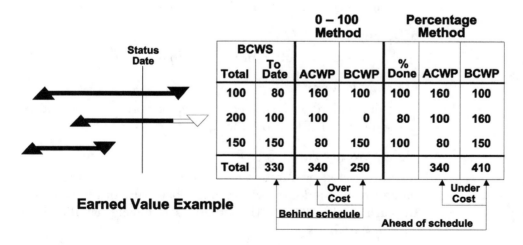

| | | | 0 – 100 Method | | Percentage Method | | |
| | BCWS | | | | | | |
Status Date	Total	To Date	ACWP	BCWP	% Done	ACWP	BCWP
	100	80	160	100	100	160	100
	200	100	100	0	80	100	160
	150	150	80	150	100	80	150
Total		330	340	250		340	410

Earned Value Example

Over Cost — Behind schedule — Under Cost — Ahead of schedule

Earned Value System

A performance measurement system used to plan and status schedule and cost performance of a project and entities within the project. Formerly called Cost/Schedule Control System Criteria or C/SCSC.

economic life

The time period during which a project provides economic benefit.

economic value

The project value in terms of the expected financial returns and contribution to achieving its strategic objectives.

economies of scale

Reductions in the unit cost of production as quantities are increased.

effectiveness

A measure of how well the solution meets expectations and satisfies the objectives.

effectiveness analysis

The assessment of how well a proposed solution will respond to the anticipated operational scenarios.

effectiveness criteria

The value algorithm for solution efficiency.

efficiency

Ratio of the useful output of a system to total input.

efficiency factor

Ratio of standard performance to actual performance. May be expressed in units of time or other quantities.

eighty-twenty rule

A term created by Pareto, an Italian sociologist, meaning that a process or methodology will accommodate 80% of the situations that arise, with 20% of the situations requiring handling on a case-by-case basis.

elaborated

Expanded to include the details necessary to fully describe the situation, especially as applied to baseline management.
See also **baseline.**

electromagnetic compatibility   EMC

Verification that system performance is not impaired by the operational electromagnetic environment and that system elements do not electromagnetically interfere with each other.

electromagnetic environment

The man made and natural electromagnetic fields that the solution will be exposed to.

electromagnetic interference   EMI

Electromagnetic emissions that adversely affect the system. Shielding often mitigates EMI.

electromagnetic susceptibility

The sensitivity to being affected by the electromagnetic environment.

electronic counter-countermeasures   ECCM

Anti-jamming systems used to mitigate opposing electronic countermeasures.

electronic countermeasures   ECM

Electromagnetic emissions to jam or disrupt opposing systems, especially communications or radar systems.

electronic warfare   EW

The concealing of friendly electronic transmissions and the mitigation of rival electronic warfare techniques.

element

(1)   An entity of a system.
(2)   Level 3 in the example system decomposition hierarchy.

embedded system

A system or function built into a host system in such a way that it cannot be removed without disassembly of the host system.

empower

Delegation of authority to act.

empowered workgroup

A team that is authorized to make decisions relative to how they will accomplish their objectives.

end article

Deliverable.

end item   **EI**

See **end article.**

end user

The person or group for whom the project's product or service was developed.

engineering

The application of scientific and mathematical principles to conceive, design, manufacture, and operate efficient and economical structures, machines, processes, and systems.

engineering analysis

The evaluation to predict technical, cost, and schedule factors of a proposed solution.

engineering change

A modification to the approved technical baseline.

engineering change notice   **ECN**

The formal release of an engineering revision to an approved baseline.
See also **engineering order (EO).**

engineering change proposal   **ECP**

A proposal submitted by the seller in response to a buyer request for an engineering change proposal to change the existing effort. Only the buyer can initiate the request for an engineering change proposal. This activity is usually preceded by a request for change. The user, buyer, or the seller can initiate a request for change, an exploratory activity.

engineering change request   **ECR**

A request to a change control board to consider a change to the technical baseline.

engineering cost estimate

Cost estimate derived by summing detailed cost analysis of the individual work packages and adding appropriate burdens. Usually determined by the performing organization's price analysts and cost accountants. Also called a bottom-up cost estimate.

engineering data

Technical information and data relative to the requirements, concepts, design-to, build-to, testing, deployment, training, operation, maintenance, and deactivation of a solution.

engineering development

See **engineering.**

engineering development model   **EDM**

A technical demonstration model constructed to be tested in a simulated or actual field environment. The model usually meets electrical and mechanical performance specifications, and either meets or closely approaches meeting the size, shape, and weight specifications. It may lack the high-reliability parts required to meet the reliability and environmental specifications, but is designed to readily incorporate such changes in the prototype and final production units. Its function is to test and evaluate operational performance and utility before making a final commitment to produce the operational units. Also called an engineering model.

engineering estimate

An estimate of labor hours, material, and computer support to accomplish a task or a group of tasks.

engineering model

See **engineering development model.**

engineering order   **EO**

Documented technical direction to change an approved baseline. The EO is proposed by the engineering organization, approved and, released through the configuration control process to manufacturing, software development, procurement, and other affected parties.

engineering process group

Specialists that develop and control common processes of the organization.

engineering release

Design data baselined and distributed for general use.

engineering release record

The record of the engineering baseline, the change record, and who has it and is using it.

engineering release system

The management method to control engineering baselines and engineering changes.

engineering review board   **ERB**

A committee of senior engineering organization personnel to assist the project manager by providing technical oversight. Also, it may be a group of experts convened by the chairperson of the project control board to fact find and provide recommendations on technical changes requested.

enhancement

A change to increase value.

enterprise project management

The application of the project management disciplines to all enterprise activities.

entitlement

A right to something. Also a claim against another.

entity

A hardware or software item.

entity relationship diagram

The interaction structure between entities.

entry criteria

Mandatory prerequisites for an activity to begin.

environment

(1) Internal and external forces which aid or restrict the achievement of the product or system objectives.
(2) The external conditions within which the system must operate.

environment, electromagnetic

Radiated and conducted electromagnetic emissions present in the subject or target environment.

environmental requirements

The environmental conditions that will affect any system solution.

environmental stress screening   ESS

The application of selected environments such as temperature and vibration during tests to disclose quality defects in parts and systems.

equitable adjustment

The price or target cost adjustment to which a contractor is entitled upon the occurrence of some special event, such as the issuance of a contract change.

equivalent staging

Equivalent staging is a target staging, created using the continuous representation that is defined so that the results of using the target staging can be compared to the maturity levels of the staged representation. [SEI]

Such staging permits benchmarking of progress among organizations, enterprises, and projects, regardless of the CMMI representation used. The organization may implement components of CMMI models beyond those reported as part of equivalent staging. Equivalent staging is only a measure to relate how the organization is compared to other organizations in terms of maturity levels. [SEI]
See also **target staging, maturity level, capability level profile,** and **target profile.**

error

Discrepancy between a computed, observed, or measured value or condition and the true, specified, or theoretically correct value or condition.

error recovery

The detection and correction of an anomaly usually by a fault tolerant or self-test system.

escalation

(1) Expected rise in uncommitted costs due to reduced purchasing power of money.
(2) Raising of problems to a higher authority for resolution.

Essentials of Project Management

The five Essentials of project management are: Communication, Teamwork, Project Cycle, Project Management Elements, and Organizational Commitment. This is an enhancement of the four Essentials (Common Vocabulary, Teamwork, Project Management Elements, and Project Cycle) in previous versions of the Visual Process Model. Communication, as the first Essential, explicitly encompasses a common vocabulary. Organizational Commitment (to the project management process), implicit in earlier versions, is the fifth Essential. [VPM]

estimate

(1) To predict quantitatively.
(2) To form an opinion about.

estimate at completion   EAC

Actual cost and schedule of work completed to date plus the predicted costs and schedule for finishing the remaining work.

estimated completion date   ECD

The predicted date for task completion.

estimated time to repair   ETR

The predicted time to correct system anomalies based on spares availability, defect accessibility, and time required to make the correction.

estimate to complete   ETC

The predicted costs and schedule to complete the remaining work.

ethical

In accordance with a code of professional conduct.

ethical, legal, and moral conduct

Ethical conduct is established by published professional standards of conduct. Legal conduct is established and authorized by law. Moral conduct is established by generally accepted standards of rightness of conduct. Considerable overlap may exist in these categories.

evaluation

The consideration and analysis of whether an item or activity meets specified criteria.

evaluation criteria

Explanation of the evaluation factors as applied in proposal evaluation.

evaluation factors

Core issues that are the basis of proposal evaluation. Usually includes technical, cost, and schedule factors and their relative importance.

event

A milestone or schedule occurrence.

evolutionary development

A serial development approach where successive versions respond to discoveries surfaced by the previous version.

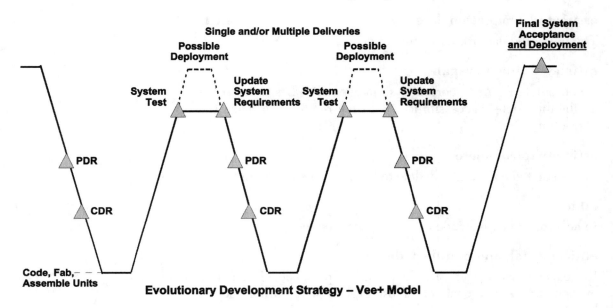

Evolutionary Development Strategy – Vee+ Model

evolutionary prototype

(1) A software or hardware model within a family of models constructed to better understand both requirements and expected performance by the experience with each evolution of the concept.

(2) The progressive maturing of a software or hardware product by building a model under appropriate process controls and developing it into the final product by the progressive introduction of required performance.

exception report

A summary of variances from the baseline.

executive control gate

A control gate identified, defined, and included in the project cycle and/or schedule by executive management.

executive management

Senior managers responsible for overall direction, policy, and priorities.

exit criteria

Mandatory prerequisites for an activity or project cycle phase to end.

expectations

The envisioned or anticipated outcome.

expected CMMI components

CMMI components that explain what may be done to satisfy a required CMMI component. Model users can implement the expected components explicitly or implement equivalent alternative practices to these components. Specific and generic practices are expected model components. [SEI]

expected outcome

A value used to rank opportunities and risks, defined as the probability for the outcome multiplied by its consequence. Also called expected value.

expected time

A PERT value of the statistically derived time for an activity.

expected value

A value used to rank opportunities and risks, defined as the probability for an outcome multiplied by its consequence. Also called expected outcome.

expert

An individual with a high competency in a subject area.

exposure time

The time a hazard exists before being mitigated.

external dependency

Reliance on factor(s) outside of the project.

external risk

Risk beyond the control of the project team.

fabrication

The building of hardware and software.

facilities

Real property, buildings, structures, improvements, and plant equipment.

facilities capital

Net book value of tangible and intangible capital assets that are amortized over time.

facilities capital cost of money   FCCM

U.S. government reimbursement for use of contractor owned facilities and capital (CAS-414). [USG]

Facility Contract Review   FCR (2)

See **Contract Review.**

Facility Performance Verification Review   FPVR

See **Performance Verification Review.**

Facility Readiness Review   FRR

See **Operational Readiness Review.**

facility scope of work   FSOW

See **statement of work.**

Facility Test Readiness Review   FTRR

See **Test Readiness Review.**

fact-finding

The discovery process to fully understand the details of an offeror's proposal. Fact-finding is usually a prerequisite to establishing a negotiating strategy and position.

factory acceptance test   FAT (1)

Verification testing at the producer's facility to determine acceptance and readiness to deploy to an operational site.

fail safe
A design approach that requires the effect of failures on the mission objectives to be minimized by innovative design practices.

failure
The inability to perform within specified limits.

failure analysis
The examination of a failure to find the root cause.

failure analysis approach
The evaluation of how to approach the examination of a failure to find the root cause without compromising the evidence.

failure catastrophic
A failure that terminates the mission.

failure cause
The root cause of a failure, such as a cold solder joint, operator error, or mistake in software code.

failure effect
The impact of the failure on the operation of the system.

failure intermittent
 Occasional anomalous performance.

failure mechanism
The failure root cause defect and how it initiates and propagates the failure.

failure mode and effects analysis   FMEA
An analysis of potential failure modes and the resulting consequences.

failure mode, effects, and criticality analysis   FMECA
An analysis of the potential failure modes, the resulting consequences, the criticality of the consequences, and actions to reduce the probability of serious failures (i.e., single point catastrophic failures).

failure rate

Number of failures per unit time, per number of operations, or other measure.

failure report

A report covering an anomaly, the investigation, conclusions, and corrective action.

failure review board   FRB

Experts convened when there is evidence of an anomaly or failure to determine the best approach to failure diagnosis and resolution.

fair and reasonable cost

Costs that are consistent with what an ordinary, prudent person in the conduct of competitive business would incur.

fair and reasonable price

Prices that are consistent with what an ordinary, prudent person in the conduct of competitive business would expect to pay.

fast track

Schedule compression by overlapping serial activities and accepting the increased risk of doing unnecessary work.

fatigue

Material weakening due to prolonged exposure to or cycling of stress.

fault

(1)   Failure to perform.
(2)   An imperfection or defect.

fault isolation

The localizing of the failure cause.

fault tolerant

The design practice of making overall performance relatively immune to failures of parts of the system.

fault tree

A decomposition of potential failure modes from top decomposition level down to the most detailed decomposition level, usually the part level.

fault tree analysis

The structured investigation of failure modes in products and processes by constructing a fault tree.

feasibility study

An evaluation to determine if something is achievable within cost, schedule, or other limitations.

feasible

Capable of being accomplished.

Federal Acquisition Reform Act   **FARA**

U.S. government Federal Acquisition Reform Act of 1996. Provides for government-wide acquisition reform, including the repeal of the Brooks Act (automatic data processing procurements), a shortening of the General Accounting Office's time for issuing bid protest decisions, a revision of the Procurement Integrity Act, and the elimination of certain regulatory certification requirements. [USG]

Federal Acquisition Regulations   **FAR**

U.S. government standards governing practices for procuring from industry. [USG]

Federal Acquisition Streamlining Act   **FASA**

U.S. government Federal Acquisition Streamlining Act of 1994. Substantially revises federal procurement law by reducing paperwork, encourages procurement of commercial items, raises the threshold for simplified acquisition procedures to $100,000, promotes electronic commerce, and encourages greater commonality and efficiency in procurement practices among the agencies. [USG]

**Federally Funded Research and
Development Center**   **FFRDC**

Private sector organizations that assist the U.S. government with scientific research and analysis, systems development, and systems acquisition by bringing together the government, industry, and academia to solve complex technical problems that cannot be solved by any one group alone. FFRDCs are operated, managed, and/or administered by either a university or a consortium of universities, another not-for-profit organization, or an industrial firm as an autonomous firm or as an identifiable separate operating unit of a parent organization. Examples are MITRE, Rand, and the Software Engineering Institute (SEI) at Carnegie Mellon University. [USG]

fee

A negotiated dollar amount to motivate and compensate contractors for performance on cost reimbursable contracts. A fee may be fixed or vary in accordance with an incentive or award formula.

feedback

(1) The transfer of critical knowledge from those having it to those needing it.
(2) The return of a portion of a process output to the process input that is then used to increase the effectiveness of the process itself.

feedback on document content

The request for and the providing of constructive critique of document based content. This can be conducted to three levels of discipline.

Level 1. Review and Comment—Reviewer prepares comments and receiver is free to accept or reject.

Level 2. Red Team—Reviewers compare to a standard, score the content and prepare a strengths and weaknesses report. Receiver endeavors to correct weaknesses. Example: Proposal review against the RFP.

Level 3. Collaborate to Consensus (CTC)—Reviewer reviews and comments and the receiver is compelled to collaborate with the reviewer until consensus is achieved on the differences.

fenced funding

An identified aggregation of resources reviewed, approved, and managed as a distinct entity.

fenced funds

Resource levels established to provide management control and influence. Fences may also be called ceilings and floors, to protect resources.

field replaceable unit

A hardware element configured to be normally replaced by field or operational personnel.
See also **line replaceable unit.**

fifty-fifty progress reporting

An earned value schedule metric that allows fifty percent of the earned value to be booked at task start and the remaining fifty percent at task completion. Can make progress appear more complete than actual.

figure of merit   FOM

Desired performance for a specified set of conditions.
See also **measure of performance** and **technical performance measurement.**

Final Contract Review   FCR (1)

The control gate held for the buyer to approve the contractor's contract closeout. [RPC]

final design

The documentation that describes the last as-delivered configuration to provide the baseline for future replication.

Final Design Review   FDR

The control gate held to approve all design documentation and to authorize construction start.
See also **Critical Design Review.** [RPC]

Final Proposal Review   FPR (1)

The seller executive control gate of the Reference Project Cycle held to ensure that a responsive proposal has been prepared, that executive management will support the effort if the company wins the competition, and to approve the proposal for delivery to the buyer. [RPC]

financial management

On-going orchestration of the funding and expendures of the enterprise or the project.

findings

The results of an audit or assessment.

firm fixed price contract FFP

A completion type contract that establishes a price that is not subject to adjustment by reason of the actual cost experience of the contractor. Appropriate for contracts where costs can be estimated with reasonable accuracy.

firmware

Computer instructions resident in read-only memory.

first article FA

The first unit of a production run.

first article test FAT (2)

First production run unit tests that are usually more comprehensive than acceptance (quality) tests performed on subsequent articles.

fiscal year FY

Any 12-month period for financial planning and reporting purposes.

fishbone diagram

An analysis tool that provides a systematic way of looking at effects and the causes that create or contribute to those effects. The fishbone diagram assists teams in categorizing the many potential causes of problems or issues in an orderly way. The problem/issue to be studied is the head of the fish. Each succeeding bone of the fish are the major categories to be studied: the 4 M's: Methods, Machines, Materials, Manpower; the 4 P's: Place, Procedure, People, Policies; The 4 S's: Surroundings, Suppliers, Systems, Skills. Dr. Kaoru Ishikawa, a Japanese quality control statistician, invented the fishbone diagram.

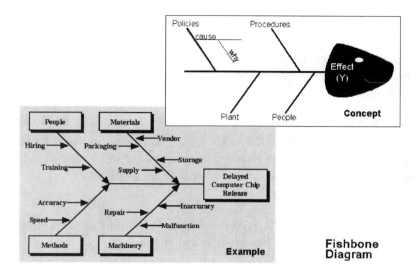

Fishbone
Diagram

fixed asset

Property or equipment used for the project.

fixed costs

Costs independent of variable factors such as overtime and production volume.

fixed price award fee   FPAF

A completion type contract that establishes a firm fixed price
with an award fee incentive to motivate contractor performance.
The amount is determined by the buyer's subjective evaluation of
the contractor's performance against predetermined and negotiated criteria. Award fee disputes cannot be adjudicated in court.

fixed price contract   FP

A completion type contract with a deliverable, a firm price, and a
defined schedule. Types of fixed price contracts are:
- Firm Fixed Price
- Fixed Price with Escalation
- Fixed Price Redeterminable
- Fixed Price Incentive
- Fixed Price Indefinite Delivery, Indefinite Quantity
- Fixed Price Award Fee.

fixed price incentive fee   FPIF

A completion type contract with a target price to complete and an incentive fee provision. The negotiated fee is adjusted based on a fee adjustment formula proportional to the risk or uncertainty within the contract.

fixed price redeterminable   FPR (2)

A completion type contract with an initial period of firm fixed price and a provision for price adjustments for subsequent periods of performance to account for potential variables.

float

The amount of time an activity can be delayed without affecting baselined schedule milestones. Also called slack.

flow chart

A diagram representing an interactive process. Also called flow diagram.

focus group

A technique for obtaining feedback on a specific issue or idea from a selected group. Often used in product management as a market research technique to observe typical consumers interacting about an existing product line or new product idea to determine true customer reaction. Observers sometimes use one-way glass windows to witness the interchange.

fog index

A measure of readability and/or efficiency of project documents. The fog index of a sentence is the percentage of words with three or more syllables. The lower the fog index, the more readable.

forecasting

Estimating in advance such as cost, schedule, and technical performance.

form, fit, and function data

Technical data pertaining to objects and processes that are sufficient to enable physical and functional interchangeability, to include hardware source identity, size, configuration, mating and attachment characteristics, hardware/software functional characteristics, and performance requirements.

formal

Official and for record, not a rehearsal.

Formal Qualification Review   FQR

A control gate held to review test and analysis data to prove the design will survive the expected handling and operational environments with margin. The FQR includes approval of the qualification certificate. Also called Qualification Acceptance Review. [RPC]

formal qualification testing   FQT

Testing in environments that include exposure to all expected conditions to be encountered in testing, shipping, handling, deployment, and operations. Conducted to demonstrate the ability to survive in its intended environment with margin.

formal test

Tests conducted in accordance with test plans and procedures approved by the customer and witnessed by an authorized customer representative.

Forming

The first stage of Tuckman and Jensen's team building model where teams meet, get to know each other, and establish a code of conduct.

forward pass

Calculation of earliest start dates in a task network, working from left to right.

forward pricing

Calculating future prices based on projected changes in costs.

forward scheduling

The calculation of the expected end date based on the durations contained in the critical path.

Freedom of Information Act   FOIA

A U.S. public law that allows citizens to obtain data from Federal and State agencies. The agency holding the data must prove "overriding national interests" to avoid disclosure. [USG]

full and open competition

The process by which all responsible bidders are allowed to compete.

full operational capability   FOC

The attainment of all specified performance in the operational environment.
See also **initial operational capability.**

full rate production

The initiation of planned production rates following satisfactory outcome of limited rate production.

fully funded

The appropriation of funds for the total estimated costs to be incurred in the delivery of a project.

function

(1) A process that converts inputs into outputs.
(2) The purpose of a system or its components.

functional analysis

(1) Examination of required functions to determine common functional groupings, functional relationships, interactions, and potential allocation to sub-functions.
(2) The process of hypothetically exercising a proposed system by simulating scenarios of what the system (and interfacing systems) must do in order to perform a defined mission.
(3) The graphical representation and interactive analysis of system functions typically described by a behavior diagram.

functional architecture

The arrangement of functions, sub functions, and interfaces (internal and external) according to the physical decomposition of the system.

functional baseline

The approved and change controlled summation of the required functions for the system or an entity along with the verification plan to demonstrate achievement of functional requirements.

Functional Configuration Audit   FCA

An engineering audit of a configuration item (CI) to verify that the test results of the as-built item satisfy the item specification. The FCA, with the results of the Physical Configuration Audit (PCA), is the decision point to confirm that the design is ready for either integration with higher assemblies or replication.

functional configuration documentation

The approved functional baseline plus approved changes usually contained in the design-to specification.

functional decomposition

Analyzing functional requirements by portraying them in an IDEF0 or behavior diagram.

functional flow block diagram   FFBD

A graphical representation of system (or component) functions that illustrates the required sequence and interactions.

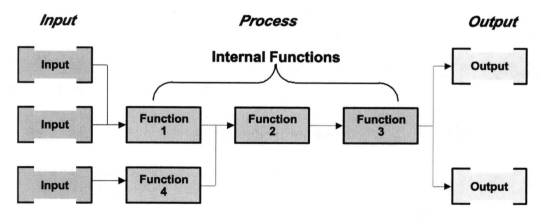

Functional Flow Block Diagram - Format

functional manager

The manager of like-disciplined personnel. For example, an electronic design-engineering manager manages electronic design engineers. Also, a manager of, or within, a functional organization.

functional organization

(1) A functional skill unit, for example, operating system software engineering.
(2) A project organizational option in which project tasks are assigned to the functional skill units.

functional requirement

A requirement relating to behavior such as detect, point, transmit, receive, and decode.

function point estimate

A software prediction and budgeting technique based on analyzing the complexity of software in terms of function points (reads, writes, system calls, and queries) rather than predicting cost based on lines of code.

function points

A software attribute that is described by inputs, outputs, master file inquiries, and system calls. Used for estimating costs, sizing maintenance, and evaluating enhancements.

funding

Money required for managing the project.

funding profile

Time-phased project funding usually displayed in spreadsheet or graphical format.

funding wedge

A rough funding estimate accompanying the initial program plan to establish an approximate budget need (Budget Aspect of the Project Cycle).

future value

An estimate of assets value over time accounting for factors such as appreciation, depreciation, and the cost of money.

Gantt chart

A time-phased horizontal bar chart representation of both planned activities and actual performance.

Project Development Schedule

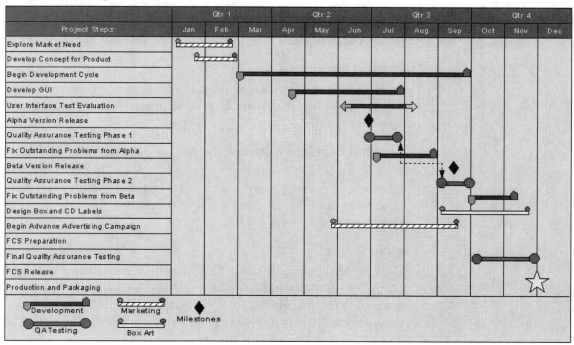

gap analysis

Evaluation of the differences between planned and actual achievement.

General Accounting Office   GAO

A U.S. government Agency of the legislative branch established by Congress in 1921, whose function is to audit all government contracts and to investigate all matters relating to the receipt, disbursement, and application of public funds. It determines whether public funds are expended in accordance with appropriations. The Comptroller General, appointed by the President with consent of the Senate, is the head of the GAO. [USG]

general accounting system GAS

The financial management system used to categorize and apportion fiscal matters.

general and administrative costs G&A

An indirect cost element, which includes expenses for the general management and administration of the business unit. Insurance, legal fees, bid and proposal, independent research and development (IR&D), and interest expenses are examples of G&A costs.

general provisions

The mandatory (by law or regulation) clauses by type of contract, sometimes called boilerplate. Unique clauses are special provisions.

General Services Administration GSA

A U.S. Federal Government agency responsible for acting as landlord for most government office buildings and specifying, procuring, and distributing routine purchases (stationery, vehicles, computers, etc.). [USG]

generic goal

Each CMMI capability level (1–5) has only one generic goal that describes the institutionalization that the organization must achieve at that capability level. Thus, there are five generic goals; each appears in every process area. Achievement of a generic goal in a process area signifies improved control in planning and implementing the processes associated with that process area thus indicating whether these processes are likely to be effective, repeatable, and lasting. Generic goals are required model components and are used in appraisals to determine whether a process area is satisfied. (Only the generic goal title and statement appear in the process areas.) [SEI]

generic practice

Generic practices provide institutionalization to ensure that the processes associated with the process area will be effective, repeatable, and lasting. Generic practices are categorized by capability level and are expected components in CMMI models. In the continuous representation, each generic practice maps to one generic goal. (Only the generic practice title, statement, and elaborations appear in the process areas.) [SEI]

GIDEP alert

U.S. government Industry Data Exchange Program that alerts users to potential problems in piece parts. [USG]

glance management

(1) A management technique for maintaining awareness of project activities, issues, and situations. Management-By-Walking-Around is one form of glance management.
(2) The ability of experts to be able to glance at a situation in their field of expertise and immediately identify improper processes, practices, and results.

glass box testing

Verification of and entity's internal behavior as well as inputs and outputs.
See also **white box testing** and **black box testing.**

glueware

The software that enables two existing software modules to functionally interact as required.

goal

The purpose or intention of an endeavor, usually supported by measurable objectives.

gold plating

The practice of embellishing beyond requirements.

go/no go

Decision points to determine whether to proceed or not.

government furnished equipment   GFE

Government owned items provided to a contractor for use on a contract.

government furnished facilities   **GFF**

Government owned building, land, or other real estate provided to a contractor for use on a contract.

government furnished information   **GFI**

Government owned data provided to a contractor for use on a contract.

government furnished material   **GFM**

Government owned material or parts provided to a contractor for use on a contract.

government furnished property   **GFP**

Government owned property provided to a contractor for use on a contract.

government off-the-shelf   **GOTS**

Existing hardware, software, or service available from a government.

government owned, contractor operated   **GOCO**

A government owned facility that is operated by a contractor under contract to a government.

government owned, government operated   **GOGO**

A facility owned and operated by a government.

government program office

A government office responsible for two or more projects within a discipline or business focus.

government project office   **GPO**

A government office responsible for a managing project.

grade

Gradations of quality.

grapevine

In project management it is jargon for the information transfer and collaboration that occurs outside of the formal visibility and statusing processes.

gross profit

Difference between revenue and cost of goods and/or services provided for the revenue.

ground support equipment   GSE

Equipment used to service or supply airborne or space borne systems. Examples are power, air conditioning, and deicing.

groupware

Software applications that facilitate collaborative interaction of groups.

growth

Increased cost or schedule due to added scope. Not to be confused with overrun.

guideline

Recommended methods to be used to achieve an outcome.

hammock

A group of related activities that are shown as one in a network.

hardware   HW

The physical portion of a system including the electrical, electronic, electromechanical, mechanical, and optical components.

hardware configuration item   HWCI

A hardware component of a system, designated for configuration management to ensure integrity. It may exist at any level in the system hierarchy where interchangeability is required. Each HWCI is to have appropriate design reviews, qualification certification, acceptance reviews, and operator and maintenance manuals.
See **configuration item.**

hardware engineering

The systematic approach to best practices for the development, operation, maintenance, and retirement of hardware.

hazard

Danger to people or systems.

hazard analysis

A study of project dangers and risks to people and equipment with recommendations to minimize them. Typically includes materials and processes hazards analysis, job task analysis, job safety analysis, and failure modes and effects analysis.

headquarters   HQ

The principal office of an organization usually housing the top management and their staff.

heuristic problem solving

(1) Exploratory problem solving by experimental techniques, and especially, trial and error techniques.
(2) Trusted, time-tested guidelines for problem solving, based on abstractions of experience (from Rechtin and Maier, *The Art of Systems Architecting*).

hierarchy

A ranking or ordering of items by level in which each item has only one superior and any number of subordinates.

histogram

A frequency distribution illustrated as bars on a horizontal axis to graph occurrences and occurrence density.

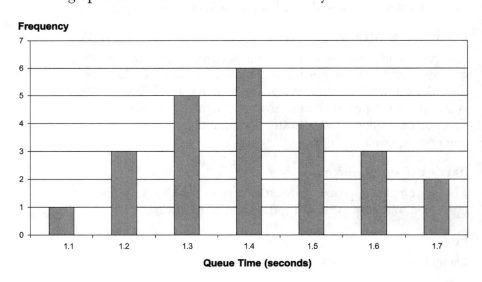

hold point

An interrupt in a process or procedure requiring an input or an approval to proceed.

House Appropriations Committee   HAC

A U.S. government House of Representatives committee responsible for oversight of the use of government funds. [USG]

House of Quality

A mapping technique for relating the ability of design features to satisfy prioritized requirements. A matrix of cells appearing like a house has rows containing the requirements and columns containing the design features. The intensity of the cell hue indicates the degree of requirements satisfaction. The plus and minus symbols in the cells of the triangular house roof highlights strong or weak correlation in the satisfaction of requirements by multiple design features. See also **quality function deployment.**

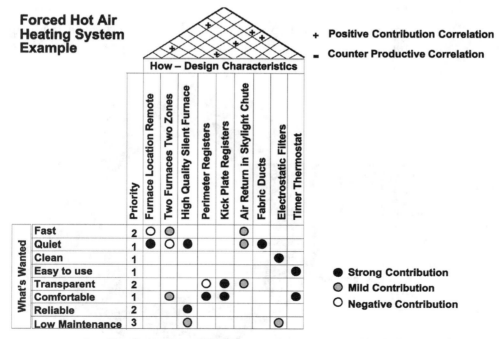

Quality Functional Deployment - House of Quality

human computer interface   HCI

The shared boundary between the human operator and the computer system. The computer hardware and software as seen and experienced by the human operator.

human engineering

The science of designing and managing user/machine interfaces.

human factors

The systematic application of relevant information about human abilities, characteristics, behavior, motivation, and performance. It includes principles and applications in the areas of human engineering, anthropometrics, personnel selection, training, life support, job performance aids, and human performance evaluation. This area also addresses the human-machine and human-computer interface, including the graphical user interface.

hypothesis

A theory or tentative explanation.

IDEAL   IDEAL

An organizational improvement model that serves as a roadmap for initiating, planning, and implementing improvement actions.

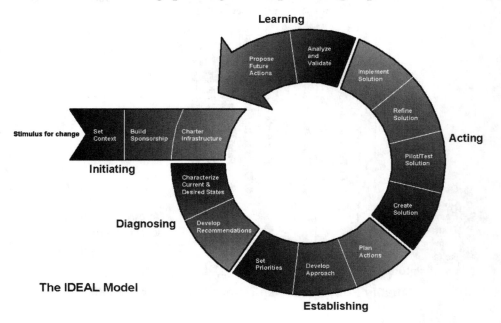

The IDEAL Model

The IDEAL model is named for the five phases it describes: initiating, diagnosing, establishing, acting, and learning. [SEI IDEAL Web page]

identifier ID (1)

An alphanumeric code depicting a name or hierarchical member.

ilities

Availability, maintainability, vulnerability, reliability, logistic supportability, operability, etc.

implement

To carry out a plan.

Implementation Period

The second period in the Reference Project Cycle, the first being the Study Period and the third, the Operations Period. In the Implementation Period, the supplier(s) are selected and the system is produced and delivered to the customer. The phases of the Implementation Period are Source Selection, Development, and Verification. [RPC]

Implementation Phase

See **Development Phase** and **Verification Phase.**

implementation plan

See **project implementation plan.**

implementation planning

The process of converting all requirements into a logically sequenced set of Project Work Authorizing Agreements and subcontracts that define and authorize all work to be performed for the project.

implementation practices

The processes and procedures to accomplish the Implementation Plan.

impossibility of performance

A common law concept that a contract is not enforceable when subsequent events cause the contract performance to be infeasible.

This does not apply if performance is merely inconvenient or is the cause of a loss from one party to the other.

in accordance with   IAW

A term used to imply that an activity, course of action, or statement complies with a law, regulation, standard, or reference document.

incentive contract

A negotiated pricing arrangement that motivates the contractor in monetary terms to deliver a product that achieves stipulated goals that may include improvements in

- Performance and quality.
- Contract schedule.
- Substantially reduced costs of the work.
- A weighted combination of the above.

Conversely, the arrangement may also provide monetary penalties for under-performing in prescribed areas.

Incentive contracts include:

(1) Contracts where the fee adjustment is made in accordance with a pre-established formula, such as fixed price incentive (FPI) and cost plus incentive fee (CPIF). Incentive fee is subject to the disputes clause provision and disputes can be resolved in court.

(2) Contracts where the fee adjustment is made by unilateral determination of the buyer such as cost plus award fee (CPAF). Award fee is unilateral and is not subject to the disputes clause provision.

incomplete process

A process that is not performed or is only performed partially (also known as capability level 0). One or more of the specific goals of the process area are not satisfied. [SEI]

increment

One of a series of planned additions and contributions.

incremental

A series of planned additions or contributions.

incremental development

A hardware/software development process that produces a partial implementation and then gradually adds preplanned functionality or performance in subsequent increments.

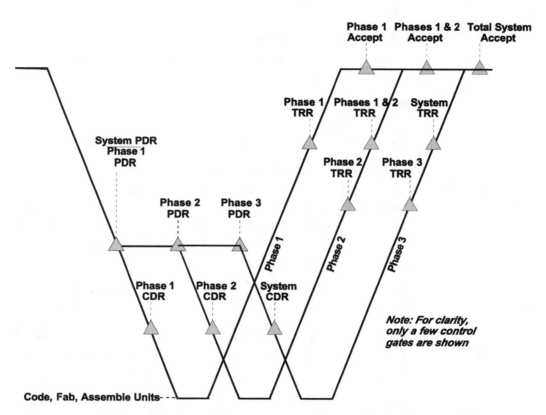

Incremental Development Strategy – Multiple Deliveries – Vee+ Model

incremental funding

The provision (or recording) of budgetary resources for a project based on estimated obligations for one fiscal period when such estimation will cover only a portion of the obligations to complete the project. This differs from full funding, where budgetary resources are provided or recorded for the total estimated obligations in the initial period of funding. Most commonly used for research and development (R&D) as opposed to production, which must be fully funded. Also, financial resources made available based on elapsed time or on specific milestone achievement.

indefinite delivery contract ID(3)

Unit price is negotiated and deliveries are scheduled on an as-needed basis.

indefinite quantity contract IQ

Unit price is negotiated and required quantities are ordered on an as-needed basis.

indemnify

(1) To compensate for loss.
(2) To secure against a potential loss

independent cost analysis/estimate

An evaluation of the projected cost of a project developed by knowledgeable personnel independent of the project. The independent cost estimate is used to confirm estimates made by the project staff and to ensure that planned project funding is appropriate.

independent development ID (2)

Technical activities funded by a company to enhance its competitive posture.

independent government cost estimate IGCE

The last of the Study Period should-cost estimates to be used as the baseline for evaluating proposals. [RPC] [USG]

independent research and development IR&D

Technical effort not sponsored by or required in performance of a contract. Includes:
• Basic and applied research
• Technology development
• Systems and other concept formulation studies.

independent verification and validation IV&V(1)

The process of proving compliance to specifications and user satisfaction by using personnel that are technically competent and managerially separate from the development group. The degree of independence of the IV&V team is driven by product risk. In cases of highest risk, IV&V is performed by a team that is totally independent from the developing organization.

indicator

Any sensory alert mechanism that reveals the status of something.

indirect costs

Contractor allowable costs that cannot be directly attributable to a specific project such as management salaries, employee fringe benefits, holiday pay, taxes, utilities and facility costs, and similar expenses. Indirect costs can vary between companies according to their cost accounting standards. Also called overhead cost.

inflation

A persistent increase in the level of consumer prices or a decline in the purchasing power of money caused by an increase in available currency and credit beyond the proportion of available goods and services.

informal

Not for record.

informal review

Off the record.

informal test

A test conducted only for information gathering and will not be used to prove verification of the system.

information engineering   IE

The application of management and engineering techniques for planning, analyzing, designing, and implementing information systems.

informative CMMI components

CMMI components that help model users understand the required and expected components of a model. These components may contain examples, detailed explanations, or other helpful information. Subpractices, notes, references, goal titles, practice titles, sources, typical work products, discipline amplifications,

and generic practice elaborations are informative model components. [SEI]

in-house

Work done with an organization's own employees as opposed to
using those of an independent supplier.

in-house visibility meetings

See **visibility meetings.**

initial operational capability   IOC

The first attainment of specified performance in the operational
environment.
See also **full operational capability.**

in-process validation

The practice of routinely getting user approval to each elaboration of the baseline. This technique keeps the user involved and
committed to the incremental elaboration of the approach and the
incremental verification results.

input process output

The depiction or explanation of any behavioral process sequence.
Can be hardware, software, operations, or all three.

in scope

Within the limits of the contract changes clause.
See also **contract changes.**

in-scope work

A contractual term signifying that the work being considered is
either already covered by the contract terms or is within the general scope of the contract and can be added. Under the latter, a
contract adjustment would be required as opposed to a new contract for work that is out-of-scope or not within the general provisions of the contract.

insight

Giving the customer access to the providers internal project planning and status systems so as to provide on-going continuous visibility into the provider's progress. The intent is to provide

on-going visibility to the customer into the health of the project without requiring any additional systems or methods other than those used internally by the provider.

inspection

Verification of compliance to requirements that are easily observed such as construction features, workmanship, dimensions, configuration, and physical characteristics such as color, shape, software language used, etc. Inspection also includes simple measurements such as length or weight. In general, requirements specifying function or performance are not verified by inspection.

inspection by attributes

The determination by inspection of acceptable or not acceptable without regard to the reason.

inspection by variables

The determination by inspection of degrees of compliance to prescribed standards.

inspection plan—system and CI

The document that defines the use of inspection to verify quality.

Inspector General   IG

An independent U.S. government organization, reporting informally to an agency head and formally to Congress, tasked with investigating areas of concern and the management practices of an agency. [USG]

Institute of Electrical and Electronics Engineers   IEEE

A professional organization dedicated to the disciplines of electrical and electronic engineering including software engineering. Members exchange technical information, promote standards, and otherwise advance the knowledge base of their disciplines.

institutionalization

The building and installation of organization behavior so that it persists as a culture rather than as dictated by management.

insurable risk

Risk that can be mitigated by an insurance policy.

integrate

To join with something else.

Integrated Definition for Functional Modeling   IDEF0

A multiple page (view) model of a system that depicts functions and information or product flow. Boxes illustrate functions and arrows illustrate information and product flow. Alphanumeric coding is used to denote the view.

IDEF0—system functional model

IDEF1—informational model

IDEFX—semantic data model

IDEF2—dynamic model

IDEF3—process and object state transition model

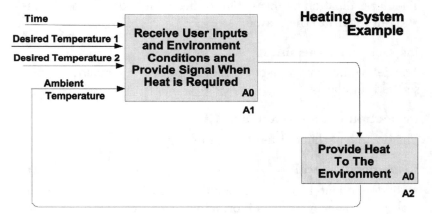

Integrated Definition for Function Modeling - IDEF0

integrated logistics support ILS

A composite of all support elements necessary for effective and economical support of a system over its life cycle. Includes:

- Maintenance planning.
- Supply support.
- Technical data.
- Facilities.
- Manpower and personnel.
- Training and training support.
- Support equipment.
- Computer resources support.

- Packaging handling, storage and transportation.
- Design interfaces.

integrated product and process development

The early consideration of all aspects of the product's life cycle to ensure completeness of design, optimum manufacturing, efficient verification, ease of operations, minimum maintenance, and ease of disposal. Includes integrated development of both the product and the processes need to produce and field the product.

integrated product teams   IPT (1)

Multidisciplinary teams responsible for all aspects of developing, delivering, and supporting a product. Designed to implement concurrent engineering and simultaneous product and process development.

integrated project teams   IPT (2)

Multidisciplinary teams responsible for all aspects of developing, delivering, and supporting a project. Designed to implement system engineering on an on-going basis.

integrated schedule commitment   ISCO

The project team development of, and commitment to, the overall and detailed schedules of the project.

integration

The successive combining and testing of system hardware assemblies, software components, and operator tasks to progressively prove the performance and compatibility of all components of the system.

integration and test

The successive combining and testing of system hardware assemblies, software components, and operator tasks to progressively prove performance and compatibility of all components of the system. In the Vee development model, the right side of the Vee which depicts the integration and verification sequence.

integration requirements

Constraints specifying how the solution will be installed into the operating environment.

integration, verification & validation — IV&V(2)

The combining of system entities, the proving the system works as specified, and the confirming that the right system has been built and that the customers/users are satisfied.

integrity

(1) Unimpaired, sound. In projects, the congruency and soundness of the business, budget, and technical baselines.
(2) Steadfast adherence to a code of ethics.

intellectual property

Products of the human intellect deemed to be unique and original and to have marketplace value and thus to warrant protection under the law.

interchangability

The feature of an entity to be able to replace another and achieve the same result.

Interest/No Interest — INI

The company control gate held to determine if funds and effort should be expended to remain cognizant of an expected business opportunity. [RPC]

interface

A common physical and/or functional boundary between different organizations, systems, products, or components. It is often defined by an interface specification and managed by a system integration organization.

interface agreement

See **interface control plan.**

interface control document — ICD

See **interface specification.**

interface control plan — ICP

The documented approach to interface management. Includes approach to management of interface specifications and interface control working group meetings. Usually part of the systems engineering management plan.

interface control working group   ICWG

The forum managed by the system integrator to discuss interface status and resolve issues involving interface compatibility.

interface design document   IDD

In some software environments, the interface is defined by the interface requirements specification (IRS). The interface design document contains the detailed design in response to the IRS. Typically, there are two IDDs for a given interface; together, they compose the detailed design for both sides of the interface. In other environments the interface specification and design description document provide this same information.

interface requirements

The physical and functional inputs and outputs across entity boundaries.

interface requirements specification   IRS

A document sometimes used to define the interface between computer software configuration items and other configuration items within the system. This document is identical to the interface specification or intraface specification.

interface specification   IS

The specification that defines the physical, functional, and operational characteristics of the interfaces between entities of a system.

intermittent failure/fault

A failure that occurs momentarily without an apparent pattern.

internal rate of return   IRR

A metric for comparing project opportunities and deciding capital investments. The calculated financial return expressed as percentage relative to expenditures or investment for processes or activities within an organization. IRR is the interest rate that makes net present value of all cash flow equal zero.

International Council on Systems Engineering   INCOSE

A nonprofit professional society formed in 1991 to promote the discipline and professionalism of systems engineering internationally.

International Organization for Standardization   ISO

The International Organization for Standardization (ISO), established in 1947, is a worldwide federation of national standards bodies from some 130 countries. The mission of ISO is to promote the development of standardization and related activities in the world with a view to facilitating the international exchange of goods and services, and to developing cooperation in the spheres of intellectual, scientific, technological and economic activity. ISO's work results in international agreements that are published as International Standards. An example is the universal size and configuration of the credit card so as to be usable worldwide.

interoperability

The characteristic of a system to be able to operate effectively with other systems. For instance a software product is interoperable if it can run on both the Apple Macintosh and Microsoft Windows operating systems.

interorganizational transfers

The authorization of work to be performed by a different organization within the same company, with the requesting organization acting as the customer. The work is considered a subcontract only if it is performed by a unit that has an "arm's length" financial relationship to the buying organization. However, the organization performing such work should be managed like a subcontractor regardless of the legal relationship.

intraface

A common physical or functional boundary within a project. It usually exists between assemblies and/or software components, is defined by an intraface specification, and is usually managed by the contractor's design integration function within systems engineering or design engineering.

intraface specification

The specification that defines the physical, functional, and operational characteristics of the interfaces between entities within a single organization.

intranet

A private network based on the Internet TCP/IP protocol, often connected to the Internet by a router and/or firewall.

invitation for bid   IFB

A formal request for fixed priced bids on well understood and defined work.

Ishikawa Diagram

A fishbone diagram analysis tool that provides a systematic way of looking at effects and the causes that create or contribute to those effects. The fishbone diagram assists teams in categorizing the many potential causes of problems or issues in an orderly way. The problem/issue to be studied in the head of the fish. Each succeeding bone of the fish are the major categories to be studied: the 4 M's: Methods, Machines, Materials, Manpower; the 4 P's: Place, Procedure, People, Policies; The 4 S's: Surroundings, Suppliers, Systems, Skills. Dr. Kaoru Ishikawa, a Japanese quality control statistician, invented the fishbone diagram.

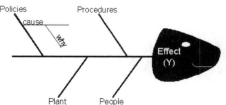

ISO 9000

Internationally recognized standard for quality system processes controlled by the International Organization for Standardization.

item

A single article, entity, or unit.

jargon

The specialized language of a trade.

job description

A summary of the comprehensive responsibilities of an individual.

job shop
(1) A manufacturing capability devoted to producing small quantities of special or urgently needed items to minimal documentation.
(2) An organization providing skilled personnel, such as engineers or programmers, for temporary support, usually at the buyer's facility.

joint control gate
A preplanned accomplishment demonstration event jointly conducted by both buyer and seller to approve and baseline the achievements and the approach to proceed.

joint venture
An agreement between two or more organizations to engage in a business partnership for a specific purpose and a limited time.

justification and approval
A document required by the U.S. government Federal Acquisition Regulation (FAR) that justifies and obtains approval for contract solicitations that use other than full and open competition. Justifications must (1) identify the agency, the contracting activity, the action being approved, the supplies or services sought, and the statutory authority permitting the action; (2) demonstrate that the proposed contractor's unique qualifications or the nature of the acquisition require the action; (3) describe the efforts made to ensure that offers were solicited from as many potential sources as practicable; (4) determine that the cost will be fair and reasonable; (5) describe the market surveys conducted; and (6) describe any other facts supporting the use of other than full and open competition. [USG]

just-in-time
The logistics management approach where material arrives at the needed location just in time for immediate use. Also applicable to the delivery of services.

Kepner-Tregoe
The authors of The Rational Manager, The New Rational Manager, and the analytical decision analysis process that uses

weighted decision criteria and scoring to achieve weighted scores to select from alternatives. Their books also describe a disciplined approach to problem solving.

key personnel

Those persons assigned by name to a project whose replacement must be approved by the buyer.

kick-off meeting

A workshop to assemble the team, accomplish teambuilding, and to plan the project.

known unknowns

Estimations or predictions where it is only possible to partially plan or predict. For example, schedule changes that are certain to occur, but the extent and nature of which are unknown in advance.

labor hour contract   L/H

A variation of the time and materials contract where materials are not required of the contractor.

latent defect/fault

A substandard condition not discovered by normal verification techniques.

leadership

Inspiring and motivating individuals and teams in their attitude to their work.

learning curve

The improvement in process efficiency as workers become familiar with a process and become proficient over time and/or in proportion to the number of repetitions of the process. This is an important factor in predicting future costs of a production run.

legacy system

An existing system that will be part of the new system.

legal, ethical, and moral conduct

Legal conduct is established and authorized by law. Ethical conduct is established by published professional standards of conduct.

Moral conduct is established by generally accepted standards of rightness of conduct. Considerable overlap may exist in these categories.

lessons learned

(1) Management principles that are based on, and developed from both positive and negative experiences.
(2) An inferior work practice or experience captured and shared to preclude repetition.

See also **best practice.**

lessons learned document

Documentation of positive and negative lessons learned with recommendations for improvement on similar future projects.

letter agreement

A formal, brief agreement, sometimes in the form of a letter written on the initiating party's letterhead and signed by all parties, which depends on clear statements of intent rather than on specific details.

letter contract

A temporary written contractual instrument that authorizes the immediate commencement of activity under its terms and conditions, pending definitization of a fixed-price or cost-reimbursement contract. Most letter contracts contain a not-to-exceed (NTE) dollar ($) amount that caps the amount of money a contractor may spend prior to definitization of the contract. In such cases, the schedule should provide for definitization within 180 days or before completion of 40 percent of the work, whichever occurs first.

letter of intent   LOI

A buyer's letter to a seller indicating possible future business involvement if certain prerequisite events happen. There is usually no legal implication but the agreement motivates early planning and preparation by the seller.

level of effort   LOE

A predetermined headcount level of qualified personnel over time to accomplish assigned tasks or operations.

level of effort contract

A contract that authorizes the use of personnel at a predetermined level over a stated period of time, for work that can only be stated in general terms. Payment is based on effort expended at the authorized level and skill.

level of effort team

The team providing the level of effort services.

liability period

The length of time following delivery that a supplier is liable for specified aspects of the product.

license

Legal grant of permission to use another's intellectual property.

life cycle

See **Project Cycle.**

life cycle cost   LCC

The total cost of implementation and ownership of a system over its useful life. It includes the cost of development, acquisition, operation, maintenance, support, and, where applicable, disposal.

life cycle environmental profile

The natural and induced environments experienced by a system over its life time.

limited competition

Soliciting proposals from as many sources as possible after certain conditions are met to narrow the field (i.e., capability, security).

line of balance

A graphical portrayal of time-phased requirements for piece parts and components needed to produce a higher level product. The display includes actual part or component availability against the dates needed. The purpose is to give early warning of possible shortages so timely corrective action can be taken to prevent delay in completion of the end product. Used when a repetitive process exists within the contract's work scope such as controlling production operations.

line of business LOB

A part of a company organization dedicated to a functional area, market segment, or type of support. A large electronics-aerospace firm might compete in three areas: tracking systems, communications satellites, and ground to air missiles. Each is a line of business.

line replaceable unit

A hardware element configured to be normally replaced by field or operational personnel.
See also **field replaceable unit.**

lines of code LOC (1)

A measure of the size of software programs. Both source statement lines and comment lines are used in the determination. This measure is effective if recording rules are consistent, if it includes deleted and changed lines, and if only one language is used.

liquidated damages

A contract provision of the amount the seller will pay the buyer if the seller fails to deliver as promised.

local area network LAN

Computers within a small geographical area, typically a building or campus, linked to share information and applications.

logic

(1)   Valid reasoning.
(2)   The underlying principles and structure of reasoning

logic diagram

A diagram depicting the sequential and parallel interrelationships (functions or data) between entities or activities. Often used to show system functionality, software functionality, hardware system interactions, and project management serial and parallel sequences and interactions. Behavior diagrams, functional flow diagrams, data flow diagrams, and project schedule networks are examples.
See also **network diagram.**

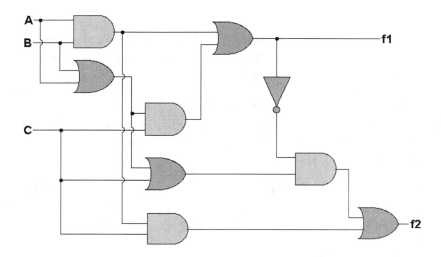

logistics

Services and supplies necessary to the deployment and support of a system.

logistics operations center   LOC (2)

The control center for logistics planning and management.

logistics support

Services provided to deploy, operate, and maintain systems. Typical services include transportation, maintenance, supply, training, spares, data management, operations and maintenance personnel, computer resources, packaging and handling, interface management, and support equipment.

long lead procurement

The early procurement of material or parts to accommodate early use or long procurement spans. Contractors may choose to seek buyer-approved pre-award commitments of funds to meet the long lead requirements.

lot

A group of products all built with the same material, processes, and personnel and assumed to be identical with respect to expected performance and failure modes. Recalls are usually lot based.

low ball

An artificially low bid submitted to significantly improve chances of winning, usually with the intent to recover financially on related business or by charges for changes.

lowest responsive, responsible bidder

The bidder that has adequately satisfied all requirements and at the same is the lowest in price. The likely winner in open competition, such as U.S. government-sponsored proposals.

low rate initial production   LRIP

Limited rate production to prove the product and processes before scaling up to full rate production.

maintainability

The ability to be conveniently serviced and repaired over the expected system lifetime.

maintenance

Service to prevent and correct defects.

maintenance reports

A record of the maintenance conducted.

major facility project

A project category where the deliverable is a multipurpose facility resulting from new construction or major renovation.

major facility project cycle

A project cycle customized to incorporate terminology, documents, and activities required to perform a major facility project. See the tailoring example for the Reference Project Cycle. [RPC]

make or buy

The management decision to either internally produce an item (hardware or software) or to purchase from others to ensure the lowest overall cost and technical risk. A buyer may reserve the contractual right to review and agree on a seller's make or buy decisions. Make or buy decisions are driven by an organization's line of business.

malfunction

See **anomaly.**

management

The control and orchestration of objectives, planning, and execution to achieve the desired results.

management by objectives   **MBO**

A technique used to manage people and teams based on documented, measurable results mutually agreed to by both the manager and the staff member(s). Progress is periodically reviewed, and in the most effective implementations, staff remuneration is tied to performance.

management by walking around   **MBWA**

Part of the Hewlett-Packard legacy and popularized by management theorist Tom Peters, MBWA works on the assumption that a manager must circulate to fully understand the teams' performance and problems. The best managers, according to Peters, spend 10 percent of their time in their offices, and 150 percent of their time talking and working with their people, their customers, and their suppliers.

See also **glance management.**

management information center   **MIC**

A location or source where project information and status, such as work breakdown structure (WBS), project network diagram, master schedule, and the top ten problems list, is available to provide broad visibility into the health of the project.

management information system   **MIS**

Data retrieval systems, presentation systems, and productivity tools designed to increase the effectiveness of the enterprise.

management plan

The approach to achieving the objectives, usually preceded by a modifier such as Quality, Security, Manufacturing, and Implementation.

management reserve   **MR**

An amount of the total allocated project funding and schedule withheld for management control to be used for omissions, contingencies, and errors in estimating. Management reserve is not part of the performance measurement baseline.

manufacture

The application of resources on material to produce products.

manufacturing

(1) The organization that manufactures and assembles.
(2) The process of producing, using the application of resources on material to produce products.

manufacturing plan

The plan that describes the project's approach, processes, and risks for manufacturing the product.

manufacturing resource planning   **MRP (1)**

Management techniques and tools to maximize the efficiency of production by planning and managing personnel, equipment, and materials. MRP is usually implemented by computer systems.

margin

(1) Design margin—the amount of designed-in performance above expected operating performance.
(2) Qualification margin—the measure of demonstrated performance above that required for anticipated handling and operations.

market research/survey

The collection and analysis of data from potential sources to determine the capability of satisfying a requirement. The testing of the marketplace may range from written or telephone contact with knowledgeable experts regarding similar requirements, to the more formal request for information (RFI).

markup

(1) The overhead and profit added to a cost estimate to determine price.

(2) Line-by-line review and approval/disapproval/modification of the U.S. government defense budget by congressional committees. [USG]

master project schedule   MPS

The highest-level summary schedule for a project, depicting overall project phasing and all major interfaces, contractual milestones, and project elements. Same as master schedule.

master schedule

The highest-level summary schedule for a project, depicting overall project phasing and all major interfaces, contractual milestones, and project elements.
See **master project schedule.**

material

The substances out of which a thing is, or can be, made.

material resource planning   MRP (2)

A method for planning the human, material, and equipment resources of manufacturing based on known or predicted demand, leads times, and existing inventories.

material review board   MRB

The team that reviews discrepant material and determines to use-as-is, repair, scrap, or return to vendor. The MRB usually has at least three members: the buyer's representative (usually on-site quality assurance); the seller's representative (usually from quality assurance); and the seller's engineering liaison. Other specialists participate as required. Non-conformance reports (NCR), which document problem areas and require a description of the corrective action, trigger MRB action.

materials management

The logistics processes for the ordering, storage, and movement of material.

material specification

The written specifics of raw materials such as chemical compounds, metals, and plastics, or semi-fabricated material such as electrical cable used in the fabrication of a product.

matériel

Systems, equipment, stores, supplies and spares, including related documentation, manuals, computer hardware and software.

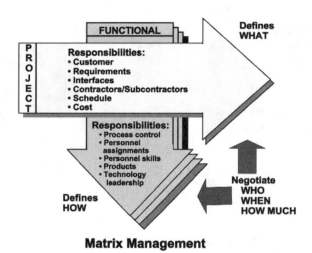

Matrix Management

matrix management

A cooperative organizational approach in which the project office defines "what is required and when it is required" and the functional organizations define "how it is to be done" and perform the required work. The project manager often actually "buys" the services using project funds.

matrix organization

An organization where the project office contracts for work from functional or product organizations. Participants from all organizations sometimes collocate to facilitate communication.

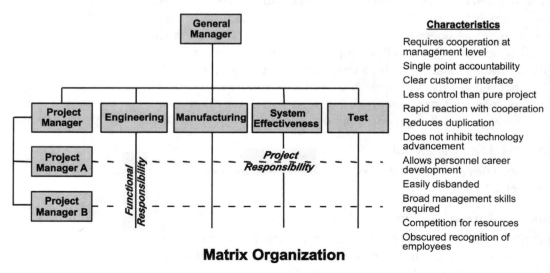

Matrix Organization

216

maturity level

(1) The measure of capability achievement ranked on a scale of required proficiency.

(2) Degree of process improvement across a predefined set of process areas in which all goals within the set are attained.

See also **capability level** and **process area.** [SEI]

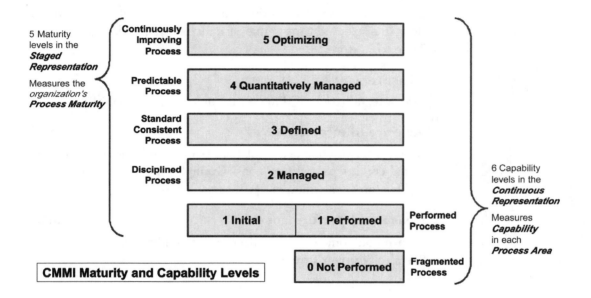

maximum fee

The ceiling fee that a contractor can receive on a fee-bearing contract.

maximum practicable competition

Solicitation from the maximum number of qualified sources.

mean down time   MDT

A measure of maintainability, derived by dividing the total time during which the system is unavailable due to failures by the number of occurrences over a selected time frame, usually one year.

mean time between failures   MTBF

A measure of maintainability derived by dividing total time between system failures by the number of samples over a selected time frame, usually one year.

mean time to repair   MTTR

A measure of maintainability derived by dividing total time to perform all corrective actions, by the number of corrective actions in a selected time frame, usually one year. Also called Mean Time to Restore

measurement

The determination of dimensions, quantity, or capability.

measure of effectiveness   MOE

A quantifiable comparison of results obtained under specific external conditions and decisions. Examples include profit, quality, and customer satisfaction.

measure of performance   MOP

Desired outcome for a specified set of conditions.
See also **figure of merit.**

mediation

The process of resolving a dispute by conferring with an impartial mediator for advice. Unlike binding arbitration, the mediator has no authority to enforce a settlement.

memorandum of agreement   MOA

A document that describes the background, assumptions, and agreements between two parties. In a contractual agreement, the buyer and seller often create a MOA at the conclusion of contract negotiations.

memorandum of understanding   MOU

A document that describes an agreement for cooperative effort between two separate organizations.

mentoring

The practice of using experts to coach others.

method

Steps and rules that provide repeatable performance in accomplishing something.

metric

A standard of measurement.

milestone

A significant measurable project event or control gate, such as Contract Award, Preliminary Design Review (PDR), successful test completion, or shipment. [RPC]

milestone dictionary

A description of exactly what is required to satisfy each milestone.

milestone status

The comparison of the actual and planned achievement of important events. A periodic or cumulative measure of schedule accomplishment.

Military Interdepartmental Purchase Request   MIPR

The U.S. government DoD internal billing system used to move funds between DoD service organizations. [USG]

military specification   MIL-SPEC

U.S. government Department of Defense (DoD) specifications and drawings for common DoD purchases. MIL-Specs are product-oriented, and describe the "what." For example, there is a MIL-SPEC for fruitcake (MIL-F-1499F). [USG]

military standard   MIL-STD

A U.S. government Department of Defense document that provides guidelines for the design, test, and manufacture of items to be procured by the DoD. [USG]

minimum fee

The least fee that a contractor can receive on a fee-bearing contract.

mission

The overall project purpose and goal.

mission analysis

The evaluation of the desired mission, the mission environment, and the expected operational scenarios. The analysis results in the user concept of operations.

mission profile

The planned time sequenced events that will occur to accomplish the mission objectives.

mission requirements

The stakeholder requirements, expectations, and context for the project.

mitigation

(1)   Alleviation.
(2)   Risk management action that either reduces the probability or the impact or both.

mock-up

A physical or virtual demonstration model, built to scale, to verify proposed design fit, critical clearances, and operator interfaces. In software, screen displays are modeled to verify content and layout.

mode

A selectable set of operating characteristics.

model

A representation of the real thing used to depict a process, investigate risk, or to evaluate an attribute, such as the Vee Model (process), technical feasibility model (risk), and physical fit model (attribute). Models may be physical or computer based, for example, thermal model, kinetic model, and finite element model.

model—advanced development model

A term for a research model that is built to prove a concept.

model—brassboard

See **brassboard** and **model—technical demonstration model.**

model—breadboard

See **breadboard** and **model—technical demonstration model.**

model—engineering model

A technical demonstration model constructed to be tested in a simulated or actual field environment. The model meets electrical and mechanical performance specifications, and either meets or closely approaches meeting the size, shape, and weight specifications. It may lack the high-reliability parts required to meet the reliability and environmental specifications, but is designed to readily incorporate such changes into the prototype and final production units. Its function is to test and evaluate operational performance and utility before making a final commitment to produce the operational units. Also called engineering development model.

model—hardware and software feasibility model

A hardware or software model constructed to prove or demonstrate technical feasibility.

model—interface simulation

A hardware or software interface simulation model used to verify physical and functional interface compatibility.

model—manufacturing demonstration

A sample to demonstrate the results of a critical process. The objective is to confirm the ability to reliably manufacture using the process and to achieve the required results. Results are often provided as evidence at the Critical Design Review.

model—mock-up

A physical or virtual demonstration model, built to scale, used to verify proposed design fit, critical clearances and operator interfaces. Mock-up verification results should normally be available at Preliminary Design Review. [RPC]

model—pre-production model

Entity built to released drawings and processes, usually under engineering surveillance, to be replicated by routine manufacturing. Provides manufacturing with a model to demonstrate what is intended by the documentation.

model—production model

A production demonstration model, including all hardware, software, and firmware, manufactured from production drawings and made using production tools, fixtures and methods. Generally, the first article of the production unit run initiated after the Production Readiness Review (PRR). A prototype model, also built from production drawings, may precede the PRR to provide confidence to authorize fabrication of the production model. [RPC]

model—requirements understanding

A software or hardware model developed by a provider to demonstrate the understanding of a buyer's problem or to help in resolving what the buyer wants.

model—risk reduction

All models are used to reduce the risk in some area of concern.

model—technical demonstration model

An experimental device constructed and operated in a laboratory environment to demonstrate application of a scientific or engineering principle. Sometimes called a breadboard model. A more elaborate model, sometimes called a brassboard is used where certain physical properties, such as dimensions are critical to performance as in RF devices.

model—test simulator

A functional replication of a system that is used to verify that interfaces or modifications to the system function properly before installing them into the real system.

modification

Changes to an approved baseline.

module

A physical or software component of a system.

Monte Carlo analysis

A statistical technique to estimate the likely range of outcomes from a process by simulating the process a large number of times with random values.

When applied to static PERT scheduling it helps predict how the real schedule might behave. Random durations are applied to each activity in the network and the probability is calculated for each activity being on a critical path. In a complex schedule it provides insight into which activities should receive special attention to ensure they occur as planned. Also referred to as Monte Carlo Simulation

monthly status review

The process of reviewing a project's technical, cost, schedule, material, and corrective action status against the implementation plan in a monthly review for the purpose of identifying situations needing corrective action.

moral, ethical, and legal, conduct

Moral conduct is established by generally accepted standards of rightness of conduct. Ethical conduct is established by published professional standards of conduct. Legal conduct is established and authorized by law. Considerable overlap may exist in these categories.

most likely time

The most probable time an activity will require based on PERT analysis.

most probable cost

A cost estimate based on an in-depth cost analysis of each candidate's proposed approach. The objective is to establish a realistic cost projection of each approach for funding and management reserve sizing. It is developed by a team of procurement, contract administration, cost audit, and engineering experts and will include team-determined adjustments for the contractor's understating and overstating estimates. The Most Probable Cost, rather than the contractor's proposed cost, may be used to determine the low bidder. Not to be confused with should-cost.

motivation
Instigation, inducement, encouragement to move to action.

multi-attribute value analysis
Quantitative assignment of weights to conflicting issues to represent value or priority.

multi-year appropriation
A U.S. Congress act permitting federal agencies to incur obligations and to make payments out of the treasury for specified purposes. Appropriation Acts make funds available for obligation for one fiscal year (annual appropriations), for a specified number of years (multiyear appropriations), or for an unlimited period (no-year appropriations). [USG]

multi-year contract
A special type of U.S. government contract covering more than one year but not more than five years, even though the total funds to be obligated are not available at the time of contract award. They are intended to help achieve economies of scale and standardization. Each program year is annually budgeted and funded and, at the time of award funds need only have been appropriated for the first year. If funds do not become available for the succeeding years the contract must be canceled. [USG]

multi-year funding
Two or three year U.S. government funds which cover one fiscal year's requirement, but permit the executive branch more than one year to obligate the funds. [USG]

multi-year procurement   MYP
A project type that requires funds for more than one fiscal year.

Myers-Briggs Type Indicator

The testing and categorization of people according to four scales relative to human behavior. Extrovert/Introvert, Sensing/Intuitive, Thinking/Feeling, and Judging/Perceiving. A specific implementation of personality typing defined by Carl Jung.

N^2 diagram or chart

A graphical depiction of the functions within a system, together with the one-way interactions between each function ordered in a matrix, with functions or entities on the center descending diagonal cells. Since functions occupy each diagonal cell, the total number of cells is equal to the square of the number of functions, hence the name. Interface functions and constraints are shown in the cells that correlate to both interfacing entities and the graphic is read clockwise. For example, cell A1 would output to cell B2 and cell B1 would contain the interface functions. Blank cells indicate that there are no interfaces between those two entities.

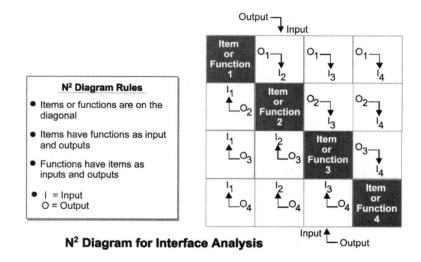

N^2 Diagram Rules

- Items or functions are on the diagonal
- Items have functions as input and outputs
- Functions have items as inputs and outputs

- I = Input
  O = Output

N^2 Diagram for Interface Analysis

narrative findings

In proposal evaluation, findings in narrative form that provide the basis for numerical ratings.

natural bounds

The inherent process reflected by measures of process performance, sometimes referred to as "voice of the process." Techniques such as control charts, confidence intervals, and prediction intervals are used to determine whether the variation is due to common causes (i.e., the process is predictable or stable) or is due to some special cause that can and should be identified and removed. [SEI]

near critical activity

A noncritical path task with little float.

need

An identified capability shortfall or additional feature to enhance capability or reduce cost.

negative cash flow

Cash outgo exceeding cash income.

negative float

When the earliest projected delivery date is later than the required delivery date.

negotiation

A bargaining process between two or more parties seeking to reach a mutually acceptable agreement.

net book value   NBV

The dollar amount shown in the accounting system for assets, liabilities, or equity. When comparing firms, the net book value is the excess of total assets over total liabilities.

net present value   NPV

A metric for comparing the value of money now with the expected value of money in the future. When used for evaluating project opportunities and deciding capital investments, the future cash flow from a product is discounted by projected future financial factors such as inflation and/or interest to obtain the present value of cash

inflow, which is then subtracted from the present value of cash outflows.
See also **internal rate of return.**

network chart/diagram

A project task sequence diagram consisting of activities (shown in nodes or along arrows) with linkages to all predecessor and successor activities. When the duration for each activity is defined, the critical path can be determined.
See also **precedence diagram.**

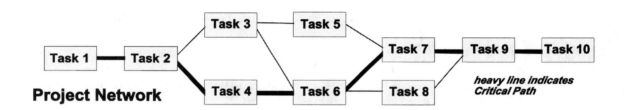

network path

A series of connected activities within a network diagram.

new initiative

A project that does not yet have U.S. government congressionally appropriated funds but for which a requirement exists and resources have been requested. [USG]

news flash meeting

A brief meeting routinely convened by the project manager (usually at the start of the day or start of the shift) to understand and resolve important project issues in real time.

no cost settlement

Termination of a contract with no monetary awards to either the buyer or the contractor.

node

An intersection of two or more lines within a network diagram.

no later than   NLT

The last acceptable date, used in conjunction with scheduling and critical path analysis.

nominal group technique

A team approach to brainstorming and achieving consensus on issues, problems, and solutions. Individuals develop their positions in isolation and then share with the group without confrontation. The six stages in Nominal Group Technique are: 1. Statement of problem, 2. Problem formulation, 3. Silent generation of ideas, 4. Idea collection / Notation, 5. Clarify / Rephrase / Group ideas, 6. Vote on ideas / Prioritize

nonappropriated funds

Monies derived from sources other than U.S. government Congressional appropriations. [USG]

nonbinding arbitration

Arbitration or a dispute without the final decision being binding on either party.

noncompetitive justification

A document citing the rationale for limiting the issuance of solicitation documents to only one source. Also called sole source justification.

nonconformance

Not in accordance with relevant standards.

non-conformance report   NCR

A quality organization's document that identifies discrepant items and requests corrective action from engineering, software developers, or manufacturing.

non-development item   NDI

Hardware and software available with little or no development effort required by the buyer, usually with the intention of reducing cost or risk. An NDI is distinguished from commercial off the shelf (COTS), in that an NDI is not commercially available.

nondisclosure agreement

A legal agreement that defines what information is not to be shared with others without consent of the controlling party. Important when considering teaming agreements and alliances that require sharing proprietary technology or business strategy within the team.

nonrecurring

A task or expenditure that does not recur during the life of the project, for example a design or verification task as opposed to a repetitive manufacturing task.

nonrecurring costs

One time costs of a production type project such as equipment design or analysis as opposed to repetitive costs such as materials used in the on going replication of the product.

normative model

The ground rules framing an issue to be resolved.

Norming

The third stage of Tuckman and Jensen's team building model where conflicts are resolved and a team starts to emerge.

not applicable   **N/A**

A contract term used to indicate that a standard clause or phrase does not apply.

not invented here   **NIH**

An attitude that prevents consideration of ideas of others because of pride, ego, or other personal or group bias.

not more than   **NMT**

A term used in cost estimating to define the highest possible estimate.

not to exceed **NTE**

A cost or schedule estimating term that defines the highest realistic estimate.

N-squared diagram

See **N² diagram.**

nuclear hardness

The resistance of a system to degrade in a nuclear environment.

nuclear survivability

The ability of a system to remain functional during and/or after exposure to a nuclear environment.

numerical control **NC**

Manufacturing process or machining operations controlled by software rather than human interaction.

objective evidence

Materials, information, and records based on observation, measurement, test, or analysis that can be verified as factual.

objective review

Evaluation of evidence against standards or by applying rules to minimize subjectivity and influence of bias.

object-oriented analysis **OOA**

Analysis based on considering the system as an assemblage of objects (entities, relationships, and attributes).

object-oriented design **OOD**

A development method that defines, organizes, relates, and links objects of known and stable characteristics to achieve system performance.

obligation (funding)

A commitment that legally encumbers a specified sum of money to be paid in the future. An obligation is incurred as soon as an order is placed or a responsible authorized individual awards a contract. See also **commitment.**

obsolete

No longer current.

Occupational Safety and Health Administration   OSHA

An agency of the U.S. government charged with promoting and ensuring safety in the workplace. [USG]

off core

The term used to represent (1) the pursuit of opportunity and risk investigation downward off the Vee+ Model core to justify baseline decisions made at the Vee+ core and (2) the securing of in-process validation by upward off core discussions with the customer.

offer

A response to a solicitation that, if accepted, binds the bidder to perform to the resulting contract. Responses to invitations for bids are offers called bids; responses to requests for proposals are offers called proposals; responses to requests for quotations are not offers and are called quotes.

Office of General Council   OGC

The senior legal advisor in U.S. government agency matters. Provides legal support to Contracting Officers and project managers. [USG]

Office of Management and Budget   OMB

U.S. government executive branch agency responsible for preparing the national budget and for responding to congressional questions relative to the budget. [USG]

off-the-shelf item

A product or service made available before receiving orders or contracts for its sale.
See also **non-development item (NDI), commercial off-the-shelf (COTS)** and **government off-the-shelf (GOTS).**

one-year appropriations

U.S. government appropriations that must be obligated in the fiscal year of the appropriation. [USG]

ongoing initiative

A multi-year U.S. government project, which has been authorized by congress and has received congressionally appropriated funds. An ongoing initiative becomes a base project two fiscal years beyond FOC. [USG]

on-the-job training   OJT

Training by acquiring direct experience in the job environment. Usually implemented by a team or mentoring approach.

open architecture

A system design approach that encourages independent parties to provide additions through the use of standard interfaces and published specifications.

open system

Design that fosters interconnectivity and reuse by providing simple and compatible interfaces for others to use.

operational acceptance

The official act of transferring responsibility for system operation to the final user.

Operational Acceptance Review   OAR

The control gate held to approve the system as operational and ready for routine operations conducted by the operators. [RPC]

operational assessment

An evaluation of operational effectiveness usually performed by an independent and objective organization.

operational availability

Ratio of system uptime to total required time.

operational concept

See **concept of operations.**

operational constraints

See **user concept of operations.**

operational demonstration

The process of operating the system in its normal environment, using trained operators and standard operating procedures, to verify the system is ready for normal operations. Also referred to as an operational readiness exercise or operational test and evaluation.

operational demonstration plan

The document that describes the required approach to operational demonstration in the operational environment. The Operational Procedures must be responsive to this plan.

operational demonstration procedures

The documents that define the detailed step-by-step instructions to be followed by trained operators to demonstrate system performance in the operational environment.

operational effectiveness

The ratio of mission objectives achieved to the total opportunities for the objectives.

operational environment

See **user concept of operations.**

operational readiness certificate   **ORC**

The documented summary of evidence verifying that the system is ready to be transferred to normal operations.

Operational Readiness Review   **ORR**

A control gate held to approve the readiness of both the system and operators to conduct the operational demonstration designed to prove readiness for routine operations. {RPC]

operational requirements document   **ORD**

A document that defines user expectations usually in user terminology from the user's perspective.
See also **user requirements statement** and **user concept of operations.**

operational scenario

A description of one or more expected behavior sequences of a system with its stakeholders.

operational test and evaluation   OT&E

Realistic field tests by objective evaluators to determine potential system effectiveness and value.

Operational Validation Review   OVR

A control gate held to confirm user satisfaction with a facility.

operations and maintenance   O&M

Usually covers field operations, training, repair, logistics support, upgrades, and other items.

operations and maintenance manual

A document that describes the required operations and maintenance procedures for an entity or a system.

Operations and Maintenance Phase

The ninth of ten phases of the Reference Project Cycle and the second phase in the Operations Period. It is the phase in which the system is operated and maintained for the benefit of the operational user. System validation procedures, system validation report, maintenance reports, annual operational reports, deactivation plan and deactivation procedures are produced in this phase. [RPC]

Operations Period

The third of three periods of the Reference Project Cycle, in which the system is fielded, operated, maintained, and deactivated. Its phases are (1) Deployment, (2) Operations and Maintenance, and (3) Deactivation. [RPC]

operations period plan

Describes the overall approach to deployment, achieving initial operational capability, on-going operations, maintenance, and ultimately deactivation.

operators

The personnel who functionally operate the system.

operators manual

A document providing instructions on how to operate the system.

opportunities

The potential for improving the value of the project results. The project itself is the paramount opportunity and lower decomposition level opportunities to select superior solutions should be pursued on an on-going basis to maximize project value.

Opportunities and Risks

One of ten Project Management Elements. Includes identification, analysis, probability, impact, causative, preventive, and contingent actions. [VPM]

opportunity cost

If an opportunity is not pursued the potential value of that opportunity is lost and is considered the opportunity cost.

optimal

The most favorable among alternatives.

optimization

(1) The process of progressively making something as effective or functional as possible.
(2) The mathematical determination of the best solution in an environment with multi-attribute goals and constraints.

optimizing process

A quantitatively managed process that is improved based on an understanding of the common causes of variation inherent in the process. A process that focuses on continually improving the range of process performance through both incremental and innovative improvements.
See also **quantitatively managed process, defined process, and common cause of process variation.** [SEI]

organization

A reporting structure in which individuals function as a unit to conduct business or perform a function.

organizational breakdown structure   OBS

The project organization structure. The OBS can be diagrammed to intersect with the work breakdown structure (WBS) resulting in a task responsibility matrix that identifies organizational responsibilities for performing each task.

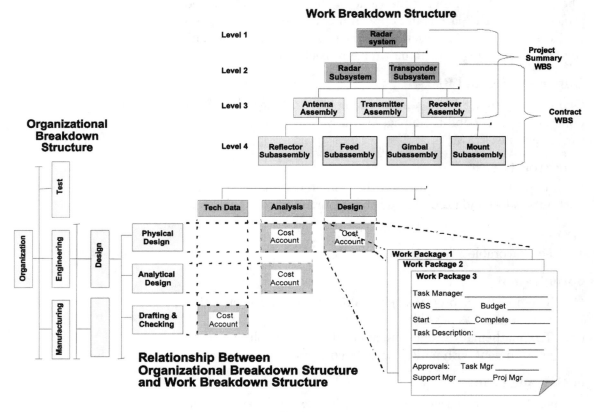

Relationship Between Organizational Breakdown Structure and Work Breakdown Structure

Organizational Commitment

The fifth Project Management Essential. The supporting foundation that includes: 1) the project manager's charter to do the job; 2) an organizational culture responsive to the project manager's orchestration of the project; 3) the financial and other resources necessary to accomplish the job; and 4) the appropriate tools and training for efficient execution. [VPM]

organizational conflicts of interest

A condition that exists when the nature of the contract work may result in a future unfair competitive advantage or may impair a contractor's ability to remain objective and impartial in serving the buyer.

organizational maturity

The extent to which an organization has explicitly and consistently deployed processes that are documented, managed, measured, controlled, and continually improved. Organizational maturity may be measured via appraisals. [SEI]

organizational policy

Management principles, usually rooted in ethics, established to guide personnel behavior and influence decision-making.
See also **legal, ethical, and moral conduct.**

organizational unit

A functional entity within the organization.

That part of an organization that is the subject of an appraisal (also known as the organizational scope of the appraisal).

An organizational unit deploys one or more processes that have a coherent process context and operates within a coherent set of business objectives. An organizational unit is typically part of a larger organization, although in a small organization, the organizational unit may be the whole organization. [SEI]

organization chart

A diagram of an organization's reporting structure.

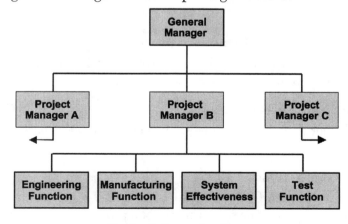

Project Organization

Organization Options

One of ten Project Management Elements. Includes options such as functional, project, matrix, co-located matrix, integrated project teams, and integrated product teams. [VPM]

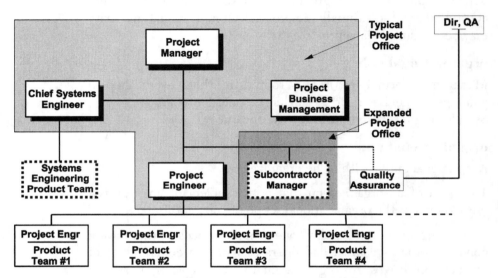

Typical Project Team Organization

organization's measurement program

Definition of an organization's measurements, methods, and practices to support process improvement.

organization's set of standard practices

Processes that are applicable across the organization and are expected to be implemented without tailoring.

other direct costs   ODC

Costs other than labor and materials that are directly charged to a contract.

other transactions

A form of contract for basic, applied, advanced research, and prototype development projects that is not a procurement contract, a

grant, or cooperative agreement and is not subject to many of the statutes and regulations governing those instruments.
See United States Code Title 10 sections 845 and 2371. [USG]

out of scope

Requirements not included in the current contract and beyond the limits of the change clause.
See also **contract changes.**

output

The result of a process or activity.

outsourcing

The practice of purchasing goods or services from specialty suppliers.

overhead   OH

The costs of operating a facility or organization that cannot be charged directly to a single contract or single product. Overhead costs are described in the contractor's disclosure statement setting forth cost accounting practices. Overhead or indirect cost does not include the general and administrative (G&A) cost.
See also **indirect costs.**

overrun

To exceed a limit. In project management, overrun is typically the amount a cost target has been exceeded because of reasons other than change based cost growth.

oversight

Watchful care or management; supervision. Also, the process of a buyer to require a seller to furnish status information and reports as designed and scheduled by the buyer.
See also **insight.**

pairwise comparison

The process of ranking items by comparing all pairs, and through mathematical analysis, determining the relative ranking.
See also **analytical hierarchy process.**

parameter

One of a set of measurable factors or characteristics, such as length or temperature or maximum speed, that defines a system and determines its behavior, and are varied in an analysis or experiment.

parametric analysis

The development and understanding of a range of performance of a function as other function variables are adjusted over ranges of interest. Used to help determine flow down of requirements in system decomposition.

parametric cost estimating

Appraising the costs of a project based on knowledge gathered from similar, but different projects. Typically uses parameters such as weight, power, lines-of-code, or other characteristics of the system to estimate or to scale development cost or schedule. System complexity and team maturity are also influencing factors.

Pareto Chart

A column chart where each column represents a type of defect and column height is frequency of occurrence. Used to pinpoint

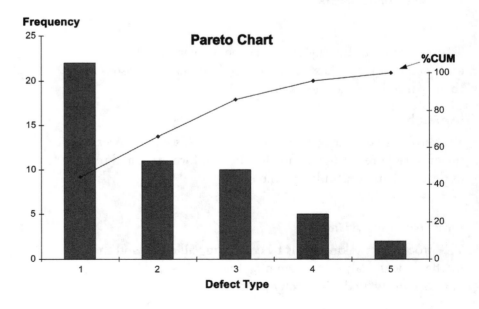

where corrective should be applied to most effectively improve quality by reducing the greatest number of defects.

Pareto's Law

The conclusion that, in quality, a small number of causes will produce the majority of defects. Improvement is focused on the high impact causes.

parse

To decompose or break apart into smaller units of a type such as components.

part

A single piece that cannot be disassembled without destruction or impairment of use, such as resistors, integrated circuit chip, or gears. The lowest level in the example system decomposition hierarchy.

part derating

The practice of using parts well within their proven capability to reduce stress and increase reliability.

partial termination

Buyer initiated discontinuance of a portion of contract work.

partnering

Joining with another for a common interest.

parts, materials, and processes   PM&P

Manufacturing elements, each of which must be controlled to have a predictable and reliable result.

path

The series of connected activities within a project schedule network with a single beginning and a single end.

pedigree

The documented heritage of material or components usually created by tracing from the raw material to the finished entity.

peer review

Objective critique of anything by peers with substantive knowledge. An effective technique for sharing ideas and improving the overall quality of an output. However, sometimes resisted because of personal pride. The failure review of a number of high-profile project failures has identified lack of peer review during development as one of the contributing causes.

percent complete

The amount a task is complete as measured by the ratio of work accomplished to the total work.

performance

Achievement as in technical achievement, schedule achievement, and cost achievement.

performance analysis

The examination of performance behavior over a specified range of circumstances.

performance based contracting

A method of acquisition in which all aspects of the acquisition are structured around the purpose of the work rather than either the manner by which it is to be done or imprecise statements of work. Encourages respondents to propose innovative solutions to solving a problem.

Performance-based contracting emphasizes objective, measurable performance requirements and quality standards. These must be reflected in the statements of work, in selecting contractors, in determining contract types and incentives and in performing contract administration.

NOTE: U.S. government regulations require that federal agencies use performance-based contracting wherever practicable when acquiring services.

performance improvement plan

The approach to improving performance deficiencies.

performance management

The approach to improving performance by setting objectives, measuring performance against the criteria, and rewarding achievement.

performance measurement baseline   PMB

The time-phased project cost and schedule plan against which contract performance is measured. The PMB does not include fee, profit, or management reserve.

performance measurement system   PMS

A project planning and status system that periodically measures variances (usually cost and schedule) and requires documented corrective action to eliminate the variances that exceed predetermined thresholds.
See also **earned value.**

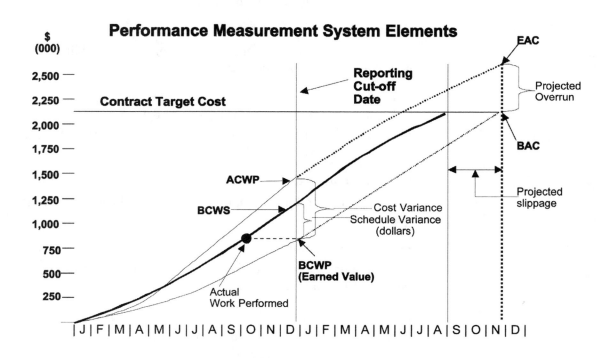

Performance Measurement System Elements

performance objective

Measurable outcome that can be a significant measure of achievement in an area of desired improvement.

performance parameters

Metrics used to manage processes and to identify areas requiring corrective action.

performance requirement

Requirements are usually both function and performance. Function is qualitative and performance is quantitative. A functional performance requirement might be to weigh (function) to an accuracy of 1 gram (performance).

performance specification

See **system specification.**

performed process

A process whose goals are satisfied.

Performing

The fourth stage of Tuckman and Jensen's team building model where emphasis is on the assigned tasks.

Period

The highest level division of the project cycle. Typically there are three periods; Study, Implementation, and Operations. There are multiple phases within each period. [RPC]

personal computer   **PC (1)**

A desktop or notebook computer typically dedicated to a single user.

personal development plan

An individual's action plan for new or improved capability for the benefit of the organization.

personality types

Categories of personalities as depicted by the Wilson learning Model or the Myers Briggs Model.

personal work processes

The individual's approach to accomplishing work tasks.

Phase

A portion of the project cycle that accomplishes a major project milestone, such as concept definition within the Concept Definition Phase of the Study Period. [RPC]

physical architecture

The structured decomposition of the entities of a system.

physical characteristics

Descriptions of the features and properties of anything. Can include dimensions, color, texture, etc.

physical configuration audit   **PCA**

An engineering and quality inspection of a configuration item (CI) (from component level to the system) to verify that the item as-built conforms to the build-to documentation. Results of the PCA are part of the Acceptance Review at each level. [RPC]

physical model

A three dimensional representation built of material as opposed to a computer-displayed model.

piece part

A component that cannot be disassembled without destruction.

pilot

A tentative model for future development or deployment.

pilot production

The initial limited-quantity production used to confirm readiness for full quantity production.

plan

A scheme determined beforehand for how an objective will be accomplished.

planned process

A process with a process description and a plan for implementation.

planning

Determining beforehand how an objective will be accomplished.

planning package

A logical group of work within a cost account, that is identified and budgeted in early baseline planning but is not yet subdivided into work packages.

plan violators meeting

A meeting between the project manager and a task manager to discuss technical, cost, and/or schedule deviations from the plan and the actions necessary to correct the deviation.

point of contact **POC**

The individual(s) identified to be the communications interface between two interfacing organizations.

policy

Management principles, often rooted in ethics, established to guide personnel behavior and influence decision-making.
See also **legal, ethical, and moral conduct.**

portfolio

A group of projects of a common type or purpose.

post-award conference

The first meeting after contract award to orient all personnel (buyer and contractor) to the project and the contractual implications of the project.
See also **Contract Implementation Review (CIR)** and **System Requirements Review (SRR).**

practice

A customary way of doing something based on experience and lessons learned.
See also **best practice.**

pre-award survey

A survey by buyer representatives of a seller's capability that is focused on the RFP requirements and the claims in the seller's proposal.
See also **pre-solicitation survey.**

precedence

To occur or to exist before. Also a ranking or priority.

precedence diagram

A project task sequence diagram consisting of activities (shown in nodes or along arrows) with linkages to all predecessor and successor activities. When the duration for each activity is defined, the critical path can be determined.
See also **network diagram.**

predecessor

Something that has been succeeded by another.

preliminary design

The portion of the development process where systems are subdivided into elements of the system and the concepts, behavior, performance, interactions, and interfaces of the elements are specified.

preliminary design documentation

Concept definition, design-to specifications, verification plans, analyses, flow diagrams, data sheets, pictorials, schematics, and other documents that convey the technical and operational requirements of the system or entities (CIs) of the system.

Preliminary Design Review   PDR

The series of control gates held to approve the concepts, design-to specifications, associated verification plans, and approaches to developing build-to and code-to documentation for all configuration items (CIs). All hardware, software, support equipment, facilities, personnel, and tooling should be reviewed in descending order of system to assembly. More appropriately called Performance Guarantee Review since it must be proven that the specified performance is achievable. This is usually done by laboratory tests, analytical models, or field tests. At this review the project details should be sufficiently well defined to predict the project completion costs within 15%. The National Aeronautics and Space Agency (NASA) has implemented a Cancellation Review to be implemented after PDR that is convened ad hoc if at any time the project cost estimate at completion (EAC) exceeds the 15% growth bound. At the Cancellation Review the project manager must show cause why the project should not be terminated. [RPC]

pre-planned product improvement   **PPPI**

Provisions that anticipate and provide for future increased capability. This may require the predecessor versions to have excess capability or special provisions to accommodate the subsequent enhancements.

pre-production article

See **model—pre-production.**

pre-proposal conference

A meeting hosted by the buyer contracting organization to assist prospective bidders in understanding the request for proposal (RFP).

pre-solicitation survey

A survey by buyer representatives of a seller's capability that is focused on the specific need.
See also **market survey.**

preventive action

Actions to eliminate the probability and/or seriousness of risk or the recurrence of an anomaly.

preventive maintenance

Services designed to reduce the probability of a system failure.

previously developed products   **PDP**

Existing products that may or may not be available off the shelf. Offers the potential of reduced development risk. Previously

Developed Products include Commercial-Off-The-Shelf (COTS) items, Government-Off-The-Shelf (GOTS) items, and non-development items (NDI).

prime contractor

The organization that enters into contracts with the highest-level buyer. When there are multiple prime contractors they are also called associate contractors. When this is the case, a system integrator is usually required to manage the interfaces among the associate contractors. The system integrator may also be both a prime contractor and an associate contractor or this function may be performed by the buyer organization.
See also **contractor.**

principal contracting officer   PCO (2)
See **contracting officer.**

prior year   PY
The preceding fiscal or calendar year.

privity of contract

A relation between parties that is held to be sufficiently close and direct to support a legal claim that views the parties as one. For instance a prime contractor has privity of contract with its subcontractors and the buyer has privity of contract with the prime, but not with the subcontractors.

proactive

Taking action to prevent, ensure, or prepare for an expected or unexpected situation.

proactive management

Taking actions to ensure future events will happen as planned. Examples include expeditors and long lead procurement.

probability

The likelihood of occurrence.

procedure

Step by step instructions to accomplish an objective.

process

A preferred and controlled method of repetitively and reliably doing something, generally involving sequential steps, techniques and tools.

process ability

The individual's ability to apply their knowledge and skills to the organization's work processes.

process action team

A team that has the responsibility to develop and implement process-improvement activities for an organization as documented in the process-improvement action plan. [SEI]

process area

A process area is a cluster of related practices in an area that, when performed collectively, satisfy a set of goals considered important for making significant improvement in that area. All CMMI process areas are common to both continuous and staged representations. [SEI]

process assessment

The evaluation of an organization's practices against a recognized standard to identify strengths and weaknesses.

process context

The set of factors, documented in the appraisal input, that influences the judgment and comparability of appraisal ratings. These include, but are not limited to, the size of the organizational unit to be appraised; the demographics of the organizational unit; the application discipline of the products or services; the size, criticality, and complexity of the products or services; and the quality characteristics of the products or services. [SEI]

process control

Managing a process to a proven standard.

process database

A protected repository for all measured process data.

process description

A documented expression of a set of activities performed to achieve a given purpose that provides an operational definition of the major components of a process. The documentation specifies, in a complete, precise, and verifiable manner, the requirements, design, behavior, or other characteristics of a process. It also may include procedures for determining whether these provisions have been satisfied. Process descriptions may be found at the activity, project, or organizational level. [SEI]

process element

The fundamental unit of a process. A process may be defined in terms of subprocesses or process elements. A subprocess can be further decomposed; a process element cannot.

Each process element covers a closely related set of activities (for example, estimating element, peer review element). Process elements can be portrayed using templates to be completed, abstractions to be refined, or descriptions to be modified or used. A process element can be an activity or task. [SEI]

process flow chart

Network diagram illustrating the serial and parallel process activities.

process group

The specialists that facilitate the processes of an organization.

process improvement

(1) The continuous adjustment of process steps to improve both efficiency and results.
(2) A program of activities designed to improve the performance and maturity of the organization's processes, and the results of such a program. [SEI]

process improvement objectives

A set of target characteristics established to guide the effort to improve an existing process in a specific measurable way either in terms of resultant product characteristics (e.g., quality, performance, conformance to standards, etc.) or in the way in which the process is executed (e.g., elimination of redundant process steps, combining process steps, improving cycle time, etc.). [SEI]

process management
The oversight of process development, implementation, measurement, control, and improvement.

process maturity
The extent of process management actually realized.

process measurement
The set of definitions, methods, and activities used to take measurements of a process and its resulting products for the purpose of characterizing and understanding the process. [SEI]

process model
A representation of a process's sequential steps including inputs and outputs.

process owner
The person (or team) responsible for defining and maintaining a process. At the organizational level, the process owner is the person (or team) responsible for the description of a standard process; at the project level, the process owner is the person (or team) responsible for the description of the defined process. A process may therefore have multiple owners at different levels of responsibility.
See also **standard process.** [SEI]

process performance
A measure of actual results achieved by following a process. It is characterized by both process measures (e.g., effort, cycle time, and defect removal efficiency) and product measures (e.g., reliability, defect density, and response time). [SEI]

process performance baseline
A documented characterization of the actual results achieved by following a process, which is used as a benchmark for comparing actual process performance against expected process performance.
See also **process performance.** [SEI]

process reengineering

Critical evaluation of an existing process to eliminate low value steps and to improve the overall result.

process specification

The procedural directions for control of a process that is performed on material.

process tailoring

(1) The adapting of a process description to the needs of the organization.

(2) To make, alter, or adapt a process description for a particular end. For example, a project tailors its defined process from the organization's set of standard processes to meet the objectives, constraints, and environment of the project.

See also **process description,** and **defined process.** [SEI]

procurement

The process of acquiring, by contract, products or services for the direct benefit or use of the buyer, whether the products or services are already in existence or must be created, developed, demonstrated, or evaluated. It involves all aspects of contract administration and project management performed within the context of the project cycle. Also called acquisition.

procuring contracting officer   PCO (1)

See **contracting officer.**

producibility

The ease with which anything can be produced.

product

The output of activities.

Product Acceptance Review   PAR

A control gate held to ascertain verification and acceptance.
See also **Acceptance Review.** [RPC]

product assurance   PA

The function responsible for influencing the design as it evolves in order to achieve the required quality performance. Includes inspectability, testability, process control, and related factors.

product baseline

The hardware/software as-built configuration established at completion of development. In the U.S. government formerly called "C Specification."

product breakdown structure   PBS

The structured decomposition of the product into entities of the product. The work breakdown structure (WBS) elaborates on the PBS.

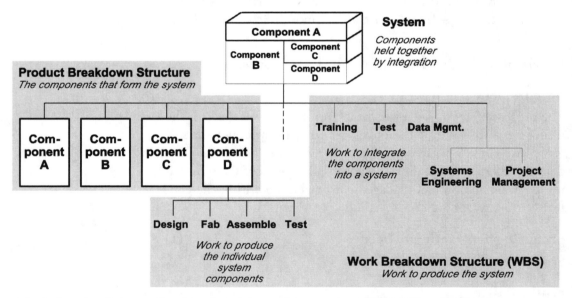

Relating the System, Product Breakdown Structure, and Work Breakdown Structure

product cycle
See **Project Cycle.**

product improvement plan   PIP
The approach to achieving increased capability over time.

product integration project

A project to deliver a system requiring mainly the integration of off-the-shelf hardware and software.

production

Application of processes to materials to realize an item of increased capability.

production article

An article produced from build-to documentation, tooling, and methods. The deliverable is intended for operational use. It usually follows the production model. Also called production unit.

production engineering

The application of manufacturing knowledge to the design and development of the configuration item to facilitate manufacturing. Includes analyses of design producibility and production operations; application of manufacturing methods, tooling and equipment; control of the introduction of engineering changes; and employment of manufacturing cost control techniques.

production model

A production demonstration model, including all hardware, software, and firmware, manufactured from production drawings and made by production tools, fixtures and methods. Generally, the first article of the production unit run initiated after the Production Readiness Review (PRR). A prototype model, also built from production drawings but under engineering supervision, may precede the PRR to provide confidence in authorizing fabrication of the production model.

production project

A project where the deliverable is replication of an existing proven design.

Production Readiness Review   PRR

A control gate to ensure all preparations to initiate production are complete. All material, processes, personnel, facilities, and design are prepared. [RPC]

production unit

An article produced from production drawings, tooling, and methods. The deliverable is intended for operational use. It usually follows the production model. Also called production article.

product line

A group of products sharing a common mission or market.

product specifications

U.S. government DoD terminology for CI build-to documentation. See also **build-to documentation.**

product user

A system user primarily interested in the output of the system.

profit

The amount received on a fixed price contract minus the cost of performance (a negative number represents a loss).

program

A coordinated group of planned undertakings (projects) having a common goal or objective. In the U.S. government, activities with a common mission. In Industry, activities in a common business area. Examples are alternative energy sources program, public transportation program, or hazardous waste management program.

program controls

The project business management function that commonly manages cost, schedule, legal, contracts, subcontracts, human resources, safety, and security. The function works closely with systems engineering to keep the technical, business, and budget baselines congruent.

Program Evaluation Review Technique
See **Project Evaluation Review Technique.**

program management

The overall direction of the project portfolio. Includes project prioritization, funding, support, and other management functions.

See also **project management.**

program management memorandum   POM

A U.S. government DoD document that details the goals and resources of a new program and requests funding. [USG]

program manager   PM (1)

The individual responsible for managing a coordinated group of
planned undertakings (projects) having a common goal or objective.
See also **project manager.**

program plan

See **project plan.**

Program Review Information for Costing and
Estimating   PRICE

A parametric model used for cost estimating. It consists of many
specialized focus segments, such as hardware, software, and mi-
croelectronics. Initiated in 1970s it is continuously updated to remain current, and is available as a software product or service
from PRICE Systems, L.L.C.

progress payments

Payments made to a fixed price contractor based on a percentage
of incurred total cost or actual direct labor and material cost. This
practice has been generally superseded by a system of payments
made on buyer acceptance of contractually identified deliverables at predetermined milestones.

project

Any undertaking to achieve a desired result within defined budget and schedule constraints.

project breakdown structure

The work breakdown structure for the project work.
See also **work breakdown structure.**

project business case

See **business case.**

project business management

The project business management function that commonly manages cost, schedule, legal, contracts, subcontracts, human resources, safety, and security. The function works closely with systems engineering to keep the technical, business, and budget baselines congruent.

project champion

An advocate within the buyer or contractor organization who works to establish a project to satisfy user requirements.

project change control board

A board established for approval of changes to the technical, operations, schedule, or cost baseline for the project.

project charter

The executive authorized document or proclamation that identifies the project, appoints the project team, delegates responsibility and authority and describes the supporting organizations and reporting relationships. This is essential to positioning the project and the project team within the organization's business environment.
See also **charter.**

Project Communications Management

One of the nine PMBOK® knowledge areas. This area includes processes to ensure timely and appropriate management of project information.
See also **Project Management Body Of Knowledge.**

Project Completion Review   PCR

A control gate held to confirm that deactivation is complete and that the project is complete. [RPC]

project configuration control board   PCCB
See **project change control board.**

Project Control

One of ten Project Management Elements. Includes all risk based proactive and reactive control systems. The project's configurations management system and related change control system are examples of proactive control. Visibility, Status, and Corrective Action are the components of reactive control. [VPM]

Project Cost Management

One of the nine PMBOK® knowledge areas. This area includes processes to ensure the project is completed within budget.
See also **Project Management Body Of Knowledge.**

Project Cycle   PC (2)

The third Project Management Essential. The highest level management logic, depicted as a series of periods and phases, each with a defined output, that guides research, development, production, and/or the acquisition of products and services. Includes control gates that approve the evolving project baseline that is elaborated in each phase. Development project cycles start with user needs and end with system decommissioning and disposal. Project cycles contain three aspects: business, budget, and technical. Sometimes called the Project Life Cycle. [VPM] [RPC]

Project Cycle—Reference

The example project cycle referenced by this dictionary consists of three periods. Study, Implementation, and Operations. The Study Period contains four phases, User Requirements, Concept Definition, System Specification, and Acquisition Preparation. The Implementation Period contains three phases, Source Selection, System Development, and Verification. The Operations Period contains three phases, Deployment, Operations and Maintenance, and Deactivation. [RPC]

Project Evaluation Review Technique   PERT

A technique for scheduling and statusing a project by constructing a network diagram of tasks and events and periodically evaluating progress against the network. Estimates are given for the most optimistic, nominal, and most pessimistic duration of each task in the network. These data allow statistical evaluation of critical paths for the project and a statistical prediction of project completion dates. The three-point estimate on each task is the primary feature that distinguishes a PERT network from a

Critical Path Method (CPM) network that uses a single estimate for the duration of each task.

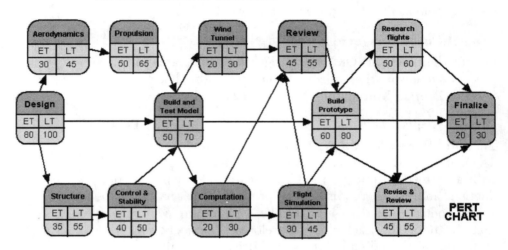

PERT CHART

Project Human Resource Management

One of the nine PMBOK® knowledge areas. This area includes processes to ensure most effective use of people.
See also **Project Management Body Of Knowledge.**

Project Implementation Plan

The plan for project implementation. It is usually developed after the Study Period. Typically the provider develops the Project Implementation Plan during the preparation of the proposal in response to the customer's Request For Proposal. This plan is the collection of all contractor project planning documentation leading to the development of a well-ordered set of project work authorizing documents and subcontracts (which are binding only on winning the contract, and are subject to customer approval).

After contract negotiation and contract award, the proposed Project Implementation Plan is updated to reflect the results of negotiation.

After contract award, the planning documentation usually includes:
- Contract documentation.
- Systems engineering management plan (SEMP).
- Project products list and fact sheets.
- Work breakdown structure and dictionary.
- Task responsibility matrix.

- Master schedule with milestones.
- Milestone dictionary.
- Risk management plan.
- Quality management plan.
- Detailed functional (or support or product center) specialty plans.
- Project network diagram.
- Detailed schedules.
- Budgets.
- Work authorizing agreements.
- Subcontracts.

Project Implementation Review   **PIR (1)**

A seller executive control gate held to secure executive approval of the project team's implementation plan and to confirm executive management support of the approach. The objective is to:
- Confirm that the proposed implementation approach is the best approach for the project, is supported by the management, and that the project is authorized to start in response to the contract.
- Approve tactical approach, opportunity and risk management, critical issues, resources and investment required, and agreed to responsibilities for executive management. [RPC]

See also **Contract Implementation Review.**

project information center

See **management information center.**

Project Initiation Review   **PIR (2)**

A control gate held for the provider's executive management to review, approve, and commit company resources to the Project Plan and approves the project start. Also referred to as the Project Implementation Review.

Project Integration Management

One of the nine PMBOK® knowledge areas. This area includes processes to ensure project elements are coordinated.
See also **Project Management Body Of Knowledge.**

project integrity

See **system integrity.**

Project Leadership

One of ten Project Management Elements. Includes instilling inspiration and motivation into the team to achieve the results as expected. [VPM]

project management

The process of planning, applying, and controlling the use of funds, personnel, and physical resources to achieve a specific result.

Project Management Body Of Knowledge   PMBOK®

The Project Management Institute's reference information consists of nine areas:
(1) Project Integration Management
(2) Project Scope Management
(3) Project Time Management
(4) Project Cost Management
(5) Project Quality Management
(6) Project Human Resource Management
(7) Project Communications Management
(8) Project Risk Management
(9) Project Procurement Management

The Project Management Institute's Project Management Professional (PMP®) certification is based on the Project Management Body Of Knowledge. Further information is available at http://www.pmi.org.

Project Management Elements

The fourth Project Management Essential. Ten categories of interactive management responsibilities, techniques, and tools that are situationally applied to all phases of the Project Cycle by all organizations participating in the project to accomplish the project objectives. These ten elements are:
(1) Project Requirements.
(2) Organizational Options.
(3) Project Team.
(4) Project Planning.
(5) Opportunities and Risks.
(6) Project Control.

(7)   Project Visibility.
(8)   Project Status.
(9)   Corrective Action.
(10) Project Leadership.

[VPM]

project management essentials
See **Essentials of Project Management.** [VPM]

Project Management Institute   **PMI®**
A nonprofit professional organization that promotes project management and certifies project managers that meet PMI® established qualifications.
See also **Project Management Body Of Knowledge.**

Project Management Process
The project cycle phases and activities that are managed by the techniques and tools of the ten project management elements to ensure that all project control gates are completed satisfactorily and that project objectives are accomplished. The formality of application is tailored to the type of project and value and risk of the project. Also referred to as the Visual Process Model. [VPM]

Project Management Professional   **PMP®**
The profession certification of practitioners awarded by the Project Management Institute (PMI®) following the satisfaction of qualifying requirements.
See also **Project Management Body Of Knowledge.**

project manager   **PM (2)**
The individual with the authority and responsibility, as defined by higher management to manage a project. The project manager is held accountable for project success.

project office triad
The three distinct roles that comprise a project office: project manager; systems engineer/manager; and business manager. Any or all of these roles may be performed by the project manager.

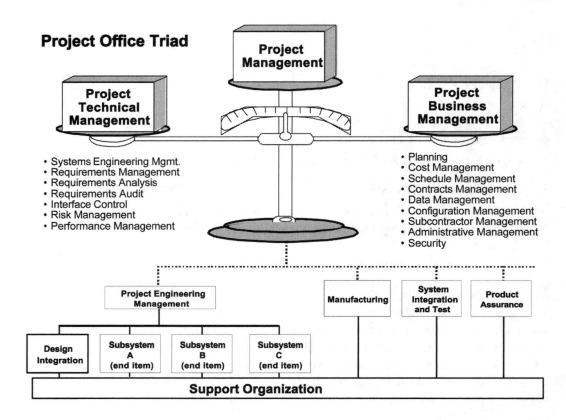

Project Office Triad

Project Management

Project Technical Management

Project Business Management

• Systems Engineering Mgmt.
• Requirements Management
• Requirements Analysis
• Requirements Audit
• Interface Control
• Risk Management
• Performance Management

• Planning
• Cost Management
• Schedule Management
• Contracts Management
• Data Management
• Configuration Management
• Subcontractor Management
• Administrative Management
• Security

Project Engineering Management

Manufacturing

System Integration and Test

Product Assurance

Design Integration

Subsystem A (end item)

Subsystem B (end item)

Subsystem C (end item)

Support Organization

project plan

The overall plan for accomplishing the project. The detailed project plans are developed as a series of separate documents, which are usually created sequentially consistent with the overall project cycle. The project plans include study period plan, acquisition plan, source selection plan, systems engineering management plan, implementation plan, verification and validation plan, deployment plan, operations plan, etc.

Project Planning

One of ten Project Management Elements. Includes converting all requirements into work authorizations using WBS development, network development, critical path analysis, scheduling, estimating, costing, and pricing. [VPM]

Project Plans Review   PPR

An executive control gate held to review, approve, and commit to support the project champion's project proposal for the start-up of a new project (new initiative). [RPC]

Project Procurement Management

One of the nine PMBOK® knowledge areas. This area includes processes to acquire goods and services from organizations external to the project.
See also **Project Management Body Of Knowledge.**

project products list   PPL

A matrix summary of what entities and services must be provided to accomplish the project including quantities required for each form of each entity. Examples: Mock-ups, field test units, deliverables, and spares. The PPL is the basis for planning, estimating, assigning, and material ordering.

project products list fact sheets   PPLFS

A narrative description of each entry of the project products list. The narrative should be written by the most knowledgeable expert and should include sufficient information to facilitate planning, estimating, and scheduling.

project proposal

A document that details the goals and resources of a new program and requests funding to initiate the procurement and project development. For U.S. government agencies, it is incorporated into each agency's program plan for each year in which resources are required.

Project Quality Management

One of the nine PMBOK® knowledge areas. This area includes processes to ensure the project satisfies the needs.
See also **Project Management Body of Knowledge.**

Project Requirements

One of ten Project Management Elements. Includes requirements elicitation, elaboration, concept selection, design-to, build-to and code-to, and verification and validation planning. [VPM]

project review board   PRB

Executive management review of projects and their progress.

Project Risk Management

One of the nine PMBOK® knowledge areas. This area includes processes to identify and manage risk.
See also **Project Management Body Of Knowledge.**

Project Scope Management

One of the nine PMBOK® knowledge areas. This area includes processes to control the project work.
See also **Project Management Body Of Knowledge.**

Project Specification Review   PSR

A control gate held to approve the system specification and verification plan for the selected system concept. The review should include evidence that the required specification values are achievable. [RPC]

project sponsor

The person or organization that owns the project's business case and champions the project's cause and keeps it sold. The sponsor may or may not have control of the project's funds but makes sure that the funds are acquired and authorized.

Project Status

One of ten Project Management Elements. Includes timely comprehensive measurement of project progress against the plan to identify variances and the seriousness of the variances if not controlled by corrective action. Earned value measurement and technical perfornace measurement (TPM) reside within this element. [VPM]

project success

Achieving the solution that does what it is supposed to; when it was is supposed to; for the predicted development, operating, and replication costs; and with the reliability and quality expected.
See also **system integrity.**

Project Team

One of ten Project Management Elements. Includes staffing the organization based on attributes, qualifications, and competencies. [VPM]

Project Time Management

One of the nine PMBOK® knowledge areas. This area includes processes to ensure timely project completion.
See also **Project Management Body Of Knowledge.**

project type organization

An organizational option in which the project manager has full responsibility for all functional and administrative personnel.

Project Visibility

One of ten Project Management Elements. Includes the means by which project personnel and management stay aware of project activity to facilitate timely statusing and effective corrective action. [VPM]

project work authorizing agreement   PWAA

The work release system document that defines and authorizes work tasks to be performed within a company for a project. The PWAAs and subcontracts are the end product of implementation planning.

The PWAA should contain the following five elements:
(1) Task description (input required, task to be performed, and output resulting from successful completion).
(2) Time-phased budget.
(3) Schedule, with appropriate intermediate milestones, and if appropriate, detailed work packages to enable earned value reporting.

(4) Signature of the task leader indicating commitment to do the task within the time and budget constraints.

(5) Signature of the project manager indicating that the task is authorized.

proposal

A contractor's written reply to a request for proposal. Usually includes technical, management, cost, and basis of estimate volumes.

proposal evaluation file

The documentation of the source selection process results. Includes technical, schedule, management, security, cost and price analysis, and other factors relative to the offeror's ability to perform.
See also **source selection evaluation file.**

proposal evaluation teams   PET

Experts temporarily assigned to evaluate proposals against the predetermined criteria of the source selection plan and to select a best value winner. Typically, there are separate teams for technical, cost, management, and security evaluation.
See also **source selection evaluation team.**

proposal preparation instructions   PPI

The buyer's instructions, usually included in Section L of the RFP if a U.S. government solicitation, that define to the bidders how to respond to the RFP. May include page count limits, proposal organization, font and font size, delivery instructions, etc.

proprietary information

Selected information of individuals and/or companies that is controlled as to access and use. The information cannot be disclosed unless the owner grants formal permission.

protest

An unsuccessful bidder's written objection to the solicitation of a U.S. government competition or the award of a contract. Protests can be made to (1) the procuring agency before or after award, (2) the General Accounting Office (GAO), within 10 calendar days after the grounds for the protest are known or should have been known, (3) the United States Court of Federal Claims, and (4) the U.S. District Court if the protester has suffered an "injury in fact" within six years of the date the cause of action arose. [USG]

prototype—hardware

A specification-compliant, production readiness demonstration model developed under engineering supervision that represents what manufacturing should replicate. All design engineering and production engineering must be complete, and the assembly must be under configuration control.

prototype—software

An imprecise term, currently with multiple meanings. A "rapid prototype" is usually a software requirements demonstration model, which provides a simulated representation of the software functionality and operator interface. The model facilitates early buyer-developer agreement on the design approach. A software prototype may also be a technical demonstration model. Except with "evolving prototypes," the code is usually discarded once the model has served its purpose.

public law   PL

Federal, State, County and other statutes.

punch list

A list of remaining work prepared close to the end of the project.

purchase order

The instrument used to transact business with a supplier selling standard items.

Pursue/No Pursue   PNP

A seller executive control gate held to approve pursuing an expected business opportunity based on receipt of the draft request for proposal. The PNP is the decision point for seller management to fund development of a core proposal team, to develop comments to the draft RFP, and optionally to begin proposal development. [RPC]

qualification

Proof that the design will survive in its intended environment with margin. The process includes testing and analyzing hardware and software configuration items to prove that the design will survive the anticipated accumulation of acceptance test environments, plus its expected handling, storage, and operational environments plus a specified qualification margin. Qualification testing usually includes temperature, vibration, shock, humidity, software stress testing, and other selected environments. Analysis may be required to extrapolate test results to the full scope of the qualification envelope. For instance, in spite of extensive model and component tests, it was impossible to do a full-scale reentry test on the space shuttle orbiter before its first flight. Analyses and tests together provided data to give the necessary confidence that the vehicle had adequate margin to permit the first launch. Qualification by similarity may be used if the item in question is sufficiently similar to a qualified item and the planned use is also sufficiently similar so as to not invalidate the previous qualification evidence and decision.

Qualification Acceptance Review   QAR

A control gate held to approve the qualification evidence and qualification certification of a CI and may include approval of a CI qualification certificate. The qualification history, failures, and corrective action, and subsequent qualification test results are reviewed and compared to the expected shipping, handling, and operational environments. [RPC]

qualification certificate

A configuration item specific document that defines the extent of the qualification of the CI. It provides subsequent users details of the qualification environments and history.

qualification test

A test of a qualification unit that is representative of production units to demonstrate that the design will survive the specified qualification environment. Environments are sized to envelop handling and operational experience to prove design margin. A qualification test must be performed on a unit that is representative of the production item, and a number of qualification units may be built and tested, each for a specific purpose. The structural qualification unit does not need the operational electronics, for instance, during structural tests.

For example, the first space shuttle test vehicle, the Enterprise (OV-101), was taken to an altitude of 11,000 meters on a Boeing 747 transporter and dropped to verify the approach and landing characteristics of the orbiter vehicle. It was intended that later the Enterprise (named after the Star Trek Enterprise) would be retrofitted to become the second orbiter in the operational fleet. While the landing tests were underway the structural design evolved, and it was decided that the Enterprise structure, built to an earlier design, was too heavy and would be too costly to retrofit. (The "earth-bound" Enterprise is to be on permanent display in the Smithsonian Museum in Dulles Airport near Washington, D.C.) However the landing drop test data were all valid, since the exterior contour correctly represented that of the operational orbiter, and weight and balance were simulated by inert objects that accurately represented the internal components. Another partial orbiter (body plus one wing), the structural test article (STA-099), was exercised through all its planned tests (operational maximum loads, followed by qualification loads to prove margin). Then, since it had the correct design for the structure, it was repaired and refurbished for flight operations, and it is the second orbiter vehicle (the Challenger, OV-099) in the operational fleet. The Challenger disaster in 1986 was caused by an O-ring failure on the solid rocket booster, and had nothing to do with the test article retrofit to flight configuration.
See also **qualification.**

qualification verification procedures

Step by step instructions leading to the qualification of an entity. Usually contain environment levels, test duration, test set up instructions, and facility instructions.

qualified products

Assemblies and components that have passed all qualification requirements and are considered low risk in operating within those environments.

qualitative

Approximate, based on referenced judgment, not measured. Subjective opinion as compared to quantitative measurements.

qualitative model

A logic representation to reveal general behavior.

quality

(1) A measure of excellence against a standard of excellence such as a hotel five star rating system

(2) A measure of conformance to requirements, usually in terms of defect rate, such as the Consumer Reports' frequency of repair ratings for vehicles.

quality assurance   **QA**

The design and implementation of design features and procedures to ensure that specifications can be verified. This includes specification analysis, quality engineering for inspectability and testability, manufacturing process control, and the use of techniques and training to implement the measurement and testing process.

quality assurance plan

A document that describes the approach to achieving and verifying quality. Includes quality engineering, inspection, audits, sampling plan (if appropriate), oversight and reporting.

quality attribute

A feature or characteristic that affects an entity's ability to conform to requirements.

quality audit

An examination of the processes used to achieve the desired quality for lessons learned and potential improvements.

quality circles

Process teams that meet to improve the effectiveness of their processes
See also **Total Quality Management.**

quality control   **QC**

The procedures and actions to ensure that the required product quality is achieved throughout development and deployment.

quality function deployment   **QFD**

The mapping of requirements satisfaction effectiveness to product decomposition entities resulting in a requirements satisfaction effectiveness map. For instance, the hefty chrome gear shift lever with hand stitched leather knob in a high priced sports car has little to do with the shifting capability of the transmission but has a large impact on the look and feel of the sports car. Similarly the "thunk" sound of the doors closing radiates quality while having little contribution to strength or safety. The QFD House of Quality effectiveness map reveals where the various desirable attributes are being realized.
See also **House of Quality.**

quality improvement

See **continuous quality improvement.**

quality indicator

Measures the show quality trends.

quality management system

The function that determines quality policy, objectives, and responsibilities, and implements quality planning, quality control, quality assurance, and quality improvement.

quality plan

The approach to achieving the quality objectives of the project.

quality planning

The activities that establish and maintain the objectives and requirements for quality and for the application of quality management.

quality system
The organizational infrastructure of procedures, processes, practices, resources and tools used to support the quality plan.

quantifiable
Capable of being measured.

quantitatively managed process
A defined process that is controlled using statistical and other quantitative techniques. The product quality, service quality, and process performance attributes are measurable and controlled throughout the project.
See also **optimizing process, defined process,** and **statistically managed process.** [SEI]

quantitative model
A representation to reveal specific numerical behavior.

quantum
The amount a claimant is entitled to under a legal claim.

quick reaction capability   QRC
A project approach directed to delivering in a shorter time than would normally be expected. Cost is usually secondary to program schedule. Sometimes called Skunk Works.

random access memory   RAM
Computer memory in which the locations can be accessed or written in any order (as contrasted with serial or rotating memory devices).

random cause
An event cause that is manifested as a one time occurrence and is outside the control band.

random failure
A one time anomaly caused by a single event with no pattern or repetition characteristics.

random sampling

Spontaneous testing for quality where any unit has an equal chance of being examined.

rapid application development   RAD

The building of software by linking together readily available functional modules of known reliability and interfaces. The process includes development of a functional flow diagram and then substituting the software module blocks into their functional flow location. RAD tools are available to facilitate the process. User participation is encouraged to facilitate this generally evolutionary development process.

rapid prototype

The quick construction of a hardware or software model or simulation to illustrate or prove an idea or theory, typically requirements understanding, critical technology, or operational concept. For software, it is often developed in a rapid prototyping facility equipped with the tools, high order languages, and stable objects suitable for point and click development.

For hardware, it is often developed in a model shop or laboratory where a wide array of skills and capability permit rapid development using a broad mix of materials, parts, and processes.

reactive management

Taking action in response to indications of trouble to avoid the impending consequences. Examples are implementing overtime or adding expert help.

read only memory   ROM (2)

Memory that can be repetitively read but not overwritten.

re-baseline

Development of a revised implementation plan with new milestone schedules. Rebaselining is required to respond to changed contract requirements, funding changes, or realization that the operative implementation plan is not achievable.

recurring cost

Costs of activities that are repeated during a project, such as the materials and repetitive labor for the manufacturing of like items.

red team

Objective peer or expert review of documentation and presentation material to identify deficiencies and recommend corrective action. A red team review is usually used to evaluate and score proposals before submittal, but is applicable to any documentation and presentation material. A red team is not the forum for a debate and the document owner decides which of the red team recommendations will be implemented.

reduction in force   RIF

An action to reduce the number of headcount through layoffs, transfers or attrition.

redundancy

Duplication of capability to increase reliability. Redundancy is used to eliminate single point failure modes. Parallel systems and back-up systems are common forms of redundancy.

reengineering

The analysis of design or process to eliminate low value content and improve the overall result. Also known as process reengineering.

reference model

A benchmark or basis for comparisons.

refurbish

The reprocessing of hardware to eliminate areas of high risk and suspicion. Usually directed to replacement of highly stressed parts and processes.

regression test

Tests to ensure that imposed corrective actions to correct a deficiency have not inadvertently altered other functions. May require complete retesting to achieve the required confidence.

reimbursable expenditure

A seller's expenditure funded by the buyer.

release

A configuration management action whereby a particular version of hardware, software, or documentation is baselined and made available for general use.

reliability

The probability that a configuration item or system will perform its intended function for a specified period of time under stated conditions; usually stated as a mean time between failure (MTBF) number.

reliability assessment

The predicted reliability based on analysis of the collective reliability of all parts and processes.

repair

To remedy by restoring to the correct condition.

replan

Schedule or resource adjustments to meet contract milestones. Re-planning does not imply re-baselining.

request for change   **RFC**

A buyer or seller request to spend contract funds on an engineering change proposal (ECP) for a change. The request states the technical or contractual issue being addressed, the impact on or benefit to the project, and an assessment of the cost and schedule impact.

request for information   **RFI**

A buyer initiated request for seller information relative to the seller's business capability.

request for proposal   **RFP**

A buyer document used to solicit proposals from potential bidders. The U.S. government request for proposal consists of a solicitation letter, instruction to bidders, evaluation criteria, statement of work, and a system specification. Contractors may issue an RFP to potential subcontractors. Contractor's RFP to subcontractors usually follows the buyer's format.

request for quotation **RFQ**

A document used to solicit price quotations from potential suppliers of standard items.

required CMMI components

CMMI components that are essential to achieving process improvement in a given process area. These components are used in appraisals to determine process capability. Specific goals and generic goals are required model components. [SEI]

requirement(s)

Needs or necessities; something demanded or obligatory. For clarification purposes, a descriptor should always precede requirements; for example, user requirements, system requirements, operational requirements, contract requirements, and test requirements.

requirement accountability

The proof of requirements satisfaction. Usually displayed in a compliance matrix that records formally proven performance against the requirements. This evidence is used to prove that the contract requirements have been satisfied.

requirements analysis

Determination of required function and performance characteristics, context of implementation, stakeholder constraints, measures of effectiveness, and validation criteria.

requirements creep

The tendency for requirements to increase as stakeholders remember forgotten issues and users decide they want increased performance. If incorporated without due process, the technical and business baselines will not be congruent.

requirements elicitation

The capturing of user expectations and stakeholder constraints.

requirements flowdown

The process of deriving and allocating requirements to all levels of system decomposition. Well-managed flowdown requires repeated application of the Decomposition Analysis And Resolution process that produces properly system-engineered solutions at each level of decomposition.[VPM]

requirements management

Management of the project business, budget, and technical baselines. The objective is to keep the three baselines congruent. The process includes baseline change management and authorization. Also included are requirements flowdown, traceability, and accountability.

requirements traceability

The management of the parent/child relationships of all requirements.

requirements traceability and verification matrix   RTVM

See **requirements traceability matrix.**

requirements traceability matrix   RTM

A document that maps the parent-child relationships of requirements. Sometimes called requirements traceability and verification matrix.

requirements verification matrix   RVM

A document that maps verification results to each requirement. Sometimes called requirements compliance matrix or verification compliance matrix.

Level	Rev	ID	Name	Make /Buy	Requirement		Predecessor	Verification			
0	0	0.0	Bike System	M	0.0.1	"Light Wt" - <105% Competitor	"User Need" Doc ¶1	0.0.1	Assess Competition	Auditor	Date
0	0	0.0	Bike System	M	0.0.2	"Fast" - Faster than any other	"User Need" Doc ¶2	0.0.2	Win Tour de France		
1	0	1.1	Bicycle	M	1.1.1	8.0 KG max weight	0.0.1, Marketing	1.1.1	Test (Weigh bike)		
1	0	1.1	Bicycle	M	1.1.2	85 cm high at seat	Racing rules ¶3.1	1.1.2	Test (Measure bike)		
1	0	1.1	Bicycle	M	1.1.3	66 cm wheel dia	Racing rules ¶4.2	--	*Verif at ass'y level*		
1	0	1.1	Bicycle	M	1.1.4	Carry one 90 KG rider	Racing rules ¶2.2	1.1.4	Demonstration		
1	0	1.1	Bicycle	M	1.1.5	Use advanced materials	Corporate strategy ¶6a	--	*Verif at ass'y level*		
1	0	1.1	Bicycle	M	1.1.6	Survive FIVE seasons	Corporate strategy ¶6b	1.1.6	Accelerated life test		

Requirements Verification Matrix

research

Scientific investigation.

research and development   **R&D**

Technical pursuit of a new technology or design to support a strategic goal.

research, development, test, and evaluation   **RDT&E**

The process used to develop and verify systems to meet mission requirements.

reserve

To retain for future use or for a special purpose.

resource allocation

Funds and material distributed according to a plan.

resource leveling

The process of smoothing the fluctuations and discontinuities of required headcount for a project by adjusting task schedules within their available slack.

resources

The means and assets used for achieving project objectives, such as money, personnel, material, facilities, and tools.

responsibility matrix

A matrix that maps WBS tasks to the organizations and individuals assigned as responsible and those supporting those responsible. Also called task responsibility matrix.

retrofit

Modernizing or expanding with new parts and/or software.

return on investment   **ROI**

Profit expressed as an annualized percentage return relative to the investment made.

reuse

The use of a product previously developed for another system.

review

A formal examination of a document or product for comment and approval.

revision

A change to a document or design.

reward

Something given to compensate for positive performance.

rework

Corrective action to a discrepant item to make it acceptable to use.

risk

The potential for not achieving the project strategic opportunity or internal tactical opportunities as planned.

risk analysis

The examination of risk to determine the probability of the occurrence and the seriousness of the resulting consequences. Follows risk identification.

risk assessment

See **risk analysis.**

risk avoidance

Taking action to reduce the probability of the risk to zero.

risk identification

The identification of programmatic and product risks relative to the project opportunity or opportunities within the project.

risk management

Actions that include risk assessment, risk analysis, and risk control. To control risk, preventive and/or contingent actions with triggers are defined and incorporated into the implementation plan. Risk management is applied throughout the project cycle.

risk mitigation

Actions to reduce, transfer, or eliminate risk.

risk reduction model

Any model used to mitigate project risk.
See also **mock-up, model—technical demonstration,** and other terms beginning with **model.**

risk transference

Actions to shift the consequences of risk to others as with insurance.

robust design

Design that provides for anticipated manufacturing variations, performance drift, and component aging during mission life without compromising mission performance.

robustness

The ability to survive environments beyond that expected. Sometimes called design margin.

rolling wave planning

Cost and schedule planning where details are developed as far out as information is available, and these are established as the baseline. General allocations and judgments are made for future periods. As information becomes available for the future periods, detail planning is incorporated, and the baseline is extended. Rolling wave planning is often done on a monthly basis to keep the plans as current as possible. (The baseline is continuously extended by this process; it is not to be confused with rebaselining, where the established baseline is revised.)

root cause

The source of a defect that, when removed, removes similar future defects.

rough order of magnitude   **ROM (1)**

Estimated cost based on approximate cost models or expert analysis. It is usually based on top-level requirements, concepts, and specifications, and an overall estimation of work required. The ROM is usually used for financial planning purposes.

safety

Reducing the risk of harm by reducing the probability or seriousness of a harmful event.

safety critical function

An action or device to manage the control of harm to personnel or equipment such as a flashing red warning light during hazardous operations or a switch guard on a critical switch.

safety integrity

The condition of achieving safety under defined operational conditions.

sample

One or more units from a batch or lot according to a sampling plan. Representative sample.

sample plan

The predetermined sample sizes to be examined against acceptance criteria relative to quality.

sampling

Evaluating the characteristics of a population by analyzing a portion of the units drawn from it.

scenario

The arrangement of incidents in a hypothetical happening. Typically used in creating test cases against which to test and judge system performance.

schedule

Activities and events with associated time spans and due dates. It may be graphically displayed.
See also **Gantt chart** and **Critical Path Method.**

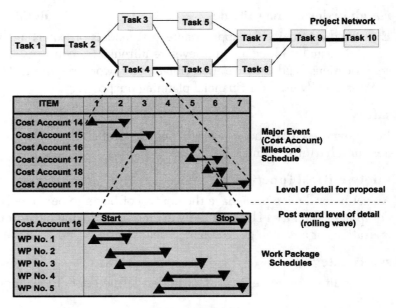

Schedule Development

schedule baseline

Approved project schedule under change control used for status and reporting.

schedule performance index   SPI

In the earned value system, the ratio of actual schedule achievement (budgeted cost of work performed or BCWP) to the planned schedule achievement (budgeted cost of work scheduled or BCWS) for a specified period. SPI = BCWP/BCWS. An SPI of 1.0 indicates that schedule progress is according to plan. An SPI of less than 1.0 indicates that the project is progressing slower than planned. An SPI of more than 1.0 indicates that the project is progressing faster than planned.

schedule variance   SV

In the earned value system, budgeted cost of work performed (BCWP) minus budgeted cost of work scheduled (BCWS) provides schedule variance in dollars. A negative value indicates that the project is behind schedule.

scheduling

The development of the time for required activities and the dates required for events.

schema

A conceptual framework for organizing information and knowledge. The method for describing a database for use by a database management system.

schematic

A relationship diagram especially of an electrical or mechanical system where graphic symbols represent entities and lines represent the interfaces between the entities.

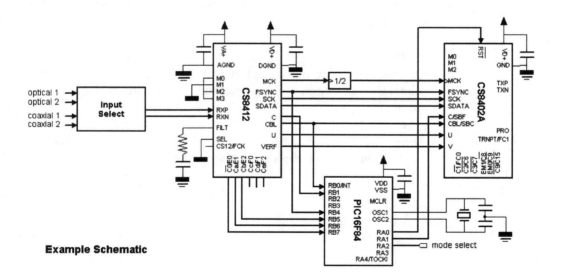

Example Schematic

scientific wild anatomical guess   SWAG

A rapid estimate based on personal experience. Sometimes used in cost and schedule predictions.

scope

(1)   The total of the products and services to be provided.
(2)   The breadth of a project, opportunity, or function

scope creep

On-going requirements increase without attendant cost and schedule adjustment.

scoring

Rating one against another using numerical values to denote ranking.

scoring plan

Scoring plans provide guidance to proposal evaluators to ensure an orderly and uniform approach for evaluating proposals. It is part of the source selection plan.

screening

To examine, based on rules or standards, in order to determine suitability and acceptance.

s-curve

Graphical display of project resources against time showing a relatively flat beginning and end and a high rate of usage in the center.

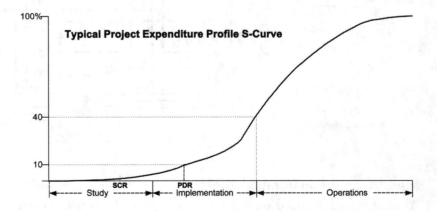

sealed bid

A competitive bidding process where all sealed bids are opened at a prescribed time.

second source

A redundant qualified supplier held in reserve as risk management to ensure a source for critical material or service.

security

(1) Methods for preventing unauthorized access to a system and/or for ensuring secrecy.
(2) Methods for ensuring freedom from danger
(3) Measures adopted to prevent espionage, sabotage, or attack.

segment

A grouping of functionally related elements at a common location. Level 2 in the example system decomposition hierarchy.

self directed work teams

Process-intensive teams controlled by process rather than a supervisor. Process improvements require team consensus.

self inspection

Inspection of work by the performer of the work rather than by an independent inspector.

seller

(1) The organization that exchanges something for money or something of value.
(2) The provider of project deliverables to the buyer or customer. To generalize the concept, the buyer and seller may be members of the same project team working at different levels of the system decomposition hierarchy. For example, the person responsible for a computer software configuration item (CSCI) who needs a computer software component (CSU) is the customer and buyer for the CSU developer, who is the seller.

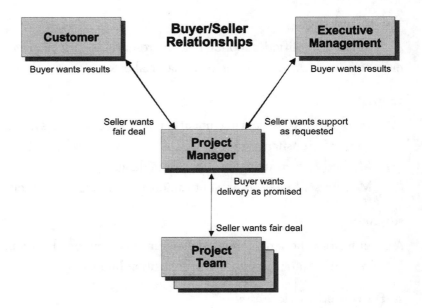

semantics

The relationship between words or symbols and what they represent.

sensitivity

The degree of response to an input.

sensitivity analysis

(1)   The analysis of response over a range and types of inputs to understand the relationships. Selecting appropriate decision criteria and weights is important to the results.

(2)   Determining how much a solution changes when input parameters are changed, to understand the significance of the system drivers.

service life

The expected duration of usefulness for an entity or a system.

severity

A qualitative measure of the seriousness of the consequences of a potential hazard event.

shelf life

The maximum rated storage time without degradation beyond specification limits.

should-cost estimate

A pre-RFP estimate, developed by or for the buyer, of the anticipated cost of a project. The estimate is based on cost models or expert analysis. It is first developed within the User Requirements Definition Phase as a rough estimate. More substantive cost estimates are required as part of the Concept Definition Phase to aid in the best value trade-off of the concepts under consideration. The estimate is also used by the buyer to secure budget for subsequent funding of a contract effort. The funding must be available before an RFP can be released. [RPC]

should-take estimate

A pre-RFP estimate developed by or for the buyer, of the anticipated schedule of a project based on schedule models or expert analysis. It is first developed within the User Requirements Definition Phase as a rough estimate. More substantive schedule estimates are required as part of the Concept Definition Phase to aid in the best value trade-off of the concepts under consideration. [RPC]

show cause

An action initiated by the buyer to notify the contractor of unsatisfactory performance and the consideration of termination for default. The contractor is requested to "show cause" why the contract should not be terminated. The notice may state that failure of the contractor to show cause may be taken as admission that there is no valid cause and that the contract should be terminated.

show cause letter

A written delinquency notice by the buyer to the contractor. It documents the contractor's failure to perform to the specified terms of the contract and indicates that the buyer is considering terminating the contract for default. Pending a final decision by the buyer, the contractor is afforded the opportunity to "show cause" why he should not be terminated for default; that is, to present documented, factual evidence proving excusable cause. This may also be used between a prime contractor and a subcontractor. Also called Show Cause Notice

show stopper

A problem so serious that, if not fixed, it will cause the project to fail.

significant variance

A variance from the plan that exceeds a predefined threshold and therefore requires variance analysis complete with corrective action recommendations.

silo

A tall cylindrical structure used for storage. In project management it is jargon for the virtual barriers between functional disciplines that inhibit communication.
See also **stovepipe.**

simulation

Representation of a system, system behavior, scenario, or situation.

simulator

An apparatus or software that simulates an entity or a condition.

single point failure mode

Physical or functional failure points that will cause mission failure or compromise if they occur. They include hardware, software, and operational failures and errors. Prevention methods include fail-safe systems, redundancy, self test and correction, fault tolerant systems, double checking.

Experience indicates that we do not think broadly enough when seeking single point failure modes in a design. The three-engine DC-10 passenger plane had built-in redundancy for the hydraulic flight control system, with three independent hydraulic loops to operate vital controls to avoid single point failures. Catastrophe struck on a flight over Iowa when turbine blades ruptured from the rear engine, punching through the "fail-safe" engine shroud. The pilot lost all control over the aero surfaces, and had to fly the plane on differential thrust of the two remaining engines. It was later discovered that the fan blades cut through the common connection point for the three independent hydraulic loops, proving that the fail-safe design was flawed. In another instance a company built its reputation and business in fast support to stock market "day traders" who demand up-to-the-minute, accurate price data, and must have immediate response to buy-sell orders. To protect their customers and their own reputation, the company installed four ground-based satellite antennas to avoid the single-point failure mode of antenna failure. What they did not anticipate was that the geosynchronous satellite would fail. When it did, their system went down for days because all four antennas were pointed at the same satellite, another example of a "fail-safe" system that wasn't because of an overlooked single point failure mode.

single source

Relying on only one supplier for a product or service.

situational

Responsive to conditions and circumstances.

Six Sigma program/method

A quality program developed by Motorola. To achieve Six-Sigma quality equates to allowing no more than 3.4 defects per million opportunities. It requires continuously improving high use processes until no defects result.

skunk works

A collocated project environment, usually isolated from other operations and/or distractions, to shorten communication paths and to keep highly skilled functional contributors close to one another and to the project activity centers.

slack

The amount of time an activity can be delayed without affecting any milestone. Normally, activities on the critical path have zero slack. Also called float.

Small Business Administration **SBA**

A U.S. government agency charged with assisting small businesses by providing loans, business and technical consulting. Small businesses generally have less than 1000 employees. [USG]

software **SW**

A sequence of instructions suitable for processing and execution by a computer. Software may reside in various forms of memory and media.

software architecture

The decomposition structure of the software design into CSCIs (computer software configuration items), CSCs (computer software components), and CSUs (computer software units).

Software Capability Evaluation **SCE**[SM]

A method for independently evaluating the software process of an organization to gain insight into its software development capability. [SEI Software Capability Evaluation (SCE) Version 2.0 Team Members' Guide]

software complexity metrics

Measures of software complexity expressed in quantitative terms such as numbers of entities, function points, branches, nodes, or lines of code.

software component

See **computer software configuration item.**

software design document **SDD**

The primary product of the detailed design activity for software that describes the CSCI in terms of requirements, concept, functions, and interfaces.
See also **design-to documentation.**

software development

The process by which user needs are translated into software requirements; software requirements are translated into design; the design is implemented in code; and the code is tested, documented, and certified for operational use.

software development file   SDF

A repository for materials pertinent to the development or support of software. Contents typically include (either directly or by reference) design considerations and constraints; design documentation and data; schedule and status information; test requirements; test cases; test procedures; and test results. The developer is required to establish an SDF for each computer software unit (CSU) or related group of CSUs, each computer software component (CSC) or related group of CSCs, and each computer software configuration item (CSCI) or related group of CSCIs.

The Therac-25 radiation couch development illustrates the importance of these software development files. The radiation couch holds cancer patients in position during radiation treatment. After the couches were in use for several years, a series of six accidents over 18 months exposed patients to radiation 75 times higher than planned and 15 times higher than a fatal level. It was determined that in certain circumstances the software safety interlocks failed. The code to operate the system had been written by one person who was no longer at the firm, and little documentation was available to the failure investigating team. There was an apparent lack of software specifications or software test plan. As a result the investigation, which began after the second accident, took far longer (over 2 years) than it might have to pinpoint the problem. One of the cited reasons for the failure was the lack of software discipline and associated documentation. (Reference: Leveson and Turner, IEEE Computer Journal, July 1993.)

software development library   SDL

A controlled collection of software, documentation, and associated tools and procedures used to facilitate the orderly development and subsequent support of software. The SDL includes the development configuration as part of its contents. An SDL provides storage of, and controlled access to, software and documentation in human-readable form, machine-readable form, or both. The library may also contain management data pertinent to the software development project.

software development plan   SDP

A document describing a developer's plans for conducting software development. The software development plan (SDP) is used to provide the buyer insight into the organization(s) responsible for performing software development and methods and procedures to be followed. The SDP is used by the buyer to monitor the procedures, management, and contract work effort of the organizations performing software development.

Software Development Specification Type B5

Included for reference only. Defined by the U.S Department of Defense and no longer required.
See also **specification types.**

software engineering

(1) The systematic approach to best practices for the development, operation, maintenance, and retirement of software.
(2a) The application of a systematic, disciplined, quantifiable approach to the development, operation, and maintenance of software. [SEI]
(2b) The study of approaches as in (2a). [SEI]

software engineering environment

The personnel, tools, language, platform, model, strategy, and code of conduct to be used for software development.

Software Engineering Institute   SEI

A federally funded laboratory operated by Carnegie-Mellon University under contract to the U.S. Department of Defense. The SEI mission is to advance the practice of software engineering and to make the acquisition, development, and sustainment of software-intensive systems predictably better. The SEI uses its capability maturity models, People-CMM, SW-CMM, and CMMI, to carry out its primary mission. For more information see http://www.sei.cmu.edu.
See also **Capability Maturity Model** and **Capability Maturity Model Integration.**

software life cycle
See **Project Cycle.**

software management and assurance program　　SMAP

An initiative led by the Chief Engineer of the National Aeronautics and Space Administration (NASA) to improve software quality. Started in 1985, the program has produced standards for software life cycles and documentation. [USG]

software problem report　　SPR

The description of an error or a perceived error in a software product. SPRs can be fixed on an emergency or periodic basis, acknowledged but not fixed, or found to be a problem not related to the software (for instance, user error). Also known as a bug report.

software product specification　　SPS

Consists of the software design document and source code listing for a computer software configuration item.

Software Product Specification Type C5

No longer required U.S. government nomenclature for software code-to specifications. [USG]
See also **specification types.**

software programmers manual　　SPM

A document that provides the information needed by a programmer to understand the instruction set architecture of the specified host and target computers. The software programmer's manual (SPM) provides information that may be used to interpret, check out, troubleshoot, or modify existing software on the host and target computers.

software quality

The measure of the software as to its development environment and meeting all functional specifications.

software quality assurance　　SQA

The control of the development environment to produce quality code.

software requirements analysis

The portion of the development process where system requirements are allocated and flowed down to the software elements of the system.

software requirements specification   SRS

A document that describes the performance requirements for computer software configuration items (CSCI). The requirements include function, performance, constraints, and quality. Same as design-to specification.

software sizing model   SSM

A computer application that predicts the probable size of software. The model requires estimates of least, probable, and largest size, example module size, and multiple estimators as inputs. The model tells the expected size and a standard deviation for each module, and an overall system size and confidence factor. The model is most accurate when the system has been decomposed into software components.

Software Specification Review   SSR

A control gate held to approve the specifications of the software and firmware. Preliminary software development specifications are reviewed at the SSR. Software development specifications for the computer software configuration item(s) are released after approval at the Preliminary Design Review (PDR).

If warranted by software risk factors, the SSR is a separate control gate; otherwise these items are addressed in the Project Specification Review (PSR), Project Implementation Review (PIR), Design Concept Review (DCR), and Preliminary Design Review (PDR).

software support

The activity necessary to ensure that implemented and fielded software continues to fully support the operational mission of the software.

software support environment   SSE

A system of computers, tools, methods, and personnel to facilitate efficient software development.

software testing

Verification of behavior over a range of inputs and interactions.

software test report   STR

A record of the verification results of any verification testing of a computer software configuration item (CSCI).

software users manual   SUM

Provides user personnel with instructions for executing the software, the expected output, and the measures to be taken if error messages appear.

sole source

The only qualified source possessing a unique and singularly available capability for the purpose of a contract award.

sole source acquisition

A contract that is entered into after soliciting and negotiating with the sole source. This is frequently referred to as a noncompetitive acquisition.

sole source justification

A document citing the rationale for restricting or limiting the issuance of solicitation documents to only one source. Also called noncompetitive justification.

solicitation

A request for proposal (RFP), invitation for bid (IFB), or request for quotation (RFQ) from a buyer to contractors or from a contractor to subcontractors.

source evaluation board   SEB

The team formed to evaluate proposals in accordance with the source selection plan. Also known as the source selection evaluation board.

source inspection

Buyer inspection of a product, in process or upon completion, at the seller's facility.

source list

A list of contractors judged capable by the procuring organization from which bids, proposals, or quotations may be solicited. Verification of contractor capability typically involves review of financial status and past performance, as well as on-site review of facilities and personnel.

source selection

The process of competitive solicitation, proposal evaluation and fact-finding, and selection of a contractor.

source selection advisory council   SSAC

A team of senior officials appointed by the source selection authority to act as advisors to the source selection process, to approve the source selection evaluation board and to review the evaluation criteria.

source selection authority   SSA

The senior contracting officer (government) or senior contract administrator (contractor) designated to direct the source selection process, approve the source selection plan, and with the source selection official select the source for negotiations.

Source Selection Authorization Review   SSAR

A control gate held to approve the results of the source selection process, the ranking and acceptability of the offerors, and to authorize proceeding with contract negotiation. [RPC]

source selection board (contractor)

A contractor team formed to manage the subcontractor selection process.

source selection decision memorandum

The document that records the source selection decision, the authority for the decision, and the rationale for the decision.

source selection evaluation board   SSEB

See **source evaluation board.**

source selection evaluation file

The records of the source selection evaluation team. Includes all formal and informal competition related documents and notes.

Important to the justification of an award and in the defense of a protest.
See also **proposal evaluation file.**

source selection evaluation team

Experts temporarily assigned to evaluate proposals against the predetermined criteria of the source selection plan and to select a best value winner. Typically, there are separate teams for technical, cost, management, and security evaluation.
See also **proposal evaluation team.**

Source Selection Initiation Review   SSIR

A control gate held to approve the request for proposal and source selection plan and to authorize release of the RFP to the bidders on the bidders list. [RPC]

source selection official   SSO

The senior official responsible for the acquisition activity with the authority to appoint or approve members of the source evaluation board, concur in the source selection plan, and with the source selection authority, select the offeror.

Source Selection Phase

The fifth of ten phases of the Reference Project Cycle and the first phase of the Implementation Period. This phase is dedicated to selection of the best supplier for the solution. The request for proposal, source selection plan, source selection evaluation file, source selection decision memorandum, and contract are all prepared in this phase.

Source Selection Plan   SSP

Defines the solicitation and award process to be used by the buyer's procuring organization for a specific procurement.

span of control

Number of subordinates a manager can manage effectively. Usually about seven plus or minus two.

spares and repair parts

Assemblies and piece parts available for use in preventive maintenance and failure repair.

special cause of process variation

A cause of a defect that is specific to some transient circumstance and not an inherent part of a process.
See also **common cause of process variation.** [SEI]

special test equipment   STE

Nonstandard test equipment. Procurement of authorized STE is an allowable direct contract cost.

specification

The concept-dependent document that defines the quantitative technical performance and other technical requirements such as interfaces and verification methods. All criteria must be achievable and verifiable.

specification change notice   SCN

A document used to propose and communicate specification changes.

specification traceability matrix

See **requirements traceability matrix.**

specification tree

The document hierarchy that controls the technical aspects of the system and all of the system entities. Usually maps to the architecture.

specification types

Included for reference only as defined by the U.S. Department of Defense and no longer required.

Type A System Specification defines the system's functional and performance baseline in terms of quantitative technical performance parameters and is required to be included in the RFP statement of work for system acquisition.
See also **system specification.**

Type B Development Specifications or design-to specifications define the system allocated baseline requirements of lower level configuration items. The specified performance is determined through system analysis and tradeoffs driven by the Type A system

specification. Preliminary Type B Specifications are released after approval at the Configuration Item Specification Review (CISR) (also known as the Hardware Specification Review (HSR) and/or Software Specification Review (SSR)). Final Type B Specifications are released after approval at the Configuration Item Preliminary Design Review(s).
See also **development specifications.**

Type C Product Specifications or build-to specifications define the build-to and as built requirements of lower level configuration items, the performance of which has been determined and verified through the product development cycle including successful Physical Configuration Audit (PCA) and Functional Configuration Audit (FCA) reviews. Preliminary Type C Specifications are released at the Critical Design Review (CDR) and Final Type C Part II as-built specifications are released after the PCA and FCA.
See also **product specifications.**

Type D Process Specifications are procedural directions for control of processes that are performed on material or a product.

Type E Material Specifications are specifics of raw materials such as chemical compounds, metals, and plastics, or semi-fabricated material such as electrical cable used in the fabrication of a product.

specific goal

Specific goals apply to a process area and address the unique characteristics that describe what must be implemented to satisfy the process area. Specific goals are required model components and are used in appraisals to help determine whether a process area is satisfied. [SEI]

specific practice

A specific practice is an activity that is considered important in achieving the associated specific goal. The specific practices describe the activities expected to result in achievement of the specific goals of a process area. Specific practices are expected model components. [SEI]

Spiral Model

A software development method authored by Dr. Barry Boehm in 1980 to promote the management of requirements, feasibility, and operational risk prior to proceding with traditional phased software development. The method also encourages user and stakeholder involvement in early risk resolution. Although conceived for software development the model is also applicable to hardware development.

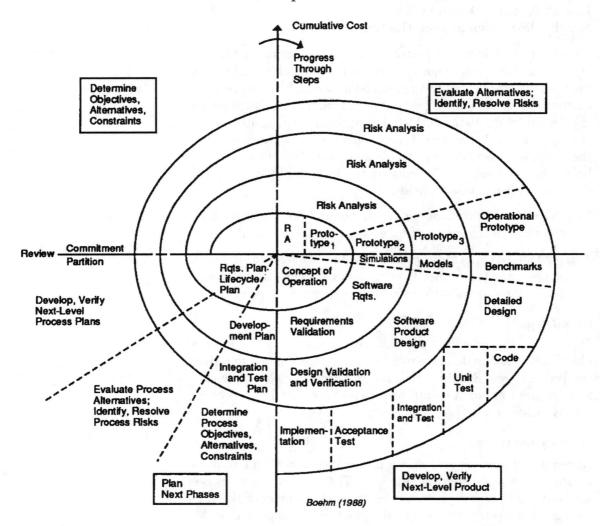

sponsor

The individual or group responsible for funding the acquisition.

sponsor's program plan

An annual response to the U.S. government's Budget Call that summarizes the funding required for base requirements, ongoing initiatives, and new initiatives. [USG]

stable process

The state in which all special causes of process variation have been removed and prevented from recurring so that only the common causes of process variation of the process remain.
See also **special cause of process variation, common cause of variation, standard process, statistically managed process,** and **capable process.** [SEI]

stage

See **Period** and **Phase.**

staged representation

A model structure wherein attaining the goals of a set of process areas establishes a maturity level; each level builds a foundation for subsequent levels.
See also **process** and **maturity level.** [SEI]

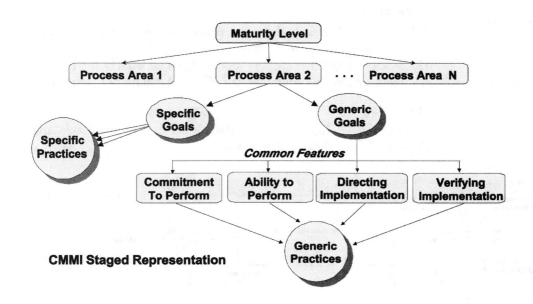

CMMI Staged Representation

stakeholder

Any individual, group, or organization that is affected by, or can affect, the project. Stakeholders, other than users, usually provide constraints to the project's requirements.

standard deviation

Standard deviation is a measure of the dispersal or uncertainty in a random variable about its mean. (Bell Curve) One standard deviation includes 68% of the samples, two includes 95% and three includes 99%.

standard operating procedure   SOP

Detailed step-by-step instructions for repetitive operations. Examples are aircraft takeoff and landing procedures.

standard process

An operational definition of the basic process that guides the establishment of a common process in an organization. [ISO/IEC 15504–9]

A standard process describes the fundamental process elements that are expected to be incorporated into any defined process. It also describes the relationships (e.g., ordering and interfaces) between these process elements. [SEI]

standards

(1) Lessons learned and best practices documents that prescribe proven approaches to minimize risk.
(2) Criteria approved by a recognized professional body that provides rules and guidelines for efficient conduct of business.

state diagram

A conditional behavior diagram that shows the results of available or potential conditions of behavior.

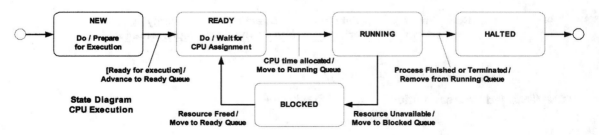

statement of work   SOW

The part of the request for proposal and resulting contract that describes the work required by the contract. Includes a description of the required tasks and the identification, quantity, and schedule of the deliverable contract end items.

state-of-the-art

Leading-edge technology that is currently available.

statistically managed process

A process that is managed by a statistically based technique in which processes are analyzed, special causes of process variation are identified, and performance is contained within well-defined limits.
See also **stable process, standard process, statistical process control, capable process,** and **special cause of process variation.** [SEI]

statistical predictability

The performance of a quantitative process that is controlled using statistical and other quantitative techniques. [SEI]

statistical process control

(1) The plotting of on-going defect data to identify whether quality control methods are achieving the desired results.
(2) Statistically based analysis of a process and measurements of process performance, which will identify common and special causes of variation in the process performance, and maintain process performance within limits.
See also **common cause of process variation, statistically managed process,** and **special cause of process variation.** [SEI]

status

The comparison of actual progress against the plan to determine variance and need for corrective action.

status report

A report that compares actual progress against the plan.

status review

An examination of project status to understand variance cause and to approve corrective action.
See also **monthly status review.**

stop work order

A contractual order by the buyer to a contractor to cease work on a contract until notified to resume. A level higher than the contracting officer must approve issuance of a stop work order.

storage life

See **shelf life.**

Storming

The second stage of Tuckman and Jensen's team building model where conflicts surface as group members try to lead and steer the methods of operation.

storyboarding

In multimedia and proposal development, the process of using a single page to summarize how a scene or a thought will be organized and depicted. Not to be confused with mock-up where each and every page of a video or proposal is structured even if it is blank at the time and is progressively filled in as the material is developed.

stovepipe

A vertical pipe usually of iron, used to contain smoke or fumes from a stove. In project management, it is jargon for the virtual barriers between functional disciplines that inhibit communication.
See also **silo.**

strategic planning

The process of examining the current state of an enterprise and then determining the desired future state as described by a set of broad goals. A tactical plan with measurable objectives is then developed to achieve the strategic goals.

strategy

The overall approach and conditions to achieving a goal.

strawman

A first draft of a document or a first concept of a system defined and presented in a way to encourage critical review and suggestions for improvement.

strength

As used in CMMI appraisal materials, an exemplary or noteworthy implementation of a CMMI model practice. [SEI]

strength/weakness report

The documented findings of the source evaluation board's evaluation of a proposal.

stress testing (hardware)

Performance testing that qualifies the hardware design in environmental conditions beyond normal expected use to demonstrate design margins. Also used to verify quality by forcing latent defects. Typical conditions are temperature, vibration, shock, humidity, and vacuum.
See also **qualification.**

stress testing (software)

Performance testing that qualifies the software design in regions and conditions beyond normal expected use to demonstrate design margins. Typical conditions are number of users, number of simultaneous transactions, inadvertent shut down, and similar tests.
See also **qualification.**

structured design

A disciplined approach to any design that responds to the logic of top down modularity and the careful allocation of requirements to the modules.

stubs and drivers

Temporary software products created to simulate unavailable parts of the system during development and testing.

Study Period

The first of three periods of the Reference Project Cycle in which the scope and direction of the project is determined.

It consists of four phases; (1) User Requirements Definition, (2) Concept Definition, (3) System Specification, and (4) Acquisition Preparation. [RPC]

subassembly

Two or more parts joined together to form a unit in an assembly, such as a printed circuit board with installed parts. Level 6 in the example system decomposition hierarchy.

subcontract   S/C

A contract between the prime contractor and a seller.

subcontract administrator   SCA

An official designated by the contractor, who has the authority to obligate contractor funds; enter into, administer, change and terminate subcontracts; and make related determinations and findings.

subcontract documentation requirements list   SDRL

The documentation required by a prime contractor from a subcontractor in the execution of a subcontract. The SDRL is usually included in the subcontract statement of work.

subcontract management team   SMT

The prime contractor's multi-disciplined team responsible for audit and corrective action guidance of a subcontractor.

subcontractor

A contractor under contract to perform work for a prime or general contractor.

subcontractor management plan

Defines how the prime contractor intends to manage specific subcontractors. Included are implementation planning, status and control techniques, use of resident representatives, and other techniques unique to management of the associated subcontractor risk.

subcontractor manager

A prime contractor team member responsible for the overall management of a subcontractor.

subprocess

A process that is part of a larger process.
See also **process description.** [SEI]

subsystem

A functional grouping of assemblies that combine to perform a function, such as electric power, command and control, guidance, etc. Level 4 in the example system decomposition hierarchy.

success

See **project success.**

succession plans

The planned approach to ensuring that qualified personnel are available to replace critical personnel should they leave for any reason.

sunk costs

Expenditures that cannot be recovered by cancellation of activities.

supplier

The provider of standard goods or services not requiring a statement of work.

supply chain

All contributors that provide material to a project. Includes production and logistics.

support

Activities necessary to field and sustain the system, including logistics, personnel, training, spares, and facilities.

support equipment

Equipment necessary to make the support function successful.

survivability

A measure of the capability of a system to live through a hostile environment without losing its ability to accomplish its mission.

sustainability

A measure of the capability of the system to remain operational under the harshest projected environment.

symbol

A representation of something by graphic or other association.

synchronous

Two are more objects that function with the same or interdependent rates of speed or events.

syntax

(1) Rules and/or patterns that govern a well-formed logical system, such as those forming sentences and phrases from words.
(2) A systematic, orderly arrangement.

synthesis

Combining separate elements to form a coherent whole.

system

A combination of any or all of hardware, software, facilities, personnel, data, and services to perform a designated function with specified results. The highest member of the example system decomposition hierarchy.

system acceptance

The act of taking custody based on satisfactory verification.

System Acceptance Review   **SAR**

A control gate held to ascertain a system's readiness for acceptance. A system-level Acceptance Review may occur twice. The first acceptance takes place at the seller's facility. A second acceptance occurs after installation at the operational site to assure no damage occurred during transportation and installation. For a single deliverable unit, the System AR consists of a Functional Configuration Audit (FCA) and Physical Configuration Audit (PCA). For a contract with repetitive deliveries of identical units, the first unit System AR will consist of a full FCA and PCA. The AR for subsequent units may consist of a subset of the first unit System AR requirements. [RPC]

system acquisition

The process of acquiring a system in response to users needs.

system acquisition plan   **SAP**

The document that describes the expected procurement approach to acquire a specific system. It will describe internal development, competitive procurement, or sole source procurement. Also called acquisition plan.

system analysis

The logical development of user requirements into system requirements, system concepts, and system specifications through the knowledgeable application of state-of-the-art technology and system evaluation criteria applied in analytical trade-off analysis.

system analysis and design

The process of evaluating alternative solution candidates against predetermined decision criteria to select a best value solution. See also **Decomposition Analysis and Resolution.**

system architecture

See **architecture.**

system architecture development

The creation of the structured decomposition of a system concept.

system as-built documentation

Drawings, material and process specifications, and software listings that document the as-built configuration of hardware and software including any required fabrication and coding fixes.

system concept

The overall system technical approach, the architecture, and system concept of operations developed to satisfy the system requirements document and user concept of operations.

system concept document

The description of the selected system concept with supporting rationale. Also known as concept definition document.

system concept of operations   **CONOPS** (3)

A description of how the selected solution is expected to operate. It typically includes a narrative description, data flow diagrams, primary operation plan, secondary operations, and timelines. A day in the life of the system. Also known as system CONOPS.

System Concept Review   **SCR**

A control gate held to approve the system concept, system concept of operations, and validation plan that have been conceived to satisfy the system requirements document and user concept of operations. [RPC]

system context

See **user concept of operations** and **system concept of operations.**

system decomposition

The hierarchical functional and physical partitioning of any system into hardware assemblies, software components, and operator activities that can be scheduled, budgeted, and assigned to a responsible manager. An illustration of the system architecture that also reflects the integration approach.

system decomposition hierarchy

A set of ranked terms defining the composition of a system. The number of levels will be determined by the complexity of the system. For very complex systems selected nomenclature may have to be repeated such as segment level 1 and segment level 2. Typical terms and the corresponding level numbers from highest to lowest rank can be:

> system,
> segment,
> element,
> subsystem,
> assembly,
> subassembly,
> part.

For software projects, computer software components (CSC) may reside at all levels below the segment level and computer software units (CSU) usually reside at Level 6 subassembly. A configuration item can be specified at any level in the system decomposition hierarchy. Also known as decomposition hierarchy, system hierarchy, system hierarchical structure, and system structure.

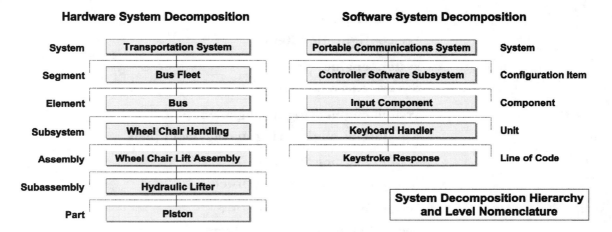

system deployment plan

The document that defines the approach to transition the system from the factory environment to a staging site or operational mode.

system deployment procedures

Step-by-step instructions to deploy the system into its operational environment.

system design

The systematic process of system decomposition and definition until all entities are defined by build-to specifications and code-to documentation.

System Design Review   SDR

A control gate held to review and approve the top-level solution concept and expected decomposition into identified hardware, software, and operator configuration items. [RPC]
See also **Design Concept Review** (DCR).

system development project

A project with a high percentage of new product design.

system effectiveness

A measure of the total project outcome with respect to requirements satisfaction and the effort to keep them satisfied such as operating and maintenance costs.

system element

See **configuration item.**

system engineering

See **systems engineering.**

system engineering management plan

See **systems engineering management plan.**

system engineering process

See **systems engineering process.**

system hierarchical structure

See **system decomposition hierarchy.**

system hierarchy

See **system decomposition hierarchy.**

system implementation phase

See **Development Phase** and **Verification Phase.**

system integration

The hierarchical upward successive combining and testing of hardware and software system components to prove compatibility and performance. The activity of the ascending right leg of the Vee Model.

system integration and testing

The hierarchical upward successive combining and testing of hardware and software system components to prove compatibility and performance. The activity of the ascending right leg of the Vee Model.

system integration plan

A document that describes the approach to system integration from the lowest hardware assembly or software unit up to the system level.

system integrator   SI

An organization responsible for managing the total compatibility of the physical, functional, and operational interfaces between associate contractors, and ensuring that all requirements of all interface specifications have been realized.

system integrity

Congruency of the business, budget, and technical baselines. A developing system has integrity when its baselines are in agreement or congruent, which results from establishing a balance among the three aspects (business, budget, and technical) at the outset of the project and maintaining that balance as changes occur to any baseline.
See also **project success.**

system interfaces

See **interfaces** and **intrafaces.**

system life cycle

See **Project Cycle.**

system O&M project

A project to improve or continue the operations and maintenance of an existing system.

system performance report

The summary and rating of system performance as compared to the operations and maintenance document requirements.

system project office   SPO

See **government project** and **project office triad.**

system requirements

The user expectations and stakeholder constraints that will be responded to by the system.

system requirements analysis/design

The high-level development process where user needs are analyzed to arrive at achievable and affordable system requirements and a viable system concept.

system requirements document SRD

The document that states what the system must do to satisfy all or a part of the user's requirements and stakeholder constraints and is traceable to the user's requirements. This document is the basis for developing the system concept and the associated System Specification.

System Requirements Review SRR

A control gate held to review and approve the user concept of operations document and the system requirements document that identifies which needs of the user requirements document will be satisfied by the proposed project. The SRR is the decision point to allow the project to proceed with the in-depth analyses and trade-offs necessary to select a preferred system concept with associated should-cost (budget) and should-take (schedule) estimates. [RPC]

system safety

The discipline of identifying hazards to the system and/or personnel and either eliminating the hazards or reducing the associated risks.

system specification

The system description, functional requirements, quantitative technical performance parameters, design constraints, interface specifications, and the criteria for acceptance. It must be formulated in terms that are quantifiable and verifiable.

System Specification Phase

The third of ten phases of the Reference Project Cycle and the third phase of the Study Period. The objective of this phase is to secure approval of the system specification and the system verification plan for the baselined system concept. The system specification, interface specifications, requirements traceability matrix, and system verification plan are prepared in this phase. [RPC]

system structure

See **architecture** and **system decomposition hierarchy**.

system test

A method of verification where the system is operated as close to expected operational conditions as practicable and measuring the actual performance against the specified performance.

system test plan   **STP**

A document that describes the approach to all development, integration, qualification, and acceptance testing. Usually part of the systems engineering management plan (SEMP).
See also **verification plan.**

System Test Readiness Review   **STRR**

A control gate held to assure readiness to initiate formal system verification in accordance with the system verification procedures. Approval means that the data collected will be applicable for verification evidence and contractual use. [RPC]

system user

The individual or group responsible for operations, and maintenance of the system.

system validation

The process of developing evidence in accordance with the user validation plan and system validation procedures to prove that the system satisfies the user's needs.

system validation plan

See **user validation plan.**

system validation procedures

Step by step instructions that implement the testing, inspection, demonstration, and analysis required by the system validation plan. They include such items as equipment to be used, calibration requirements, and facility requirements.

system validation report

The summarization of the results of system validation.

system verification

Proof of compliance with system specifications. Verification may be determined by test, inspection, demonstration, or analysis.

system verification plan

The part of the implementation plan that describes the approaches and methods of proving performance. It includes the approach to development, integration, verification, and qualification. The system verification plan may be part of the systems engineering management plan (SEMP).

system verification procedures

Step by step instructions that implement the testing, inspection, demonstration, and analysis required by the verification plan. They include equipment to be used, calibration requirements, and facility requirements.

system verification report

The summary of verification results including all discrepancies and their disposition and resolution.

system/segment design document   SSDD

A description of the system or segment design including the organization of hardware configuration items (HWCIs), computer software configuration items (CSCIs), and manual operations.

system/segment specification   SSS

A quantitative description of the system or segment function, performance, and other requirements.
See also **system specification.**

System/Segment Specifications Type A

No longer required U.S. government nomenclature for Software Development Specifications. [USG]
See also **specification types.**

systems analysis
See **system analysis.**

systems architecture
See **system architecture.**

systems engineer

The person responsible for system integrity and the advocate for orderly, systematic technical development. The responsibility begins with the identification of the user needs and ends with validation that the user needs have been satisfied. The systems engineer ensures that all appropriate technical and operational disciplines are applied to the system development process in the applicable phases, that the authorized tasks satisfy all control gate requirements, and that the technical baseline is under control and is congruent with the budget and business baselines.

systems engineering

Requirements management to include user and stakeholder requirements, concept selection, architecture development, requirements flow down and traceability, opportunity and risk management, system integration, verification, validation, and lessons learned.

systems engineering and technical assistance   SETA

Technical assistance provided by consultants and/or contractors to assist the buyer during all phases of the project cycle by performing system analysis and systems engineering oversight.

systems engineering, integration, and test   SEI&T

Technical assistance provided by consultants and/or contractors to assist the buyer during all phases of the project cycle by performing system-engineering oversight and by physically performing system integration and verification.

systems engineering management plan   SEMP

The project level system-engineering plan that describes the overall technical approach to conceiving, designing, and developing the solutions. The SEMP includes approach to development, opportunity and risk management, use of models, configuration management, verification, validation, etc.

systems engineering process

The application of scientific and engineering effort to: (a) Transform operational needs into a set of requirements with a user concept of operations (implementation concept independent), (b) select a best value concept based on weighted evaluation criteria and develop a system concept of operations (concept dependent), (c) develop the system architecture, (d) develop requirements for the lower level configuration items, (e) integrate related lower level concepts to assure the compatibility of all physical and functional interfaces and, (f) integrate the disciplines of reliability, maintainability, safety, human and other such factors into the total engineering effort.

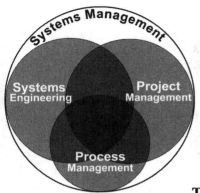

systems integration
See **system integration.**

systems management
The integration of project management and systems engineering into a seamless process that is dedicated to ensuring system integrity.
See also **system integrity** and **project success.**

Taguchi Method
Robust design method pioneered by Dr. Genichi Taguchi to produce a design that eliminates sensitivity to production variables thereby reducing defects and improving quality which is key to reaching six sigma.

tailoring
The adjustment of a proven approach or process to be responsive to the nature, challenges, and risks of the project.

target fee
The planned fee if the seller's actual costs are equal to the contract target cost in a cost plus incentive fee contract.

target profile
In the CMMI continuous representation, a list of process areas and their corresponding capability levels that represent an objective for process improvement.
See also **capability level profile** and **achievement profile.** [SEI]

target staging
In the CMMI continuous representation, a sequence of target profiles that describes the path of process improvement to be followed by the organization.

See also **capability level profile**, **achievement profile**, and **target profile.** [SEI]

task

A job or piece of work to be performed.

task definition

The WBS dictionary task descriptions for each of the WBS tasks.

task force

A team of experts tasked to investigate a problem and to develop and implement the necessary corrective action.
See also **tiger team.**

task responsibility matrix

A table showing tasks and responsible participants for the tasks. Used to ensure that work packages and task assignments are complete.

taxonomy

The division into groups or categories of a kind or type—a classification scheme.

team

A group of people sharing; (1) A common goal, (2) Acknowledged interdependency and trust, (3) A common code of conduct, and (4) A shared reward.

team building

(1) The overt process of instilling the four elements of being an effective team. Sometimes off-site events are used to facilitate the adoption of these elements.
See also **team.**
(2) According to B. W. Tuckman and M. A. Jensen, *Stages of small group development revisited* (1977), teambuilding progresses through the stages of Forming, Storming, Norming, Performing, and Adjourning.

teaming agreement

A legal agreement between cooperating parties for a business opportunity defining the roles and responsibilities of each during and after the competition. May define prime-subcontractor relationships and/or the division of work.

Teamwork

The second Project Management Essential. Positively working together to achieve a common goal, with acknowledged interdependency and trust, acceptance of a common code of conduct, and a shared reward. [VPM]

technical

Relating to specified solution performance as opposed to cost and schedule performance.

Technical Aspect of the Project Cycle

The layer of the Project Cycle dedicated to managing the technical maturation of the project solution. Can be depicted in the Waterfall, Spiral, or Vee format. [VPM]

technical baseline

The technical definition elaboration under formal change control. See also **baseline.**

technical evaluation team   **TET**

A team established to evaluate the technical aspects of a proposal.

technical exchange meeting   **TEM**

Meetings of both buyer and seller personnel to evaluate technical progress and issues. Also called technical interchange meeting.

technical interchange meeting   **TIM**

Meetings of both buyer and seller personnel to evaluate technical progress and issues. Also called technical exchange meeting.

technical leveling

In a competition, the technique of helping some offerors to bring their proposals up to the level of other proposals through rounds of discussions where deficiencies, weaknesses and corrective actions are discussed.

NOTE: This is considered to be an unfair and improper practice.

technical manual   **TM**

Written technical operating and maintenance information for the user.

technical performance measurement   **TPM**

The risk management technique of identifying and routinely measuring progress on selected critical parameters. The goal is to identify adverse trends early for timely corrective action. Typical parameters are weight, power, computer memory capacity, and similar issues.

technical reviews

See **control gates.**

technical specifications

See **specifications.**

technical transfusion

See **technical leveling.**

technique

The method or systematic procedure by which a task is accomplished.

termination

A buyer action to end all or part of the work. Termination can be for the convenience of the buyer or for default.

termination for convenience

A unilateral right of the buyer to terminate any or all of a contractual effort for any reason at any time. The parties may settle termination costs by negotiated agreement, determination of the termination contracting officer, costing out, or a combination of these methods.

termination for default

Buyer action to cancel a procurement that is not meeting contract requirements. Default relates to failure of the contractor to perform contract work within the specified time or any other provisions of the contract. If the contractor can establish, or it is otherwise determined that the contractor was not in default or that the failure to perform is excusable, the termination may be changed to termination for convenience.

termination liability

The maximum cost required to end a project based on contractual commitments and other costs necessary for orderly project shutdown. A factor in sizing the financial termination reserve if it is required.

terminology of systems management

Terms unique to the combined disciplines of project management and systems engineering.

test

An operational procedure to quantitatively or qualitatively demonstrate specification compliance.

Direct measurement of performance relative to functional, electrical, mechanical, and environmental requirements. These measurements may be obtained during or after controlled application of functional and environmental stimuli. Testing may include use of instrumentation and special test equipment not an integral part of the test article. The test activities can include data reduction and analysis. Tests for quality should include environments that will help reveal latent defects. Tests should include red line limits to protect the tested item and test personnel. Tests should result in a measurement, which can be compared against a standard either directly or through analysis.

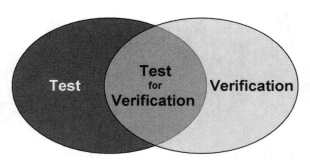

See also **verification**

test, analyze, and fix   TAAF

An approach to verification that includes testing, evaluation against specifications, and then corrective action to bring the results to expectations.

test and evaluation   **T&E**

Measurement and assessment of system performance compared to specifications.

test director   **TD**

The individual in charge of test operations.

test plan

A document that describes the approach to all development, integration, qualification, and acceptance testing. Test plan is usually preceded by one of the following modifiers: system, segment, element, subsystem, assembly, subassembly, module, etc. Usually part of the systems engineering management plan.

test procedures   **TP**

Step by step instructions for the testing to the test plan. Defines test equipment to be used, calibration requirements, test facility requirements, and other factors. It includes checks to ensure that the test article and test environments are consistent with the current baseline.

Test Readiness Review   **TRR**

The series of control gates held to demonstrate readiness to conduct formal acceptance or qualification tests during which official verification data will be produced. Since TRRs are conducted to approve the conduct of official data gathering tests, they will occur at whatever integration level the last opportunity for verification is available. For instance, items that are stowed for deployment will have to be verified before being stowed. [RPC]

test report   **TR (2)**

Documented results of testing to include discrepancies and discrepancy resolution.

then year dollars

The projected value of money based on inflation or deflation in the projected year of use.

theory of constraints   **TOC**

A factory scheduling and inventory control philosophy developed by Dr. Eli Goldratt which aims to improve factory flow and reduce inventory levels by recognizing the probabilistic nature of interdependent work stations. It applies four steps:

(1)   Identify the system/process and its constraints

(2)   Work to exploit the most critical constraint, push for maximum performance

(3)   Subordinate all others to exploiting the critical constraint

(4)   Work to facilitate new elevated performance for this constraint

Return to step one and attack the new critical constraint.

Once the critical constraint is eliminated, a new constraint will arise to take its place. The process continues until the smallest level constraint is identified that can impact the whole system. In project management, the key constraint (using TOC ideas) is the critical path of the project since it determines the length of the project and hence is the key constraint. TOC is used in the critical chain approach as an alternative to CPM or PERT for determining the length of a project by using critical resource control and application.

Three Aspects of the Project Cycle

Business, Budget, and Technical. [VPM] [RPC]

tiger team

Focused visibility, assessment of status, evaluation, and recommendations by experts relative to an area of concern.

time and materials contract   **T&M**

A contract type, wherein labor rates are negotiated to include indirect expense and profit. Materials are provided as a direct charge without the application of indirect costs and profit.

timeline

The functional timing of the solution for all modes of operations. Usually shown graphically on a horizontal time base.

time-phased estimate

A cost or schedule prediction including the monthly time phased expenditures against calendar dates. This detail facilitates the planning of funding according to the need profile over time. Construction loans on buildings are typically funded in accordance with time-phased or milestone-phased projections.

time remaining   **TR (1)**

Time between a status date and a contract milestone date.

time scaled network

A project network diagram graphically scaled proportional to the task durations.

time to complete   **TTC**

Time required from a status date to meet a contract milestone.

time value of money

The name of the concept that money changes value over time proportional to the prevailing generally accepted interest rates. A sum of money today is worth more than the same sum of money at a future date because of the interest that can be earned on the money if available now. Some sellers will discount for immediate cash because of this factor.

to be determined   **TBD**

Contract content such as dates, specifications, or criteria that have yet to be defined. Contractors cannot be expected to accurately propose to TBDs. When defined, they become the basis for a contract change.

to be resolved   **TBR**

Contractual content, such as dates, specifications, or criteria that are not final, and are to be resolved by the contractor or by the buyer as part of the development effort. When resolved, they may be a basis for a contract change.

to be supplied   **TBS**

See **to be determined.**

to complete performance index   **TCPI**

The work efficiency required to achieve a predicted estimate at completion (EAC).

tolerance

A range of values displaced from the desired value that is still considered acceptable.

top down

A method that starts at a high level and then proceeds to successively lower levels.

top down estimate

An estimate of the overall anticipated cost and schedule for a project, based on expert judgment of the key members of the project team. It may include a top down allocation to the various segments and elements of the system.

top ten problems list

A list in order of importance of critical problems with pending actions and responsible person. There may be more or less than ten.

Total Quality Management   **TQM**

An approach to quality predicated on viewing all coworkers as customers who must be satisfied and all work processes as needing continued improvement.

TQM is based on the life's work of Dr. W.E. Deming whose basic concepts are:
- Gain understanding of the product requirements,
- Assess the product against the requirements,
- Ensure that all members of the organization understand the requirements and the development process as it relates to them, and
- Improve the process continually and forever.

traceability

See **traceable.**

traceability matrix

See **requirements traceability matrix.**

traceable

The management and mapping of the parent-child relationships of all requirements. Includes: from user to system requirements;

system requirements to lower level requirements; requirements to design; design to implementation; specification to verification; and requirements to validation and the reverse.

trade-off analysis/study
See **trade study.**

trade study
A comparison of alternatives against evaluation criteria to select the best solution.

training
To coach and mentor to make proficient.

training certificates
Documented evidence of an individual's training and competency in a specified area.

trigger
An event that signals the start of other events.

triple constraint
For projects, technical, cost, and schedule objectives.

Truth in Negotiations Act
Public Law 87-653. The requirement for the submission either actually or by specific identification in writing of cost or pricing data and certification of their accuracy, completeness, and currency for the award of any negotiated contract expected to exceed $500,000. Certain exceptions apply that are tied to adequate price competition or other conditions reflecting a competitive marketplace.

Type A, B, C, D, E Specifications
No longer required U.S. government DoD nomenclature for the family of specifications usually used in defense systems. A = system performance; B = entity performance; C = build-to and code-to, and at project completion, as-built; D = process; E = material. [USG]
See also **specification types.**

unallowable cost

Contractor costs that are not attributable to the project.

unambiguous

Having only one interpretation.

underrun

Spending below budget plan for work accomplished.

understandable

The meaning is clear and without confusion.

undistributed budget   **UB**

Budget that has yet to be assigned to a specific work task.

unique

Not overlapping or redundant.

unit

A mechanical part or lowest level software element.

unit testing

Performance verification of individual hardware or software entities.

unpriced changes

Authorized but un-negotiated changes to the contract.

unsolicited proposal

(1)   A proposal submitted which is not a response to a formal RFP solicitation
(2)   A proposal submitted which is not a response to a broad agency announcement. The basic policy of the U.S. government is to encourage responses to broad agency announcements, but not to encourage proposals without an identified need. [USG]

usability

The ease or difficulty of designated users to operate the solution.

useable

Easy to learn and apply.

user

Any individual or organization that uses the system or the results of the system.

User Acceptance Review   UAR

The control gate held to ascertain that the user is satisfied with system performance and that the user accepts the system for routine use. [RPC] Also known as the initial operational capability (IOC) milestone.

user concept of operations   CONOPS (2)

The user's planned use of any solution in the operational environment. It may include the physical environment, operational environment, operating scenarios, requirements for logistics, provisioning, and maintenance. This document should be created early in the project cycle during the user requirements definition phase. Also called the operational concept document and user CONOPS.

user(s) manual

Directions of to how to operate, service, maintain, and repair a system or entity.

user product acceptance

The official act by the product user to validate that the project has fulfilled all user needs. If the final user is the system user, user acceptance occurs at operational acceptance.

User Readiness Review   URR

A control gate held to verify readiness for official system validation. [RPC]

user requirements

The user's expectations, usually expressed in user terminology. Usually a disorganized mix of musts, wants, expectations, and solutions.

User Requirements Definition Phase

The first of ten phases of the Reference Project Cycle and the first phase of the Study Period. The objective is to secure approval to initiate a new project in response to an identified user need and to initiate the funding process. The phase starts with the first recognition of a need and ends with the System Requirements Review and the program budget being included in the program plan. The user requirements statement, the initial draft system acquisition plan, project proposal, sponsor's program plan, system requirements document, user concept of operations document, and concept selection criteria, are prepared in this phase.

user requirements statement

A document prepared by the user in consultation with the procuring organization that defines the user's needs and expectations and the requirements that must be satisfied by any resulting system. Usually written in user terminology from the user's perspective.

user validation plan

The approach and methods that will be used by the user to prove user satisfaction.

validating requirements

Ensuring requirements are correct, are funded, and that they should be addressed.

validation

Proof that the user(s) is satisfied.
See also **verification.**

validation plan

The approach and methods to prove user satisfaction.

validation procedures

Step by step instructions that implement the testing, inspection, demonstration, and analysis required by the validation plan. They include equipment to be used, calibration requirements, facility requirements, etc. The procedures should include extent of user involvement.

value

Benefit divided by cost.

value added

Analysis of the value of each step within a process.

value engineering   **VE**

(1) A technique by which contractors may (a) voluntarily suggest methods for performing more economically and to share in any resulting savings or (b) be required to establish a program or to identify and submit to the government methods for performing more economically. [USG]

(2) Analysis of the functions of systems, equipment, facilities, services, and supplies for the purpose of achieving the essential functions at the lowest life cycle cost consistent with required performance, reliability, quality, and safety. Reference: FAR Part 48.

value engineering change proposal   **VECP**

A proposal to reduce overall projected cost without impairing essential functions or characteristics and usually includes savings sharing with the proposing organization. (Reference: FAR 48.103). [USG]

variance

The difference between actual and planned.

variance analysis

The analysis of the root cause of a cost or schedule deviation from the plan, and the planned corrective action to eliminate the variance. Variance analysis is an integral part of the earned value system.

variance analysis report

An earned value system report that provides the analysis of the variances, the variance causes, and explains the planned corrective action to eliminate or reduce the variances.

variance at completion   **VAC**

The difference between actual and planned cost or schedule at completion.

variance control

The detection and correction of performance considered substandard.

variance threshold

The variance level that triggers a variance analysis report. Variance thresholds differ depending on the function, level, and state of the project.

Vee Model

A software development method authored by NASA and adapted in NASA's Software Management and Assurance Program in 1988 to promote a sequentially phased development process that includes the relationship of decomposition to integration and the concept of incremental delivery. The Vee Model adds to the Waterfall Model the vertical dimension association to levels of decomposition and as a result the Waterfall shape becomes a Vee.

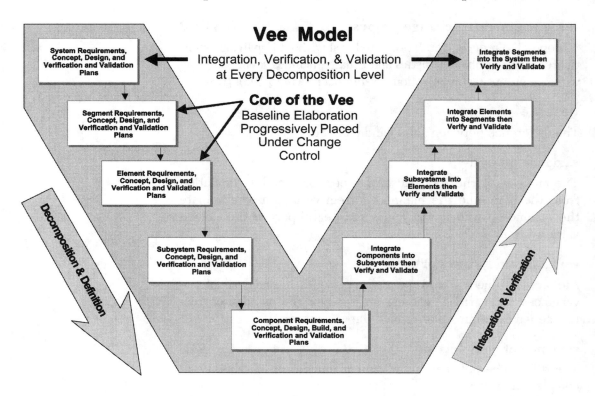

The objective was to improve the waterfall's depiction by incorporating decomposition, integration, and incremental delivery.

Vee+ Model

A system development method authored by Dr. Kevin Forsberg and Hal Mooz in 1990 to promote user/stakeholder involved phased system development, concurrent opportunity and risk management, and verification problem resolution. The approach integrates user-involved opportunity and risk management, and problem resolution into the Vee Model. The more complex the system the deeper the Vee and the thicker the Vee as it descends.

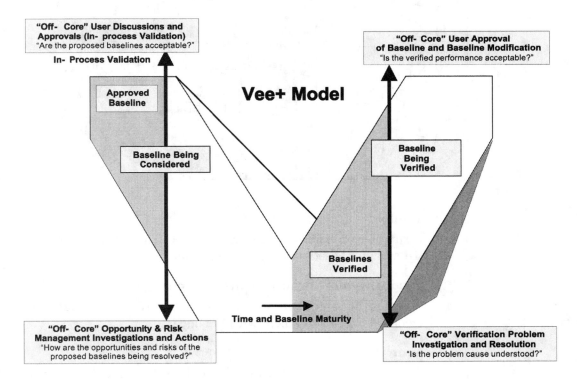

Vee++ Model

A system development method authored by Dr. Kevin Forsberg and Hal Mooz in 1993 that adds to the Vee+ method the processes of Decomposition Analysis And Resolution and Verification Analysis and Resolution. The approach provides a comprehensive model representing the integrated processes associated with system development and the pursuit of system integrity.

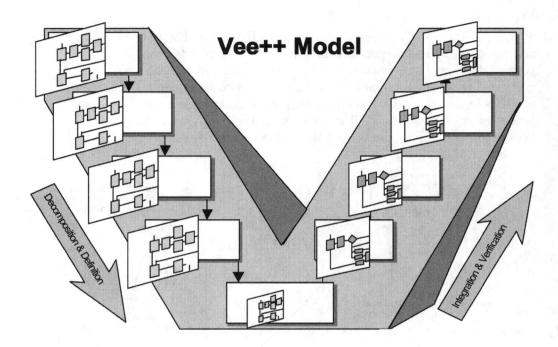

vendor

A supplier of material or services offered from a catalog or price list and purchased with a purchase order.

vendor request for information or change   VRIC

A vendor-initiated request to a buyer for information or to request a change to the agreement with the buyer.

Venn diagram

A way to illustrate logical relationships between intersecting sets, usually with overlapping circles. Named after John Venn, an English logician. See illustrations under systems management and test.

verifiable

Can be proven to be as described.

verification

Proof of compliance with specifications. Verification may be determined by test, inspection, demonstration, or analysis.
See also **validation.**

Verification Analysis and Resolution   VA&R

Anomaly driven analysis at each level of integration to ensure performance issues are resolved to user/customer satisfaction. [VPM]

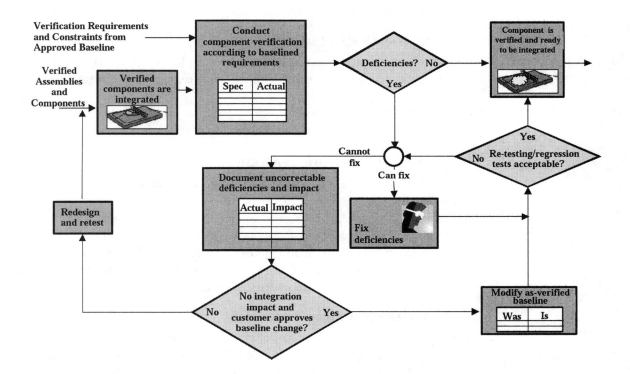

verification and validation

See **integration, verification, and validation.**

verification by analysis

An assessment of performance using logical, mathematical, or graphical techniques, or for extrapolation of model tests to full scale.

verification by demonstration

verification by witnessing an actual operation in the expected or simulated environment, without need for measurement data or post-demonstration analysis.

verification by inspection

verification of compliance to specifications that are easily observed such as construction features, workmanship, dimensions, configuaration, and physical characteristics such as color, shape, software language used, etc.

verification by test

Direct measurement of specification performance relative to functional, electrical, mechanical, and environmental requirements.

verification—design

Proof that the design meets design specifications.

verification—design margin

Proof that the design will survive in its intended environment with a specified margin.

verification matrix

A table that displays all required verification, the method of verification, and the results of verification. Also called requirements verification matrix and verification compliance matrix.

Verification Phase

The seventh of ten phases of the Reference Project Cycle in which system integration and verification takes place. This is the third and final phase of the Implementation Period. It is preceded by the Development Phase, which ends with the approval of all build-to and code-to documentation and associated verification plans and draft verification procedures. Starting at the lowest appropriate level (with verified piece-parts and computer software units for internally produced items, or higher levels for subcontracted items or purchased commercial products), the components up through system segments are sequentially verified as ready for integration. A series of qualification and acceptance reviews at succeeding levels culminate in the System Acceptance Review at either the supplier's facility or at the user's facility. [RPC]

verification plan

A part of the implementation plan that describes the approaches and methods of proving performance. Includes the approach to development, integration verification, and qualification testing, and system verification. May be part of the system engineering management plan (SEMP).

verification procedures

Step by step instructions that implement the test inspection, demonstration, and analysis required by the verification plan. They include equipment to be used, calibration requirements, facility requirements, etc. They also include precautions to ensure the test articles reflect the current baseline.

verification—quality

Proof that the producing processes faithfully replicates the design intent.

verification—reliability

Proof that the reliability specifications have been and are continuing to be being satisfied.

verification report

Documentation of the results of the verification process.

verification, validation, and test   VV&T

The methods to prove that the solution meets both specification and user requirements. This common acronym is misleading in that "test" is one of four methods of verification.

version

A specific baseline configuration of hardware or software under change control.

version control

The establishment and control of baselines and changes to the baseline.

version description document   VDD

Identifies and describes a version of a computer software configuration item (CSCI). It is used by the seller to release CSCI versions to the buyer where it is used by the buyer to track and control versions of software released to the operational environment.

virtual team

A group of people working to a common goal that are not co-located and may not have ever met each other face-to-face but function as a unit. E-communications and the internet have facilitated the efficiency and success of the virtual team.

Visibility

One of ten Project Management Elements. Includes methods of knowing what is happening on the project such as meetings, email, and resident representatives in critical work locations.
See also **management information center.**

visibility meetings

Meetings that keep personnel informed of project activities. Visibility meetings include:
* News Flash—A short meeting held for a variety of purposes; a summary of accomplishments, activities, problems, corrective action, and/or expectations. News flash meetings are often held at the start of each work shift in a multi-shift operation.
* Plan Violators—Weekly meetings with managers to review planned vs. actual. Focus is on cause of variance and corrective action.
* Project Manager's Review—Meetings at least weekly with key project and functional personnel to review project status and corrective action.

vision

A narrative description of an organization's image of their future. The vision statement helps keep teams focused.

vocabulary

A key part of Communication, the first Essential of project management. The set of words used by, understood by, or a the command of, a particular person or group. [VPM]

vulnerability

The susceptibility of a system or entity to degrade in the presence of natural or man made environments.

W Theory Management   **W-Mgt**

A software project management approach in which the project manager tries to make winners of each party involved in the software process. Its subsidiary principals are "Plan the Flight and Fly the Plan" and "Identify and Manage your Risks." Boehm and Ross suggested this theory.

waiver

Buyer action that grants contract relief from achieving specified performance. Usually applied when the required performance is not worth the cost and/or schedule to achieve full compliance. A waiver is an after the fact agreement to "use-as-is."
See also **deviation.**

walk-through

(1)   The examination of the quality of an operational procedure or test by simulating the actual execution but bypassing high risk or expensive operations. It ensures that personnel and equipment are ready to carry out the real thing.

(2)   A peer group mentally stepping through software design and logic flow with test cases to identify errors.

warrant

An authorization or certification usually given by a superior. A contracting officer has a warrant to make commitments on behalf of the government.

war room

A central location for display of project plans and status and for meetings relative to both. Originally implemented by General Dwight Eisenhower during World War II.
See also **management information center.**

warranty

Assurance that goods are as represented or promised.

Waterfall Model

A software development method authored by Dr. Win Royce in 1969 to promote a sequentially phased software development process. The model promotes knowing the requirements before designing and designing before coding, etc. The objective was to provide a repeatable process to the then undisciplined (generally ad hoc) software development environment. Although developed for the software profession the model is also applicable to hardware development.

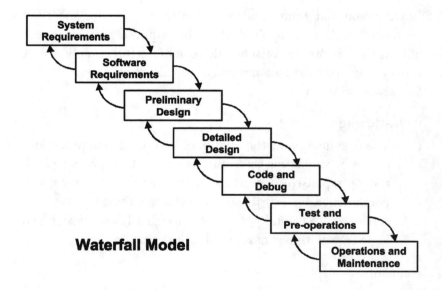

Waterfall Model

weakness

As used in CMMI appraisal materials, the ineffective, or lack of, implementation of one or more CMMI model practices. [SEI]

wearout

The condition of not performing as expected due to failures caused by exceeding the useful life of the system or entities of the system to where they under perform or fail.

weighted factor scoring

In decision analysis the process of comparing alternatives by assigning relative scores against each weighted criteria resulting in a total weighted score to reveal the highest scoring choice.
See also **Kepner Tregoe.**

weighted guidelines

The U.S. government's negotiation method of using the contractor's incurred risk to influence allowed fee or profit. Factors include nature of the work, facilities investment, productivity, independent development, and others.

weighting

Assigning numerical values to represent relative importance within a group. For example, weights from one to ten with ten being the most important.

white box testing

Verification of an entity's internal behavior as well as inputs and outputs.
See also **black box testing** and **glass box testing.**

wide area network   WAN

Computers throughout a large geographical area, such as a country or worldwide, linked to share information and applications.

workaround

A method of reducing the impact of a problem by using a different approach to accomplish the same result.

work authorization

The method of assigning and authorizing work in an organization.
See also **project work authorizing agreement.**

work breakdown structure   WBS

The hierarchical decomposition of a system into elements of the system and the associated work tasks. The form may be a structured decomposition tree diagram or may be an indented outline. The structure should also depict how the system will be integrated.

For services, the decomposition is the subdivision of the services to be provided.

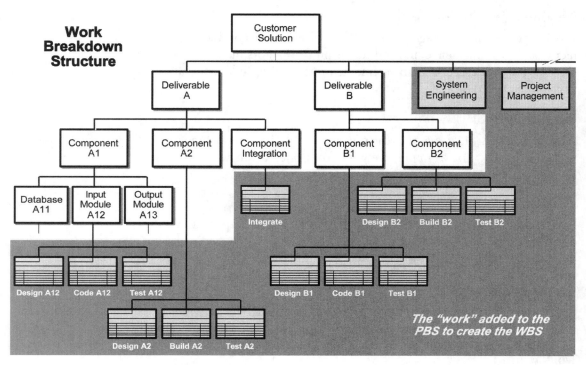

Work Breakdown Structure

work breakdown structure dictionary

A narrative description of each WBS element written by the most knowledgeable person so that it is sufficiently informative to provide the basis for planning, scheduling, and estimating.

work order/work authorization   WO/WA

An alphanumeric identifier used to code time charges to specific projects and work breakdown structure (WBS) work tasks.

work packages   WP

Work tasks required to be performed or material items required to be purchased. Characteristics are: (a) represents units of work where work is performed; (b) clearly distinguished from other work packages; (c) assignable to a single organization; (d) has start and completion dates, and, as applicable, interim milestones; (e) establishes total cost for labor, material, and other required items.

work product

A result produced by a process.

work remaining   **WR**

The work tasks still to be done to complete the project.

worst case scenario

The conditions that posses the greatest challenges for a solution to handle.

X Theory (or authoritative) Management   **X-Mgmt**

X management assumes that people dislike work, will avoid it if they can, and therefore must be induced to perform by threats and/or bribes. Authors on this subject include MacGregor and Townsend.

Y Theory (or supportive) management   **Y-Mgmt**

Y management assumes that people work when properly rewarded and motivated and that work is as natural as play or rest. Authors on this subject include MacGregor and Townsend.

Z Theory (or participative) Management   **Z-Mgmt**

Z management assumes that people need goals and objectives, motivation, standards, the right to make mistakes, and the right to participate in goal changing and process improvement. Authors on this subject include Arthur and Ouchi.

zero dollar contract

A contract, usually for one dollar, that establishes a legal relationship to facilitate transfer of items or data between the parties.

6

ACRONYMS

A&E	architecture and engineering	**ASCR**	Annual System Certification Review
AACE	American Association of Cost Engineers	**AT**	acceptance test
ABC	activity based costing	**ATE**	automatic test equipment
ACO	Administrative Contracting Officer	**ATP**	acceptance test procedure
		AUW	authorized unpriced work
ACV	At-Completion Variance	**B&P**	bid and proposal funds
ACWP	Actual Cost of Work Performed	**BAA**	broad agency announcement
ADP	automated data processing	**BAC**	Budget At Completion
ADPE	automated data processing equipment	**BAFO**	best and final offer
		BCE	baseline cost estimate
ADR	Arrow Diagramming Method	**BCWP**	Budgeted Cost of Work Performed
AF	award fee	**BCWS**	Budgeted Cost of Work Scheduled
AFR	air force regulation	**BIT**	built in test
AGE	auxiliary ground equipment	**BITE**	built-in test equipment
AHP	analytical hierarchy process	**BNB**	Bid/No Bid
AIS	automated information system	**BOA**	basic ordering agreement
ANSI	American National Standards Institute	**BOE**	basis of estimate
		BOM	bill of material
AOA	activity on arrow	**BPA**	blanket purchase agreement
AON	activity on node	**BY (1)**	base year
APR	Acquisition Plan Review	**BY (2)**	budget year
AQL	acceptable quality level	**C/SCSC**	cost/schedule control system criteria
AR	Acceptance Review		
ARB	acquisition review board	**C/SSR**	cost/schedule status report
ARC	Appraisal Requirements for CMMI	**CA**	contract administrator
ARO	after receipt of order	**CAAS**	contracted advisory and assistance services
asapm	American Society for the Advancement of Project Management		
		CAC	cost at completion
		CAD	computer aided design

CADM	computer aided document management	**CITRR**	Configuration Item Test Readiness Review
CAIV	cost as an independent variable	**CLIN**	contract line item numbers
CAM (1)	computer aided manufacturing	**CM**	configuration management
CAM (2)	cost account manager	**CMM**	Capability Maturity Model
CAR	Contract Acceptance Review	**CMMI**	Capability Maturity Model Integration
CAS	cost accounting standards		
CASE (1)	computer aided software engineering	**CMO**	configuration management officer
		CMSEP	contractor management systems evaluation program
CASE (2)	computer aided systems engineering	**CO (1)**	change order
CAT	computer aided testing	**CO (2)**	Contracting Officer
CBD	Commerce Business Daily	**COCOMO**	constructive cost model
CBJ	congressional budget justification	**CONOPS (1)**	concept of operations
CBJR	Congressional Budget Justification Review	**CONOPS (2)**	user concept of operations
		CONOPS (3)	system concept of operations
CCA	change control authority	**COR**	contracting officer's representative
CCB (1)	change control board		
CCB (2)	configuration control board	**COTR**	contracting officer's technical representative
CCN	contract change notice		
CCO	contract change order	**COTS**	commercial off-the-shelf
CCP	contract change proposal	**COW**	cards on the wall planning
CDCG	Contract Data Classification Guide	**CPA**	Certified Public Accountant
		CPAF	cost plus award fee
CDD	Concept Definition Document	**CPC**	computer program component
CDR	Critical Design Review	**CPCI**	computer program configuration item
CDRL (1)	contract data requirements list		
CDRL (2)	contract documentation requirements list	**CPFF**	cost plus fixed fee
		CPI (1)	continuous process improvement
CEO	chief executive officer	**CPI (2)**	Cost Performance Index
CET	cost evaluation team	**CPIF**	cost plus incentive fee
CFE	contractor furnished equipment	**CPM**	Critical Path Method
CFSR	contract funds status report	**CPNF**	cost plus no fee
CI (1)	configuration item	**CPO**	contractor project office
CI (2)	continuous improvement	**CPR**	cost performance report
CIAR	Configuration Item Acceptance Review	**CPU**	central processing unit
		CPVR	Construction Performance Verification Review
CICA	Competition In Contracting Act Of 1984		
		CQI	continuous quality improvement
CID	commercial item description	**CRADA**	cooperative research and development agreement
CIR (1)	Contract Implementation Review		
CIR (2)	contract inspection report	**CRWG**	computer resources working group
CIT	component integration and test	**CSC**	computer software component

CSCI	computer software configuration item	**DTS**	design-to schedule
CSE	chief systems engineer	**DVR**	Documentation Verification Review
CSOM	computer system operators manual	**EAC**	Estimate At Completion
CSSR	contract system status report	**ECCM**	electronic counter-countermeasures
CSU	computer software unit		
CTC (1)	collaborate to consensus	**ECD**	estimated completion date
CTC (2)	contract target cost	**ECM**	electronic countermeasures
CTC (3)	cost to complete	**ECN**	engineering change notice
CTP	contract target price	**ECP**	engineering change proposal
CV	cost variance	**ECR**	engineering change request
CWBS	contract work breakdown structure	**EDM**	engineering development model
CY	calendar year	**EI**	end item
DA&R	Decomposition Analysis And Resolution	**EMC**	electromagnetic compatibility
		EMI	electromagnetic interference
DAR	Deactivation Approval Review	**EO**	engineering order
DARPA	Defense Advanced Research Projects Agency	**ERB**	engineering review board
		ESS	environmental stress screening
DCAA	Defense Contract Audit Agency	**ETC**	Estimate To Complete
DCAS	Defense Contract Administration Service	**ETR**	estimated time to repair
		EV	Earned Value
DCN	documentation change notice	**EW**	electronic warfare
DCR	Design Concept Review	**FA**	first article
DD 250	DD 250	**FAR**	Federal Acquisition Regulations
DDT&E	design, development, test, and evaluation	**FARA**	Federal Acquisition Reform Act
		FASA	Federal Acquisition Streamlining Act
DID	data item description		
DLA	Defense Logistics Agency	**FAT (1)**	factory acceptance test
DMO	documentation management officer	**FAT (2)**	first article test
		FCA	functional configuration audit
DP	data processing	**FCCM**	facilities capital cost of money
DPAS	Defense Priorities And Allocation System	**FCR (1)**	Final Contract Review
		FCR (2)	Facility Contract Review
DPRO	Defense Plant Representative Office	**FDR**	Final Design Review
		FFBD	functional flow block diagram
DR	discrepancy report	**FFP**	Firm Fixed Price contract
DRD	documentation requirements description	**FFRDC**	Federally Funded Research And Development Center
DRR	Deployment Readiness Review	**FMEA**	failure mode and effects analysis
DSMC	Defense Systems Management College	**FMECA**	failure mode, effects, and criticality analysis
DT&E	development test and evaluation	**FOC**	full operational capability
DTC	design-to cost	**FOIA**	Freedom Of Information Act

FOM	figure of merit	**IDD**	Interface Design Document
FP	Fixed Price Contract	**IDEAL**	IDEAL
FPAF	Fixed Price Award Fee	**IDEF0**	Integrated Definition for Functional Modeling
FPIF	Fixed Price Incentive Fee		
FPR (1)	Final Proposal Review	**IE**	information engineering
FPR (2)	Fixed Price Redeterminable	**IEEE**	Institute of Electrical and Electronics Engineers
FPVR	Facility Performance Verification Review		
		IFB	Invitation For Bid
FQR	Formal Qualification Review	**IG**	Inspector General
FQT	formal qualification testing	**IGCE**	independent government cost estimate
FRB	failure review board		
FRR	Facility Readiness Review	**ILS**	integrated logistics support
FSOW	facility scope of work	**INCOSE**	International Council on Systems Engineering
FTRR	Facility Test Readiness Review		
FY	fiscal year	**INI**	Interest/No Interest
G&A	general and administrative costs	**IOC**	Initial Operational Capability
GAO	General Accounting Office	**IPT (1)**	integrated product teams
GAS	general accounting system	**IPT (2)**	integrated project teams
GFE	government furnished equipment	**IQ**	indefinite quantity
GFF	government furnished facilities	**IR&D**	independent research and development
GFI	government furnished information		
GFM	government furnished material	**IRR**	internal rate of return
GFP	government furnished property	**IRS**	Interface Requirements Specification
GOCO	government owned, contractor operated		
		IS	interface specification
GOGO	government owned, government operated	**ISCO**	integrated schedule commitment
		ISO	International Organization for Standardization
GOTS	government off-the-shelf		
GPO	government project office	**IV&V (1)**	independent verification and validation
GSA	General Services Administration		
GSE	ground support equipment	**IV&V (2)**	integration verification & validation
HAC	House Appropriations Committee		
HCI	human computer interface	**L/H**	labor hour contract
HQ	headquarters	**LAN**	local area network
HW	hardware	**LCC**	life cycle cost
HWCI	hardware configuration item	**LOB**	line of business
IAW	in accordance with	**LOC (1)**	lines of code
ICD	Interface Control Document	**LOC (2)**	logistics operations center
ICP	Interface Control Plan	**LOE**	level of effort
ICWG	interface control working group	**LOI**	letter of intent
ID (1)	identifier	**LRIP**	low rate initial production
ID (2)	independent development	**MBO**	management by objectives
ID (3)	Indefinite Delivery Contract	**MBWA**	management by walking around

MDT	mean down time	**ORR**	Operational Readiness Review
MIC	management information center	**OSHA**	Occupational Safety and Health Administration
MIL-SPEC	military specification		
MIL-STD	military standard	**OT&E**	operational test and evaluation
MIPR	Military Interdepartmental Purchase Request	**OVR**	Operational Validation Review
		PA	product assurance
MIS	management information system	**PAR**	Product Acceptance Review
MOA	memorandum of agreement	**PBS**	product breakdown structure
MOE	measure of effectiveness	**PC (1)**	personal computer
MOP	measure of performance	**PC (2)**	Project Cycle
MOU	memorandum of understanding	**PCA**	physical configuration audit
MPS	master project schedule	**PCCB**	project configuration control board
MR	management reserve		
MRB	material review board	**PCO (1)**	procuring contracting officer
MRP (1)	manufacturing resource planning	**PCO (2)**	principal contracting officer
MRP (2)	material resource planning	**PCR**	Project Completion Review
MTBF	mean time between failures	**PDP**	previously developed products
MTTR	mean time to repair	**PDR**	Preliminary Design Review
MYP	multi-year procurement	**PERT**	Project Evaluation Review Technique
N/A	not applicable		
NBV	net book value	**PET**	proposal evaluation teams
NC	numerical control	**PIP**	product improvement plan
NCR	non-conformance report	**PIR (1)**	Project Implementation Review
NDI	non-development item	**PIR (2)**	Project Initiation Review
NIH	not invented here	**PL**	public law
NLT	no later than	**PM (1)**	program manager
NMT	not more than	**PM (2)**	project manager
NPV	net present value	**PM&P**	parts, materials, and processes
NTE	not to exceed	**PMB**	performance measurement baseline
O&M	operations and maintenance		
OAR	Operational Acceptance Review	**PMBOK®**	Project Management Body Of Knowledge
OBS	organizational breakdown structure		
		PMI®	Project Management Institute
ODC	other direct costs	**PMP®**	Project Management Professional
OGC	Office of General Council	**PMS**	performance measurement system
OH	overhead	**PNP**	Pursue/No Pursue
OJT	on-the-job training	**POC**	point of contact
OMB	Office of Management and Budget	**POM**	program management memorandum
OOA	object-oriented analysis	**PPI**	proposal preparation instructions
OOD	object-oriented design	**PPL**	project products list
ORC	operational readiness certificate	**PPLFS**	project products list fact sheets
ORD	Operational Requirements Document	**PPPI**	pre-planned product improvement
		PPR	Project Plans Review

PRB	project review board	**SDP**	software development plan
PRICE	Program Review Information for Costing and Estimating	**SDR**	System Design Review
		SDRL	subcontract documentation requirements list
PRR	Production Readiness Review		
PSR	Project Specification Review	**SEB**	source evaluation board
PWAA	Project Work Authorizing Agreement	**SEI**	Software Engineering Institute
		SEI&T	systems engineering, integration, and test
PY	prior year		
QA	quality assurance	**SEMP**	Systems Engineering Management Plan
QAR	Qualification Acceptance Review		
QC	quality control	**SETA**	Systems Engineering and Technical Assistance
QFD	Quality Function Deployment		
QRC	quick reaction capability	**SI**	system integrator
R&D	research and development	**SMAP**	software management and assurance program
RAD	rapid application development		
RAM	random access memory	**SMT**	subcontract management team
RDT&E	research, development, test, and evaluation	**SOP**	standard operating procedure
		SOW	Statement Of Work
RFC	request for change	**SPI**	Schedule Performance Index
RFI	Request For Information	**SPM**	software programmers manual
RFP	Request For Proposal	**SPO**	system project office
RFQ	request for quotation	**SPR**	software problem report
RIF	reduction in force	**SPS**	software product specification
ROI	return on investment	**SQA**	software quality assurance
ROM (1)	rough order of magnitude	**SRD**	System Requirements Document
ROM (2)	read only memory	**SRR**	System Requirements Review
RTM	requirements traceability matrix	**SRS**	software requirements specification
RTVM	requirements traceability and verification matrix		
		SSA	source selection authority
RVM	requirements verification matrix	**SSAC**	source selection advisory council
S/C	subcontract	**SSAR**	Source Selection Authorization Review
SAP	System Acquisition Plan		
SAR	System Acceptance Review	**SSDD**	system/segment design document
SBA	Small Business Administration	**SSE**	software support environment
SCA	subcontract administrator	**SSEB**	source selection evaluation board
SCAMPI	Standard CMMI Appraisal Method for Process Improvement	**SSIR**	Source Selection Initiation Review
		SSM	software sizing model
SCE[SM]	Software Capability Evaluation	**SSO**	source selection official
SCN	specification change notice	**SSP**	Source Selection Plan
SCR	System Concept Review	**SSR**	Software Specification Review
SDD	Software Design Document	**SSS**	system/segment specification
SDF	software development file	**STE**	special test equipment
SDL	software development library	**STP**	System Test Plan

STR	software test report	**TTC**	time to complete
STRR	System Test Readiness Review	**UAR**	User Acceptance Review
SUM	software users manual	**UB**	undistributed budget
SV	schedule variance	**URR**	User Readiness Review
SW	software	**VA&R**	Verification Analysis and Resolution
SWAG	scientific wild anatomical guess	**VAC**	variance at completion
T&E	test and evaluation	**VDD**	version description document
T&M	Time And Materials Contract	**VE**	value engineering
TAAF	test, analyze, and fix	**VECP**	value engineering change proposal
TBD	to be determined	**VRIC**	vendor request for information or change
TBR	to be resolved		
TBS	to be supplied	**VV&T**	verification, validation, and test
TCPI	to complete performance index	**WAN**	wide area network
TD	test director	**WBS**	work breakdown structure
TEM	technical exchange meeting	**W-Mgt**	W Theory Management
TET	technical evaluation team	**WO/WA**	work order/work authorization
TIM	technical interchange meeting	**WP**	work packages
TM	technical manual	**WR**	work remaining
TOC	theory of constraints	**X-Mgmt**	X Theory (or authoritative) Management
TP	test procedures		
TPM	technical performance measurement	**Y-Mgmt**	Y Theory (or supportive) management
TQM	Total Quality Management		
TR (1)	time remaining	**Z-Mgmt**	Z Theory (or participative) Management
TR (2)	test report		
TRR	Test Readiness Review		

INDEX

This is an index of the keywords within Parts 1 through 4. Part 5, Terms and Definitions, is alphabetized and cross referenced. Bold page numbers refer to the location of terms defined in Part 5.

ABOUT THE AUTHORS

Hal Mooz, PMP, is coprincipal and cofounder of Center for Systems Management, one of two successful training and consulting companies he founded that specialize in the disciplines associated with project management and systems engineering. Mr. Mooz has competitively won and successfully managed highly reliable, sophisticated satellite programs from concept through operations. His 22 years of experience in program management and systems engineering was followed by 22 years of experience installing project management into federal agencies, government contractors, and commercial companies. He is cofounder of the Certificate in Project Management at the University of California at Santa Cruz and has recently developed the courses for the systems engineering certificate program in conjunction with Old Dominion University. He was awarded the CIA Seal Medallion in recognition of his pioneering efforts in the field of project management and received the International Council on Systems Engineering's Pioneer Award in 2001. Mr. Mooz received his ME degree from Stevens Institute of Technology.

Kevin Forsberg, Ph.D., is coprincipal and cofounder of Center for Systems Management, which serves international clients in project management. Dr. Forsberg draws on 27 years of experience in applied research systems engineering and project management, followed by 19 years of successful consulting to both government and industry. While at the Lockheed Palo Alto, California, Research Facility, Dr. Forsberg served as deputy director of the Materials and Structures Research Laboratory. He earned the NASA Public Service Medal for his contributions to the Space

Shuttle program. He was also awarded the CIA Seal Medallion in recognition of his pioneering efforts in the field of project management. He received the International Council on Systems Engineering's Pioneer Award in 2001. Dr. Forsberg received his bachelor's degree in Civil Engineering at Massachusetts Institute of Technology and his doctorate in Engineering Mechanics at Stanford University.

Howard Cotterman is an officer and board member of Center for Systems Management and has held key posts at leading high technology and aerospace companies, most recently as vice president at Rockwell, International. Mr. Cotterman has managed a broad range of system, software, and semiconductor projects, including Intel's family of microcomputers and peripherals for the original personal computer. His 34 years of project management experience began with the development of IBM's first microprocessor in the mid-1960s and includes research, development, and manufacturing projects as NCR's Director of Advanced Development and at Leeds & Northrup where he was principal scientist. Mr. Cotterman was cofounder of Terminal Communications, Inc. and founder of Cognitive Corporation, which specializes in information management and online training. Mr. Cotterman received his BS and MS degrees in Electrical Engineering from Purdue University where he was a Sloan Fellow.